Praise for *Building a Successful Social Venture*

From Social Entrepreneurs

"Where else can one find out how to go about developing a business plan with both impact and profit in mind? Where else does one find a guide to convert intractable social problems into opportunities for realistic dreamers to tackle through effective social ventures? Jim Koch and Eric Carlson's book *Building a Successful Social Venture* provides a powerful guide for social entrepreneurs like me, who must permanently battle the tradeoffs between social impact and sustainability. The book is a treasure."
—**Martin Burt, PhD, founder, Fundación Paraguaya (2005 Skoll Awardee), Poverty Stoplight, and Teach a Man to Fish**

"The information found here is detailed and pertinent, with real-life insights into the origins and functioning of social enterprises. Step-by-step guidelines, examples, and charts offer a critical but encouraging perspective on building and scaling social impact."
—**Neelam Chibber, cofounder and Managing Trustee, Industree Crafts Foundation (2011 Social Entrepreneur of the Year India Awardee), and Schwab Fellow**

"The term 'social venture' has been notoriously ill-defined over the past decade. The authors bring much-needed definition to the space. This will be helpful for investors, regulators, and entrepreneurs alike going forward. At Kiva, we benefitted greatly from the Global Social Benefit Incubator in getting started. This work can help us take it to the next level!"
—**Matt Flannery, cofounder and former CEO, Kiva (2008 Skoll Awardee), and cofounder and CEO, Branch.co**

"The knowledge captured by the book is amazing. I wish we had a book like this for reference in 2002–03 when we went about setting up Ziqitza. Back then there was no concept of 'social venture.' I believe this is a good foundation for anyone who is looking to start a social venture. Attending GSBI was a great experience for me; I learned so much in the short time I was on campus."
—**Ravi Krishna, cofounder and Director, Ziqitza Health Care (2013 *Times of India Social Impact Awardee*)**

"A comprehensive guide and tool kit for these times. Koch and Carlson illuminate the field with research, case studies, and critical specification checklists. Their work makes it clear that social entrepreneurship has a vital role to play in the personal and collective transformation required to create a more harmonious and equitable world."
—**Ronni Goldfarb, founder and former President and CEO, Equal Access International (2016 Tech Awards Laureate)**

"Carlson and Koch have written an informative guide that shows readers the unique opportunity that social entrepreneurship offers to address complex societal challenges and offers specific, engaging, and practical guidance for those of us eager to create financially sustainable and beneficial social ventures."

—**Sara Goldman, cofounder, Heart of the Heartland**

"This book is the culmination of James Koch and Eric Carlson's dedication to mentoring hundreds of social enterprises, from formation through scale. There's never one right way to build a company, so they have aggregated and analyzed the different lessons learned from many organizations. This book is well worth the read for any aspiring or practicing social entrepreneur!"

—**Lesley Marincola, founder and CEO, Angaza (2018 Skoll Awardee and 2016 Tech Awards Laureate)**

"I have had the honor of learning many of the concepts presented in this book directly from Jim and Eric at Santa Clara. I applied many of these concepts at Husk Power Systems and raised funding to scale. This book does a phenomenal job of providing a very detailed and easy-to-follow framework for launching and scaling successful businesses focused on solving the world's biggest problems. Concrete case studies are presented in a succinct way to illustrate how these frameworks can be applied effectively. I would highly recommend both social entrepreneurs and leaders of successful social enterprises read this book and use it as a reference to continually evolve."

—**Manoj Sinha, cofounder and CEO, Husk Power Systems (2009 and 2013 GSBI alumnus)**

"An inspirational, holistic, and practical resource with real-world lessons and examples. A must-read for early stage ventures as well as ventures moving along the path to scale. I admire Jim and Eric's completeness of vision and their true and unwavering commitment to building social ventures and mentoring the social entrepreneurs who lead them."

—**Elizabeth Hausler, founder and CEO, Build Change (2017 Skoll Awardee)**

From Academic and Industry Experts

"Complementing and extending prior Base of the Pyramid work, Carlson and Koch's book provides something new and important: a business planning paradigm designed specifically for the unique opportunities and challenges facing BOP entrepreneurs. The outcome is an entrepreneurs' road map for building better social ventures."

—**Ted London, Adjunct Professor, Ross School of Business, and Senior Research Fellow, William Davidson Institute, University of Michigan, and author of *The Base of the Pyramid Promise***

"This excellent workbook takes the reader through the steps in the process of developing and running a social venture. The examples are richly described and make the concepts come alive."

—**Madhu Viswanathan, PhD, Professor, Diane and Steven N. Miller Centennial Chair in Business, and founder of Subsistence Marketplaces Initiative, Gies College of Business, University of Illinois at Urbana-Champaign, and author of** *Bottom-Up Enterprise*

"Carlson and Koch have crafted a rare primer that offers inspiration and guidance for every stage of the entrepreneurial journey. *Building a Successful Social Venture* shines as a text for undergraduate and graduate students of social innovation. The authors offer deep experiential wisdom and theory-driven frameworks built upon the practice of hundreds of social ventures. The stakes for social innovation are high for us all, and the authors place commendable emphasis on execution with a social consciousness—including actionable tools for investors, managers, and entrepreneurs who care about meaningful social change. This book is invaluable."

—**Geoffrey Desa, PhD, Associate Professor of Management and Social Innovation, San Francisco State University**

"What a wonderful overview of the field with amazing tools for not only understanding conceptually but also moving the ideas of social innovation and social venture into practice."

—**Adrienne Falcon, PhD, Associate Professor, Department of Public and Nonprofit Leadership, and Director, Master of Advocacy and Political Leadership, Metropolitan State University**

"I feel very privileged to have been part of the first ten years of the Global Social Benefit Incubator at Santa Clara University in Silicon Valley—as a mentor, coach, friend, and teacher. In their book, Eric Carlson and James Koch brilliantly capture the lessons learned from the first ten years of their accelerator, informed by a unique combination of the Jesuit commitment to social justice and Silicon Valley's entrepreneurial and innovation-driven culture. This is a must-read for all social entrepreneurs serious about scaling their impact."

—**Charly Kleissner, PhD, cofounder, KL Felicitas Foundation, Toniic, 100% Impact Network, and Social-Impact International**

"The authors have decades of experience on what it takes to build a social enterprise. It is no easy feat, and this book provides a detailed manuscript for entrepreneurs, with examples, exercises, and resources touching on each aspect of building a business. In the age of 'fail fast,' this is a book on 'build it to last.' The authors also trace the arc of shared experience and the original thesis behind creating social impact to guide both new enterprises and today's corporations in creating a better tomorrow."

—**John Kohler, Executive Fellow and Senior Director, Impact Capital, Miller Center for Social Entrepreneurship, Santa Clara University**

"Jim and Eric's book comes at a great time. Solving the world's toughest social issues—such as poverty, access to energy, health care, and education—has not occurred with top-down philanthropy. This 'Guide for Social Entrepreneurs' simplifies that process of teaching social entrepreneurship from a bottom-up perspective. It is not an academic thought piece but rather draws from the experience of hundreds of social enterprises, both successful and unsuccessful, learning perhaps as much or more from the failures as from the successes. I highly recommend it."

—Brad Mattson, Chairman, Siva Power; former Lead Mentor, GSBI; and founder and former CEO, Novellus and Mattson Technology

"This is the most practical and useful book for anyone thinking about developing a social venture that combines market-based principles with a social mission. Written by two authors who have deep experience working with hundreds of social ventures from around the world, every chapter, case study, and exercise is based on a solid foundation of lessons from more than a decade of experience with the GSBI program. This book is essential reading for social entrepreneurs, impact investors, and others interested in this sector."

—Saurabh Lall, PhD, Assistant Professor of Social Enterprise and Nonprofit Management, School of Planning, Public Policy and Management, University of Oregon

"Professors Koch and Carlson have captured the essence of what has become the gold standard for social entrepreneur success and growth. With over ten years of practical implementation, involving hundreds of social entrepreneurs, they thoroughly detail the development of sustainable, scalable social business models and plans; clearly explain 'bottom-up innovation through social ventures' and social change theory; and offer sound practical advice to overcome key challenges that all social entrepreneurs must deal with. I've been a social entrepreneur mentor for almost fifteen years, and this book is my number-one tool to accelerate the success of social businesses."

—Dennis Reker, Lead Mentor, GSBI, and former senior executive, Intel

"From the perspective of someone who, in parallel with an international business career, has devoted more than fifty years to the development of bottom-up approaches to poverty reduction and social innovation, I find *Building a Successful Social Venture* by Eric Carlson and James Koch to be a magnificent contribution to this field and an invaluable handbook for those who wish to start, grow, fund, or evaluate a social venture—whether nonprofit or for-profit. This guide creates a historic and social context within which practitioners can better understand the significance of what they are doing, and it provides them with the tools they need to become effective at doing it. I believe it should be required reading for anyone who wants to change things for the better in a sustainable way."

—Robert H. Scarlett, Board Chair, Venn Foundation; Trustee, Sundance Family Foundation; and Member, President's Circle, Accion

"The Miller Center at Santa Clara University has continued to be a source of rigorous and serious work with social entrepreneurs worldwide—contributing invaluable insights that have significantly influenced our own development and the field of social entrepreneurship. We believe that this new book based on the Santa Clara University experience will help thousands of entrepreneurs."

—**Alfred Vernis, Associate Professor of Business Policy and Strategy and cofounder, Institute for Social Innovation, ESADE Business School, ESADE–Ramon Llull University, Barcelona, Spain**

"This fantastic resource sets a framework for social ventures as essential actors in the global economy. The middle part is the recipe: the how-to for social entrepreneurs. The beginning and end position social ventures as answers to needs in society and the economy that have not been, and arguably cannot be, addressed any other way. Social ventures are simultaneously a 'new thing' in terms of their legitimacy in the eyes of academics and conventional businesspeople, and they're all around us. We all probably interact daily with, or may even already be part of, one, often without realizing it. This book illuminates the potential to improve the world in what we may already be doing and shows how we can do it even more powerfully. While newcomers to social entrepreneurship will find this an indispensable resource, it may be even more important for experienced social entrepreneurs because it will remind you of how mighty your work really is."

—**Sara Olsen, founder and CEO, SVT Group**

From Undergraduate Beta Tests of *Building a Successful Social Venture*

"University students hunger for effective theories of positive social change: *Building a Successful Social Venture* provides them a feast. Unlike most textbooks about social entrepreneurship, *Building a Successful Social Venture* challenges students to drill down into business models and how these can drive change in society. My students have drawn rich insights in enterprise-led social transformation from this book with direct application to action research projects around the world. Subsequent to using this book in two classes, four students received Fulbright Awards."

—**Keith Douglass Warner, OFM, Senior Director, Education and Action Research, and Director, Global Social Benefit Fellowship, Miller Center for Social Entrepreneurship, Santa Clara University**

From Santa Clara University MBA Students

"I really enjoyed the class and definitely will be applying it to a future social venture I've wanted to create since I was much younger. Maybe I'll see you at the GSBI in a few years!"

—**Bhargav Brahmbhatt**

"This was by far my favorite class in the MBA curriculum. I've learned so much from the weekly assignments and roundtable discussions. I just developed my first ever business plan for work, which was a huge undertaking, and I would have been so lost without this course."

—**Erin Horiuchi**

"It was a great learning experience for me and I am sure I will be using the concepts in my social venture."

—**Sijith Salim**

"I thoroughly enjoyed the class, and I learned a lot about social entrepreneurship and MoringaConnect. It was a great experience working on a business plan for a real company with founders who are trying to make a real impact on the lives of farmers in Ghana. I will definitely take the lessons learned with me, and I hope to apply them throughout my career and personal life."

—**Brooke Langer**

Building a Successful Social Venture

Building a Successful Social Venture

A Guide for
Social Entrepreneurs

Eric Carlson
James Koch

Berrett–Koehler Publishers, Inc.
a BK Business book

Berrett-Koehler Publishers, Inc.
1333 Broadway, Suite 1000
Oakland, CA 94612-1921
Tel: (510) 817-2277
Fax: (510) 817-2278
www.bkconnection.com

ORDERING INFORMATION
Quantity sales. Special discounts are available on quantity purchases by corporations, associations, and others. For details, contact the "Special Sales Department" at the Berrett-Koehler address above.
Individual sales. Berrett-Koehler publications are available through most bookstores. They can also be ordered directly from Berrett-Koehler: Tel: (800) 929-2929; Fax: (802) 864-7626; www.bkconnection.com.
Orders for college textbook / course adoption use. Please contact Berrett-Koehler: Tel: (800) 929-2929; Fax: (802) 864-7626.

Distributed to the U.S. trade and internationally by Penguin Random House Publisher Services.

Berrett-Koehler and the BK logo are registered trademarks of Berrett-Koehler Publishers, Inc.

Cover-Photo Credits
Small photo top: Equal Access International (Afghan children enjoying an educational learning session in their community)
Large photo middle left: Sankara Eye Care (Vision screening in India)
Large photo middle right: Angaza (Registering a new customer for solar light)
Small photo bottom left: Illumexico (Solar panels for village home)
Large photo bottom center: Fundacion Paraguaya (Student in Self-Sustaining Agricultural School)
Small photo bottom near right: Build Change (Retrofitting a house in Nepal)
Small photo bottom far right: Angaza (Sun King home customer)

Printed in the United States of America

Berrett-Koehler books are printed on long-lasting acid-free paper. When it is available, we choose paper that has been manufactured by environmentally responsible processes. These may include using trees grown in sustainable forests, incorporating recycled paper, minimizing chlorine in bleaching, or recycling the energy produced at the paper mill.

Library of Congress Cataloging-in-Publication Data

Names: Carlson, Eric Daniel, 1944– author. | Koch, James L., 1944– author.
Title: Building a successful social venture : a guide for social entrepreneurs / Eric Carlson & James Koch.
Description: First Edition. | Oakland, CA : Berrett-Koehler Publisher, [2018] | Includes bibliographical references and index.
Identifiers: LCCN 2018011564 | ISBN 9781523095940 (pbk.)
Subjects: LCSH: Social entrepreneurship—Textbooks. | Strategic planning—Textbooks.
Classification: LCC HD60 .C34 2018 | DDC 658.4/08—dc23
LC record available at https://lccn.loc.gov/2018011564

First Edition

25 24 23 22 21 20 19 18   10 9 8 7 6 5 4 3 2 1

Book producer: Westchester Publishing Services
Text designer: Darlene K. Swanson
Cover designer: Adam Johnson

Paul Locatelli, S. J.

September 16, 1938–July 12, 2010

This book is dedicated to Father Paul J. Locatelli, the twenty-seventh president of Santa Clara University and the first secretary of higher education of the Society of Jesus—a network of 170 institutions around the world. Paul encouraged questions that open into a search for greater purpose in life and a thirst for justice. Throughout his twenty years as president of Santa Clara he sought to bridge the secular and the sacred—the innovation-driven ethos of Silicon Valley with the traditions of Jesuit education, a Catholic religious order founded half a millennium ago. He inspired the work of centers of distinction in Jesuit education, applied ethics, and technology and society, and, through these efforts, he sought to integrate competence, conscience, and compassion as the foundations for transformative education. As president of Santa Clara University he created an environment in which the work described in this book could flourish.

Contents

PART III EXECUTION

Preface

Bangladeshi social entrepreneur Muhammad Yunus defines a social business as an enterprise that "creates goods and services that produce social benefits" where any cash "surplus generated is reinvested in the business."[1]

He also argues that a social business should operate like a profit-making business with positive cash flow (income greater than expenses), and, rather than offering equity to its investors, it should return any invested funds (investment capital) to its investors (in an amount, possibly zero, agreed to by the investors). Thus, a social business could be a for-profit or a nonprofit organization from a legal (or tax) point of view but would have a "social impact" mission and would reinvest all operating surplus in the business (after repaying the original investors an agreed-on amount).

Yunus cites Ashoka executive Bill Drayton's definition of a social entrepreneur as "one who applies creative, innovative thinking to a previously intractable social problem."[2] Yunus also posits that a social venture is a form of social entrepreneurship. He argues, however, that social ventures make up a new category of business—one grounded in a focus on social impact that represents an alternative rationality to the private wealth maximizing logic of capitalism. In a sense, a social venture truly seeks to create a "virtuous" cycle—the greater the surplus generated, the greater the benefit to society.

Accepting the premise that social ventures are essentially businesses with social missions and profit-reinvestment financial goals, the Global Social Benefit Incubator (GSBI®) at Santa Clara University was founded to help social entrepreneurs learn to manage their ventures in a way that would improve both financial sustainability and the scalability of impact. From 2003 through 2012, we were part of a leadership group that helped more than 175 social entrepreneurs develop strategic and operating plans for their social ventures through the GSBI. Groups of executive mentors were carefully selected based on their depth of relevant start-up and general management experience, financial and marketing acumen, and sensitivity to intangible qualities such as "their ability to listen with humility" to the needs of the poor in diverse cultural and economic settings. Together with the GSBI leadership, the first group of chosen executive mentors had over five hundred years of combined executive experience in the public and private sectors. Social entrepreneurs themselves were selected from a pool of applicants who submitted a value proposition, a target market statement, and a business model description for their would-be social venture. During the first ten years of its existence, over one thousand organizations applied.

Each year, for a period of about four months, selected social entrepreneurs were assigned two or three Silicon Valley executive mentors who coached them through a set of online foundational exercises designed to develop the basic information (product/service definition, market size, go-to-market plan, etc.) needed to create a business plan. After these four months of distance-based work, the entrepreneurs attended a two-week "boot camp" at Santa Clara University during which they worked intensively with their mentors and GSBI staff to develop an elevator pitch, a detailed business model, a PowerPoint presentation about their organization, and, from 2008 onward, a two-page "investment profile" (key facts sheet) for their organization. The nine months of work, from application through in-residence, were intended to help the entrepreneurs develop a strategy and plan to achieve financial sustainability (positive cash flow) and scalable impact (growing income and impact at a rate faster than the growth in expenses).

In the 2003 pilot year, seven organizations participated, with fourteen to nineteen organizations participating in subsequent years. During this period, the growing group of enthusiastic Silicon Valley mentors (eventually over one hundred) volunteered thousands of hours of their time to work with social entrepreneurs in the GSBI program. They also contributed their lessons learned as mentors to support continuous innovation in the program itself—lessons that have been incorporated into this book.

The GSBI has continued and expanded since 2012, although the processes involved have changed somewhat to accommodate the expansion. As of December 2017

- more than 800 social entrepreneurs have been served by the GSBI, including 233 by the in-residence program,

- over 200 mentors have worked in pairs or trios with the social entrepreneurs,

- GSBI alumni have positively impacted the lives of over 267 million people,

- GSBI alumni ventures have generated $525 million in impact capital investment, and

- ninety-seven Santa Clara University undergraduates have engaged in in-depth fieldwork with GSBI alumni ventures.

Influenced by lessons from his work as a cofounder of the GSBI, Professor James Koch designed an MBA course in 2005 titled Leadership for Justice and Prosperity. First offered in the winter of 2005, this course had been taken by more than 2,500 MBA students by the fall of 2016. Each of these students was required to identify technological innovations that, in combination with business model innovation, could contribute to the eradication of global poverty. Their projects applied emergent, practice-based theories from the GSBI to stimulate thinking about the "Bottom of the Pyramid" (BOP) as a new frontier for technology and business model innovation. Around the same time, Professor Eric Carlson designed an MBA course titled Social Entrepreneurship based on the paradigm described in this book. This course has been taught in the Santa Clara University Leavey School of Business every year since. In addition, the syllabus of the course was published by Ashoka University as a model "practical" course on social entrepreneurship. Professor Koch used draft versions of this book as a resource for teaching social entrepreneurship and enabling students to prepare conceptual business plans in courses at both the undergraduate and MBA levels.

How to Use This Book

This book is intended to capture the lessons learned from the first ten years of the GSBI in a guide that will help social venture leaders be more effective in working with their teams and advisors to develop business plans that are financially sustainable and more likely to create scalable impact. While this book may be most useful for those managing a social business, it is designed to assist any social entrepreneur who seeks to develop a program or business that uses financial, human, and physical resources to create a financially sustainable and beneficial social impact. Potential investors, students, or researchers might also use the book to analyze an existing social business organization's sustainability and scalability. The book has been used in both undergraduate and MBA classes as an analytic framework for fostering systems thinking and developing market-based approaches to solving social challenges.

The book consists largely of a set of lessons and exercises that, when completed, form the basis of a business plan that can help social entrepreneurs

- raise money,

- maximize the social impact of the enterprise,

- operate the enterprise with a surplus (cash flow positive),

- grow (scale) the social impact (and income) of the enterprise at a rate faster than the growth of expenses, and

- ensure their enterprises provide a needed solution to a real problem in an effective and efficient manner.

The book consists of three parts. Part I provides background information and describes the basic assumptions on which this management guide is based (i.e., a bottom-up approach, market-based discipline, and the logic of business planning). More specifically, chapter 1 compares top-down and bottom-up theories of social change. It argues that social progress is a more meaningful measure of human well-being than gross domestic product (GDP), and examines the role of social entrepreneurship as an alternative to welfare or charity as a means of poverty reduction. Social entrepreneurs may find this chapter useful in developing their own theories of social change or comparing them with others. Chapter 2 describes the "Base of the Pyramid" market and can be used by social entrepreneurs to understand the overall structure of this vast, underserved market. Chapter 3 provides an overview of alternative business planning paradigms or frameworks and their uses, including the paradigm used in this book. While each of these frameworks has been used by social entrepreneurs to develop business plans, the GSBI paradigm has inherent advantages for ventures seeking to understand and manage all of the elements that are involved in addressing intractable social problems. For those already familiar with theories of economic development, the BOP market, and business plan paradigms, the related chapter(s) could be skipped.

Part II presents the seven elements of the GSBI Business Plan paradigm. Each chapter describes one element of the business plan. It begins with an introduction that includes a summary of the assumptions and knowledge that experienced mentors thought necessary for completing the element of the paradigm described in the chapter, and concludes with a checklist for assessing the viability of a social mission business. (Note: An online companion document containing a complete set of templates for use in developing a social venture business plan has been developed to accompany this book.)

Part III describes the key execution elements that can be derived from a business plan, including financing plans and fund-raising goals, budgeting, and the creation of an operating plan. These three execution elements may be the most important reasons for having a business plan. They are the practical "so what, now what" implications, paying particular attention to the unique challenges of social businesses—businesses that simultaneously seek to achieve both financial viability and measurable improvements in the well-being of real people.

Beyond the main parts, we also include a number of pedagogical tools—tools that are useful for helping the reader easily discern the most important takeaways of a given chapter, for situating the sometimes abstract into the real world, for diving deeper into a given area, or for putting the pieces of his or her own business plan together.

Basic Knowledge and Minimum Critical Specifications Checklists

Beginning in part II, each of the business planning chapters begins with a reference to and summary of the basic knowledge that GSBI mentors felt was necessary to successfully create that element of the business plan. In essence, this basic knowledge helps frame the chapter, cluing the reader to the most basic of takeaways. Each chapter ends with a Minimum Critical Specifications Checklist reflecting the collective intelligence of mentors as to what needs to be included in that element of the business plan. In systems thinking, a minimum critical specification is a condition that is critical to the overall viability of system design. These checklists will come in handy when a would-be social entrepreneur works to build a viable path to success for his or her venture.

Social Venture Snapshots

The cumulative insights and knowledge in this book are largely derived from GSBI participant work products. In most chapters, Social Venture Snapshots serve to illustrate how different organizations realize specific elements of a social venture business plan. Because the business plans and strategies presented are about as varied as the type and number of ventures analyzed, these snapshots give the reader some insight into how a diverse set of social ventures have put principles from our paradigm into practice. Each chapter shows snapshots from three organizations:

1. The case study of Grameen Shakti as presented in Nancy Wimmer's book *Green Energy for a Billion Poor.* This case study focuses on Grameen Shakti's first ten years.

2. The case study of the Sankara Eye Care system, prepared by Danielle Medeiros, Cathryn Meyer, and Visswapriya Prabakar for Management 548, Social Benefit Entrepreneurship in Winter Term 2015 at Santa Clara University's Leavey School of Business.

3. In each chapter we present a different GSBI organization that, while at the GSBI, was thought to be innovative in the business plan element described in a particular chapter. All nine examples involve organizations that were innovators in more than one element of their business plan. For example, Fundacion Paraguaya SSAS (mission, opportunity, and strategies innovator) and Digital Divide Data (market innovator) were also business model innovators using job-related education as an income driver. All nine organizations used as examples are still thriving, and many have been for more than ten years since their GSBI experience.

End-of-Chapter Exercises and Background Resources
Finally, the end of each chapter includes a series of exercises for use in analyzing/developing the part of the social venture business plan covered in detail in that chapter. For additional reading and research, each chapter also includes a list of relevant background resources.

Compared with other books on developing a plan for a social venture, this book is unique in its coverage of (1) the external environment—the ecosystem in which a social venture operates; (2) metrics for social ventures; (3) development of a budget and operating plan; and (4) alternative forms of financing, along with a discussion of the factors to consider when determining the most useful potential funding sources. However, the unique aspect of the book is the synthesis of the knowledge of the GSBI Silicon Valley mentors with the experiences and needs of social entrepreneurs to create a comprehensive basis for building a successful social venture.

Part I

Background

Part I of this book discusses the basics of a bottom-up approach, market-based discipline, and the logic of business planning—in other words, the main assumptions on which the rest of this book rests. We start by comparing top-down and bottom-up theories of social change and critique different measures of human well-being in the process. Then we shed some light on the market at the Base of the Pyramid and its many forms and features. We conclude by presenting a number of alternative paradigms for business planning, with special emphasis on the paradigm used throughout the majority of this book.

Chapter 1

Top-Down and Bottom-Up Theories of Social Progress

Pamela Hartigan began the 2012 Skoll World Forum with an eloquent recasting of a timeless nursery rhyme, lamenting our contemporary "Humpty Dumpty world." In this world, "a good many of the king's men are struggling to put Humpty back together again," she said.[1] As you may recall, things do not quite work out for Mr. Dumpty.

Even so, Hartigan went on to herald a "phase of new thinking and experimentation" where a growing group of people "with imagination, commitment, persistence, and strong ethical fiber is working furiously to ensure that Humpty Dumpty's model is transformed and replaced with pathways that achieve economic and social justice and arrest the destruction of our planet." Far from leaving Humpty in a heap—or to the king's men to fix—Hartigan urged the forum to "seize this hugely important opportunity" and concluded with a provocative question: "How do we rewire our systems, our practices, and our mindsets so our story reflects a greater convergence rather than fragmentation of effort?"

In other words, how do we harness "the global movement of outrage on the part of ordinary citizens against an increasingly unfair and unsustainable society" and join it with "practical, creative, and committed social entrepreneurs" so that Humpty Dumpty is not simply recast the same as he was? For Hartigan, succeeding in this way is to ensure that when "our collective story is told, it will be about depicting the time that occurred when human ingenuity, empathy, and integrity rises to dominance together to address unprecedented threats."

Our world is awash in urgent environmental, human, and social challenges. Many of them—the scourge of global poverty, for instance—are interdependent, dynamic, and seemingly intractable. What we know about how to solve them is far from complete. Not only are these global challenges urgent, but their scale is also growing at rates that appear beyond the capacity of our institutions to adapt. Are governments, philanthropic groups, large companies, and the independent sector equipped for the job? Perhaps not as they are.

Conceptual Roots

The conceptual foundations for this book are rooted in contexts of deep global poverty—contexts where scale matters. In the fifty years from 1962 to 2013, the world population grew from 3.2 billion to 7.1 billion, on a growth trajectory to reach 9.2 billion by 2050.[2] Imagine our increasingly fragile planet tripling in population over the course of a single eighty-seven-year lifetime, from 1962 to 2050. Now visualize more than 95 percent of this growth concentrated in poor countries with accelerating rural to urban migrations. Imagine populations ballooning in cities like Beijing, Kolkata, and Mexico City, where millions of people are already choking in traffic congestion and air pollution, and where the combination of infrastructure and fiscal deficits renders governments incapable of meeting basic life-supporting necessities like safe water, sanitation, housing, education, and general public safety. In these contexts and others like them, the ability to develop solutions that can be replicated at scale is urgent.

Especially among refugees and youth trapped in generational poverty, it is little wonder that the world is experiencing unprecedented population migration from destitute rural areas to cities, and from the global south to the global north. Even so, the 2016 Social Progress Index, a major study of social well-being across 133 nations, illuminates what populations migrating in search of greater income opportunities will discover—namely, that geographic advantages in per capita income and human well-being are not synonymous. Just take a look at the United States. Ranked 5th in the world in GDP per capita, the United States ranks 27th out of 133 nations on the Social Progress Index for personal safety; 40th in access to basic knowledge, because too many kids are not in school; 36th in environmental quality due to greenhouse gas emissions, poor water quality, and threats to biodiversity; and

68th on health and wellness, despite outspending every nation in the world on its healthcare system.[3] Over the past twenty-five years, U.S. gains in per capita income have become increasingly concentrated in the top 1 to 5 percent of the population. Median household incomes have stagnated, income inequality has grown, and the majority of citizens have not experienced improvements in quality of life. All of this contributes to nationalist instincts and pushback from citizens who see waves of immigrants as a source of downward pressure on working-class wages and competition for increasingly scarce opportunities to join the middle class.

In the United States, the poverty threshold for a family of four in 2015 was $24,257 per year, approximately $16.50 a day per person.[4] In richer parts of the developing world, it is $4.00 a day per person. And, when purchasing power parity is taken into account, in extremely poor nations, it is $2.00 a day. At these income levels, the poor exist in a precarious state. Above these minimum thresholds, people may not appear in poverty counts, but they do not live in a world where, to paraphrase Nobel Prize–winning economist Amartya Sen, they have the freedom to make life choices that can significantly improve their hopes of a better future.[5] With respect to the hope of achieving a middle-class standard of living, Thomas Piketty's work on global capitalism has painted a pessimistic picture documenting unprecedented increases in income inequality and declining upward mobility over the last thirty years.[6]

Although in 2017 the eight richest people in the world owned more wealth than the 3.6 billion people in the bottom half of the world's population,[7] increasing wealth disparity is not unique to developing countries. The Pew Research Center finds income inequality in the United States at the highest level since 1928.[8] After accounting for taxes and income transfers like social security, the United States is second only to Chile in terms of having the highest level of inequality in the world. Moreover, wealth inequality is even greater than income inequality. In 2013, the highest-earning one-fifth of U.S. families earned 59.1 percent of all income and held 88.9 percent of all wealth. Similarly, in China and India, inequality—as measured by the Gini coefficient (which measures the statistical distribution of incomes)—grew substantially between 1990 and 2015, from 0.45 to 0.51 in India and from 0.33 to 0.53 in China.[9] A Gini coefficient of 0 indicates that citizens shared equally in national income, whereas a coefficient of 1.0 indicates perfect inequality, with one person

Figure 1.1 Social Progress Index

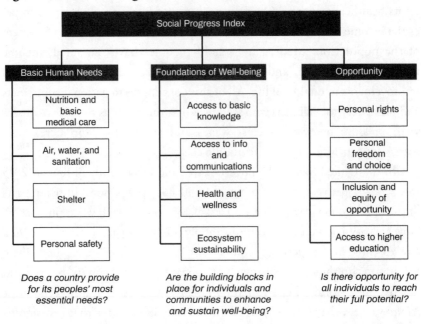

Does a country provide for its peoples' most essential needs?

Are the building blocks in place for individuals and communities to enhance and sustain well-being?

Is there opportunity for all individuals to reach their full potential?

receiving 100 percent of all income. As elsewhere, the inability of India and China to develop and sustain a rising middle class imperils future growth and social stability.

GDP growth alone does not ensure social progress or improved well-being of citizens—both of which often depend on the shifting priorities of governmental bodies. Reflecting Amartya Sen's "development as freedom" philosophy, the Social Progress Imperative movement sees the world differently, as reflected in its Social Progress Index (SPI) in Figure 1.1. It posits a more complete assessment of national wealth—one that encompasses the capacity of a society to meet its citizens' basic human needs, enhance and sustain the quality of their lives, and create the conditions for all individuals to reach their full potential.

While an in-depth examination of poverty is beyond the scope of this book, overall evidence of effective top-down solutions for fostering a more just world—be it in the form of government programs to alleviate poverty or trickle-down economic prosperity—is weak. We turn next to a brief examination of this evidence through a review of alternative approaches for eliminating poverty.

Comparing Approaches to Poverty Reduction

Since the end of World War II and the formation of the United Nations, several efforts have been mounted worldwide to help eliminate or reduce poverty. These efforts can be divided into five categories:

1. **Government programs**: National governments use tax revenues or subsidies and, in some instances, foreign aid to fund or operate programs

2. **Philanthropy**: Wealthy individuals create private foundations, charities raise money to fund or operate programs, and corporate social responsibility (CSR) funds support community initiatives

3. **Multinational corporations**: Large corporations use their resources and organization to enter and serve markets with unmet needs

4. **The informal economy**: A parallel system of economic exchange that, in some instances, uses illegal methods to address problems

5. **Social ventures**: Small organizations (both nonprofit and for-profit) focus on reducing poverty in a specific market segment

Figure 1.2 compares these five approaches to poverty reduction. We will now briefly review the first four poverty reduction approaches. The remainder of the chapter lays the foundation for the advantages of the fifth category, social ventures.

Government and Philanthropy

Although some consider government programs or aid and philanthropy to be distinct approaches to economic development, they are grouped together here because each is based on the assumption that, with adequate resources or external incentives, social systems can be changed from the outside. In the case of government, this perspective encompasses trickle-down theories of economic development, or the belief that macropolicy to stimulate economic growth will have trickle-down benefits to the well-being of those at the lowest rungs of society.[10] In the case of global philanthropy, belief systems encompass a variety of meta-theories—each reflecting alternative models of what constitutes social progress and how best to achieve it in the minds of benefactors and their foundation entities. In either instance, critical

Figure 1.2 Approaches to Poverty Reduction

Factor/Approach	Mission/Focus or Dominant Logic	Economic Efficiency	Understanding of the Problem	Resources
Government programs or aid	Multiple missions; often co-opted to strengthen power/political base; often changing	Usually high overhead, with multiple levels of bureaucracy	Many levels removed from actual clients; lack of empowerment	Finite, often changing
Philanthropic programs	Charity or wealth transfer	Usually high overhead, with at least two levels of bureaucracy	At least one level removed from clients; lack of empowerment	Finite, not often repeatable
Multinational corporations	Profitable revenue growth	Often well-developed and efficient operations, but may not work for reaching low-income customers	Often very limited knowledge of the problems of the poor and state of market development; marketing programs do not work in fractured markets	Amounts based on short-term priorities
Informal economy	Workaround poverty solution	Highly inefficient; may be corrupt	Personal, direct understanding	Limited
Social ventures	Impact on specific poverty problems	Can develop efficient solutions	Personal, direct understanding	Can grow with success of venture

resources needed for achieving social progress are externally controlled at higher institutional levels by the gatekeepers to public or private wealth.

Many economists and politicians, from J. K. Galbraith to Ross Perot and Bernie Sanders, have criticized trickle-down economics as an inefficient way to tackle urgent social needs. However, as with noteworthy success stories from the world of foundations, macropolicy can contribute to economic prosperity across economic strata. When the government invests directly in creating businesses (e.g., manufacturing in China) or accelerating the development of industry clusters in concentrated urban regions, it can have a substantial impact on economic development. For example, in China, the poverty level has dropped from around 80 percent under communism to around 40 percent under government-sponsored capitalism.[11] Similarly, where government acts to stimulate capital formation in emergent technologies (e.g., Defense Advanced Research Projects Agency [DARPA] and advances in computer networking in the United States), significant and widely shared economic benefits can result. Even so, about 14 percent of the U.S. population (about forty-six million people) still lives below the poverty level, and a poverty rate of 40 percent in China equates to five hundred million people.[12] In fact, the socialist approach to economic policy in Sweden fares no better when it comes to eliminating poverty, with 25 percent of Swedish citizens living in poverty.[13]

While targeted government programs and philanthropic initiatives to address poverty or other unmet social needs can fill the gaps in broad-based macropolicy, both are subject to a number of execution risks, including lack of accountability, failure to foster innovation, mindless pursuit of "scale" or size in the presence of inefficiency, economic waste via bureaucratic intermediaries, and the absence of impact measurement or evidence of a return on investment. Social entrepreneurship can ameliorate these risks. In its emphasis on human agency and the development of innovative capacity from the bottom up, it complements the large-scale system-changing goals of governments and global philanthropy.

The Role of Multinational Corporations:
C. K. Prahalad's Thesis

In the presence of global capitalism, business has a vital role to play in creating a more sustainable, just, and prosperous world for all people. In practice, the record is mixed. The UN Millennium Development Goals set a target of reducing the number of people living in extreme poverty by half between 1990 and 2015. Thanks in large measure to free trade, by 2015 the number of the world's seven billion inhabitants subsisting on less than $1.25 a day (the internationally accepted poverty threshold in 1990) had been reduced by half, to 1.1 billion. This definition of poverty, however, is socially constructed, and these subsistence levels of income are associated with fundamental gaps in access to the basic necessities of life—safe water and sanitation, nutrition, quality education, affordable healthcare, transportation, housing, and community safety. To paraphrase Thomas Hobbes, at these subsistence levels, life remains nasty, brutish, and short.

C. K. Prahalad's "Fortune at the Base of the Pyramid" thesis in 2004 posited an optimistic and hopeful view—one in which multinational companies envisioning the bottom four billion of the world's population as a market opportunity would become a wellspring of innovation devoted to serving the urgent unmet needs of humanity and eradicating global poverty. This thesis was challenged by Bill Davidow, founder and partner of Mohr, Davidow Ventures, at Santa Clara University's 2003 Conference "Networked World—Information Technology and Globalization" and later by Ted London in his book *The Base of the Pyramid Promise: Building Businesses with Impact and Scale.* For Davidow, corporate infrastructure is ill equipped to meet the challenging context and specific needs of the world's poor. London's research found that major business contributions beyond case studies and pilots to serve Base of the Pyramid needs have been scant. He posits that big companies have significant *advantages* in low-cost production and distribution as well as in capital efficiency because of their ability to achieve economies of scale. However, they have significant *disadvantages* when it comes to close-to-the-ground appreciations of the life circumstances of the poor, their needs, how to coinvent solutions *with* the poor, and how to overcome the daunting challenges of last-mile distribution in fragmented markets.

The Informal Economy

In the 1980s, a project begun at the University of California Berkeley defined the "informal economy" as the production and distribution of legal goods and services occurring beyond the purview of formal institutions. The project posited that the informal economy resulted from the cost of operating a business within the legal rules of an economy being greater than the costs of operating the same business illegally.[14] This project also documented the size of the informal economy in several countries.

Around the same time, Hernando De Soto, using the same definition, documented the informal economy in three market sectors (housing, retail, and transport) in Peru.[15] De Soto posited that the informal economy was still inefficient in providing goods and services because of the high costs of being "outside" the system. He argued that, to help the informal economy become both more efficient and part of the formal economy, simple laws governing business formation and operation were necessary.

Twenty years later, Prahalad defined "transaction governance capacity" as the system of rules that regulates and supports business formation.[16] Prahalad, like De Soto, felt that the informal economy would continue unless government could ensure that transaction governance costs (the costs of formal rule-based transactions) in the formal economy were less than those costs in the informal economy.

The informal economy dwarfs the formal economy, and it exists as a social institution to fill a void. It is relationship based and has its own norms centered largely on trust and reciprocity. It involves exchange relationships that encompass barter and flexible payment arrangements—arrangements that accommodate the minimal savings and uneven cash flows of the poor.[17] Unfortunately, there is no evidence that the informal economy actually reduces the poverty of its participants. Rather, it seems to be an economic system that accommodates poverty.

Theories of the informal economy are relevant to social entrepreneurs because, in many countries, that is where social ventures still operate. In some cases, social ventures may create a sustainable, scalable business in contexts where transaction governance capacity is low by focusing on how to reduce transaction costs (for example, through m-commerce or electronically mediated access to government services). These kinds of efforts can transform previously unstructured and inefficient markets, including those "subsistence economies" with impediments like a lack of infrastructure and the absence of rule of law for ventures that operate in these economies.[18]

Market Imperfections and Approaches to Poverty Reduction

As we will discuss in chapter 2, Prahalad's thesis of market-based solutions to poverty as an alternative to top-down government solutions or welfare assumed that markets, as we comprehend them, existed at the base of the economic pyramid. In reality, these markets were large—for essential products and services estimated to be $5 trillion—but extremely fragmented.[19] They existed in contexts where the rule of law and the enforceability of contracts were weak, corruption was prevalent, literacy and skill levels were low, and civil engineering deficits were extremely high. In these contexts, market intelligence, awareness of customer needs, and knowledge of the way markets worked were often extremely weak, especially among governmental, philanthropic, and multinational corporations. How barter systems, the absence of fixed pricing, and the conventions of one-to-one sales channels might influence market entry and growth was unknown. Neither were the implications of serving a customer base composed primarily of people working in the informal economy understood. In India, for example, 90 percent of the population is supported by the informal economy with irregular and unpredictable subsistence wages.[20]

In economics, the term "institutional voids" refers to an absence of the institutional arrangements and actors required to enable the smooth functioning of markets.[21] These voids can be reflected in the weak enforcement of formal regulation or contracts, as well as a lack of intermediaries and public infrastructure—factors that raise transaction costs and, as a consequence, significantly hinder market-type activity. From a transaction cost economics perspective, the absence of a fully developed institutional context—including well-defined property rights, rules of exchange, and legal recourse—undermines the emergence of well-functioning capital, labor, and product markets.[22] Where such formal institutional arrangements are lacking, they are frequently supplemented by local norms and traditions—both of which are poorly understood by major companies. This makes an understanding of the landscape of potential partners in local operating environments crucial to enterprise success.

Innovation for the Base of the Pyramid requires deep empathy with specific user needs and the constraints of their contexts. The poor are not an undifferentiated mass. For example, in her study of Grameen Shakti's approach to energy markets in Bangladesh, Nancy Wimmer discovered different design requirements for addressing various BOP income and occupational segments (e.g., farmer, fisherman, merchants, craftsmen, teachers, clinics, schools). While the scale of Shakti's off-grid lighting solutions for the poor was miniscule in comparison with offerings in developed economies, the unit size and configuration of offerings still varied substantially. At Shakti and elsewhere, distribution modalities also vary substantially depending on BOP income segments.[23]

BOP markets must be viewed on their own terms, with their own logic. Their characteristics are quite different from the well-articulated markets served by multinational and major companies in advanced economies. In some instances, the latter may be mature markets approaching saturation—a circumstance that Prahalad hypothesized would stimulate interest in serving nascent BOP markets. Still, big companies understand these well-defined markets—and it is here where their cost structures and operating styles fit most comfortably.

Advantages of Bottom-Up Innovation through Social Ventures

Taking a more proximate or bottom-up view involves migrating from a vision of "serving markets" to one of "developing these markets." This entails a process of co-creation in environments with unique traditions, customs, and ground-level dynamics.[24] For the most part, big companies have either ignored or been ineffective in these settings, whereas start-ups are beginning to chart a path to market creation. Their underlying rationales are often quite different from those of classic for-profit firms.[25] Frequently, they assume a hybrid orientation, intending to be economically viable while making a societal impact at the same time.[26] In this regard, they represent a more humanistic logic than the impersonal forms of market exchange that characterize advanced economies.[27]

In working with social entrepreneurs from developing countries, we realized that we had more to learn than we had to teach. Their proximate view as bottom-up innovators provides economies of interaction and learning that are inaccessible to big-company strategists and government technocrats—or to us in the hallways of our university setting. These entrepreneurs are in continuous dialogue with those they serve, listening to voices we may never hear. In contexts of extreme resource scarcity, they work with underserved populations to coinvent product and service solutions to some of the most difficult problems in the world. In these settings, markets must be created. Here, bottom-up approaches to social innovation and market creation have advantages in

- adapting the best practices in social marketing and behavioral change to local contexts,

- utilizing existing supply chain infrastructure to complement organizational capabilities,

- tapping local customer financing through regional banks or established microfinance institutions,

- leveraging social capital and local network acumen to access stakeholder resources, and

- combining technology advances with bottom-up innovation requirements on the basis of deep empathy with local needs.

The two examples we use in chapters 4–12, Grameen Shakti and Sankara, illustrate how these advantages work in practice. Shakti leveraged these advantages to become the world's largest solar home provider. Sankara did so to become the world's largest provider of affordable eye care. From our work with organizations like Shakti and Sankara, we believe that social entrepreneurs who can integrate their bottom-up perspectives with the knowledge of seasoned entrepreneurs about how to grow a business hold great promise for successful ventures that serve the poor.

Building a successful venture to serve marginalized populations in settings with low trust in government and outsiders requires a deep appreciation of the local customs, sociopolitical structures, and norms that form the basis for local systems of economic exchange. The bottom-up and participatory approach to enterprise development and market creation in this guide for social entrepreneurs contrasts with top-down methods that have dominated government policy and the BOP market entry strategies of multinational companies. It integrates social innovation with design for affordability as critical factors in serving the poor.[28] It is consistent with research by Jain and Koch that underscores the importance of embedding solutions in local ecosystems.[29] In their in-depth case analysis of off-grid BOP enterprises they conclude that viable solutions ultimately "involve mixing and matching state of the art technologies with indigenous knowledge, as well as an appreciation of resident absorptive capacity," a process they call "indigenization." They suggest that it is possible to address both economic viability and affordability constraints "through the development of micro-provisioning mechanisms that involve understanding unit economics across improvised value chains." And finally, they highlight the importance of having incentive plans and logistics "for last mile agent-based sales and service" when "co-producing and embedding solutions" in BOP environments. With these kinds of arrangements at the ecosystem level, "organizations can increase capital efficiency, align solutions with the informal rules of exchange, and tap into extant trust-based social structures, thereby securing legitimacy for their endeavors."

Social entrepreneurs are leading the way in discovering how to serve these distinct markets:

- They have superior knowledge of customer needs and practical knowledge of how to create compelling value equations through cost reduction or enhancing customer value.

- They possess knowledge about how culture, language, symbols, and opinion leaders shape attitudes. This knowledge enhances their ability to make effective use of local media (e.g., through imaginative soap operas for educating customers or mobile platform applications in the local language).

- They understand local distribution and how existing channels might be appropriated to reach customers.

- They understand local stakeholders and, as we address in chapter 5, how they might be enlisted to mitigate risks or leveraged through value chain innovation.

Unlike multinational companies that enter Base of the Pyramid markets from the outside, social entrepreneurs build enterprises and markets from an inside or bottom-up perspective. In settings where word of mouth is critical, they understand the bases of trust and how specific elements of brand identity influence early adoption and wider market penetration.

To Recap

In this chapter we examined top-down and bottom-up approaches to serving unmet human needs. In the context of market-based solutions, we revisited the "eradicating poverty through profits" thesis of the late C. K. Prahalad and the BOP innovation leadership role he envisioned for major companies. While there is growing evidence of innovation, social entrepreneurs, rather than major companies, are leading. Their proximate view of these unserved markets holds particular promise for producing transformative change in Base of the Pyramid communities.

The growth of social entrepreneurship as a field coincides with the emergence of a "fourth sector" that bridges the rationalities of public, private, and nonprofit or philanthropic organizations. At the nexus of this convergence, social entrepreneurship is unleashing creativity and becoming a potential wellspring of ideas for disruptive innovation. In contrast to charity, big companies that are driven by short-term profits and often viewed as extractive— or distrusted governments widely viewed as offering bureaucratic solutions gamed by incumbent actors for private gain—social entrepreneurs are rooted in local contexts and perceived as empowering local communities. They are a vital source of research and development because they are on the ground, addressing the challenges of market creation in the specific context of resource constraints and market imperfections.

Pamela Hartigan's 2012 speech at the Skoll World Forum described as outrage the response of "ordinary citizens against an increasingly unfair and unsustainable society." This outrage was reflected in a July 26, 2013, editorial by Peter Buffett:[30]

> It's time for a new operating system. Not a 2.0 or a 3.0, but something built from the ground up—a new code. What we have is a crisis of imagination. Albert Einstein said that you cannot solve a problem with the same mind-set that created it. Foundation dollars should be the best "risk capital" out there. There are people working hard at showing examples of other ways to live in a functioning society that truly creates greater prosperity for all (and I don't mean more people getting to have more stuff).
>
> Money should be spent trying out concepts that shatter current structures and systems that have turned much of the world into one vast market. Is progress really Wi-Fi on every street corner? No. It's when no 13-year-old girl on the planet gets sold for sex. But as long as most folks are patting themselves on the back for charitable acts, we've got a perpetual poverty machine. It's an old story; we really need a new one.

As many will recall from childhood memories of Humpty Dumpty, all the king's horses and all the king's men couldn't put Humpty together again. The top-down, macroeconomy approaches of governments to eradicate poverty reflect the orthodoxies of political majorities that float above the realities of impoverished communities. As with the outside-in efforts of major companies to develop market-based solutions to poverty, they often suffer from a lack of connectedness with the lives of real people. This empathy deficit undermines an appreciation of market failure and deep thinking about the factors that hold unjust equilibriums in place. In this context, macromeasures of economic well-being like GDP per capita mask the realities of inequality, widespread poverty, and the systemic barriers to social progress. In this chapter we tried to show why existing approaches (governmental, philanthropic, and corporate) have fallen short. In the next chapter, we take a closer look at the market at the Base of the Pyramid.

Background Resources

Ansari, Shahzad, Kamal Munir, and Tricia Gregg. "Impact at the 'Bottom of the Pyramid': The Role of Social Capital in Capability Development and Community Empowerment." *Journal of Management Studies* 49, no. 4 (2012): 813–842.

Battilana, Julie, and Matthew Lee. "Advancing Research on Hybrid Organizing—Insights from the Study of Social Enterprises." *Academy of Management Annals* 8 (2014): 397–441.

Bugg-Llevine, Antony, and Jed Emerson. *Impact Investing: Transforming How We Make Money While Making a Difference.* New York: John Wiley and Sons, 2011.

Coase, R. H. "The Problem of Social Cost." *Journal of Law and Economics* 3 (October 1960): 1–44.

Desa, Geoffrey, and James Koch. "Building Sustainable Social Ventures at the Base of the Pyramid." *Journal of Social Entrepreneurship* 8 (2014): 146–174.

De Soto, Hernando. *The Other Path.* New York: Harper and Row, 1989.

The Economist. "Poverty Elucidation Day." October 20, 2014.

Forbes. "America Has Less Poverty Than Sweden." September 10, 2012.

Grimes, Matthew G., Jeffery S. McMullen, Timothy J. Vogus, and Toyah L. Miller. "Studying the Origins of Social Entrepreneurship." *Academy of Management Review* 38, no. 3 (July 1, 2013): 460–463.

Hammond, A., W. Kramer, J. Tran, R. Katz, and W. Courtland. *The Next 4 Billion: Market Size and Business Strategy at the Base of the Pyramid.* Washington, DC: World Resources Institute, 2007.

Jain, S., and J. Koch. "Articulated Embedding in the Development of Markets for Under-Served Communities: The Case of Clean-Energy Provision to Off-Grid Publics." Academy of Management Annual Conference, Vancouver, BC, August 2015.

Jain, S., and J. Koch. "Conceptualizing Markets for Underserved Communities." In *Sustainability, Society, Business Ethics, and Entrepreneurship*, edited by A. Guerber and G. Markman, 71–91. Singapore: World Scientific Publishing, 2016.

Khanna, Tarun, and Krishna G. Palepu. "Why Focused Strategies May Be Wrong for Emerging Markets." *Harvard Business Review*, July-August 1997.

London, Ted. *The Base of the Pyramid Promise—Building Businesses with Impact and Scale*. Stanford, CA: Stanford University Press, 2016.

Piketty, Thomas. *Capital in the Twenty-First Century*. Cambridge, MA: Belknap Press of Harvard University Press, 2014.

Portes, Alejandro, Manuel Castells, and Lauren A. Benton, eds. *The Informal Economy*. Baltimore: Johns Hopkins University Press, 1989.

Prahalad, C. K. *The Fortune at the Bottom of the Pyramid: Eradicating Poverty through Profits*. Philadelphia: Wharton School Publishing, 2010.

Social Progress Index. "2017 Social Progress Index." Accessed March 14, 2018. https://www.socialprogressindex.com/.

Sowell, Thomas. *Trickle Down Theory*. Stanford, CA: Hoover Institution Press, 2012.

Sridharan, S., and M. Viswanathan. "Marketing in Subsistence Marketplaces: Consumption and Entrepreneurship in a South Indian Context." *Journal of Consumer Marketing* 25, no. 7 (2008): 455–462.

Viswanathan, Madhu. *Bottom-Up Enterprise: Insights from Subsistence Marketplaces*. eBookpartnership: eText and Stripes Publishing, 2016.

Williamson, Oliver E. *The Economic Institutions of Capitalism*. New York: Simon & Schuster, 1985.

Wimmer, Nancy. *Green Energy for a Billion Poor*. Vatterstetten: MCRE Verlag, 2012.

Chapter 2

The Market at the Base of the Pyramid

In his 2004 book, *The Fortune at the Base of the Pyramid*, C. K. Prahalad posited that the problems of the poor should be treated as a market—a market of potential customers with money and needs. He described this market as both urban and rural, both price-conscious and value-conscious—with a (counterintuitive) preference for brands. Without giving much detail on the size of this market, he described it as a profit opportunity for those companies that can overcome two major challenges: (1) how to provide affordable, easy-to-use solutions for the significant problems of the poor; and (2) how to provide ease of access to those solutions. Before examining this claim in greater detail, let's shed some light on the size and structure of the BOP as a market.

The Size of the BOP Market

In 2007, a couple of years after Prahalad's book was first published, the World Resources Institute (WRI) and the International Finance Corporation commissioned a study, under the leadership of Al Hammond, to try to quantify the market at the base of the economic pyramid.[1] The study estimated that the four billion poor people in the world had about $5 trillion in spending power (Figure 2.1). Since the 2007 study, the world's population has expanded from 6 billion to over 7.2 billion with the number of poor people rising from 4 to 4.5 billion. The World Bank's Global Consumption Database[2] confirms the analyses of the WRI study of how the poor spend more than $5 trillion a year (Figure 2.2).

Figure 2.1 BOP Spending

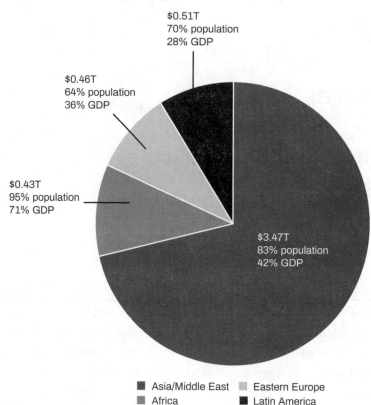

Source: A. Hammond, W. Kramer, J. Tran, R. Katz, and W. Courtland, *The Next 4 Billion: Market Size and Business Strategy at the Base of the Pyramid (Washington, DC: World Resources Institute, 2007), 28.*

Asia and the Middle East, containing both China and India, was by far the largest geographic segment. In it the poor constituted about 83 percent of the total population; their $3.47T (trillion) in spending represented 42 percent of the segment's total GDP. In Latin America, the poor represented a slightly smaller percentage (70 percent) of the population, but a much smaller portion (28 percent) of the overall GDP. This smaller percentage of GDP may account for the informal economy being much larger in Latin America than in Asia. Eastern Europe was slightly smaller than Latin America in terms of total spending and of the percentage of the population that was poor, and the poor spent slightly more of total GDP. But it was in Africa that the poor represented the largest percentage of the population (95 percent) and spent the largest percentage of the GDP (71 percent). All of this is to say that the poor do represent a potentially large

Figure 2.2 Global Poverty

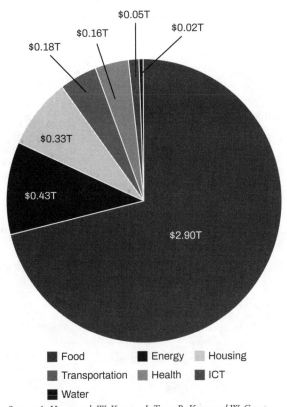

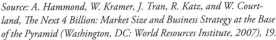

Source: A. Hammond, W. Kramer, J. Tran, R. Katz, and W. Court-land, The Next 4 Billion: Market Size and Business Strategy at the Base of the Pyramid (Washington, DC: World Resources Institute, 2007), 19.

market, both in terms of total spending and in terms of the percentage of the GDP that such spending represents. And while much of the discussion in this chapter surrounds countries that can largely be classified as part of the BOP market, such markets can also be found in so-called developed countries (such as the United States) where the majority of the market is not part of the BOP market.

The WRI study also reported on vertical market segments, or particular categories of spending. While there was some variation by geography, in general, the study found that the poor spent their money in seven main categories: food, water, energy, housing, transportation, health, and information and communication technology.

It should come as no surprise that food represented over half of spending. More surprising is that energy (for lighting and cooking) was the

Figure 2.3   ICT Spending Growth

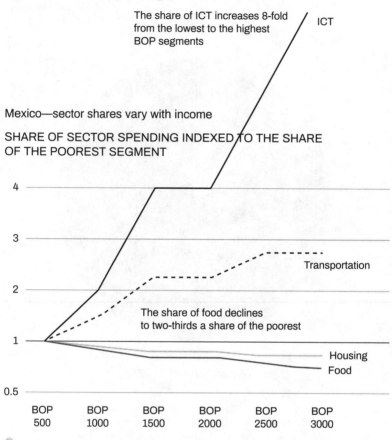

The share of ICT increases 8-fold from the lowest to the highest BOP segments

ICT

Mexico—sector shares vary with income

SHARE OF SECTOR SPENDING INDEXED TO THE SHARE OF THE POOREST SEGMENT

Transportation

The share of food declines to two-thirds a share of the poorest

Housing
Food

| | | | | | |
| BOP 500 | BOP 1000 | BOP 1500 | BOP 2000 | BOP 2500 | BOP 3000 |

WORLD RESOURCES INSTITUTE

Source: A. Hammond, W. Kramer, J. Tran, R. Katz, and W. Courtland, The Next 4 Billion: Market Size and Business Strategy at the Base of the Pyramid (Washington, DC: World Resources Institute, 2007), 14.

second-largest area of spending—ahead of both housing and transportation.

In the area of information and communication technology (ICT), a significant amount of spending is for cell phones or cell phone time. For instance, in 2015, cell phone penetration in Africa exceeded 80 percent.[3] This has enabled the market for mobile banking to explode and accelerated the diffusion of household solar solutions through pay-as-you-go business models. Here and elsewhere, as individuals move from the poorest of the poor to mid and higher segments of the BOP, spending on ICT grows dramatically (Figure 2.3).

A similar pattern exists in energy consumption, where simple solar lanterns represent an entry-level product. The poor are seen migrating away from entry-level products to more expensive solar home systems as they move from the BOP 1000 to the BOP 3000. The economic benefits of access to energy are well documented, so it comes as little surprise that a rapidly growing market exists for the targeted use solutions of organizations like Grameen Shakti in a wide variety of occupations—from farmers to fishermen, merchants, craftsmen, and nurses in rural health clinics. In these and many other contexts, access to energy increases productivity and incomes. The correlation between energy access and income suggests that the BOP market for energy may be much greater than the estimated $433 billion derived from year 2000 household expenditures for kerosene and other inferior sources of energy. With the discovery of a host of specific energy market segments by social entrepreneurs and rising incomes in developing countries, it is estimated that this energy market now exceeds $1 trillion.[4]

So, the BOP market, as first sized by the WRI study, represents at least $5 trillion in annual spending on essential products and services, with seven major segments. We next examine the urban/rural nature of the BOP market and its dynamics since the WRI study.

Poverty as a Concentrated Problem

Within the countries with the greatest concentrations of extreme poverty—particularly Asia, Latin America, and Africa (Figure 2.4)—the percentage of people living in extreme poverty is substantially greater in rural areas than in urban centers. This is one factor driving migrations to major cities and peri-urban areas—areas often lacking the essential water, sanitation, housing, and transportation services to accommodate the influx. Similarly, civil war and high percentages of poverty in the global south are driving migration to the global north.

Despite this reality, some still see reason to cheer the "unprecedented economic growth" that has pulled more than a billion people "out of poverty in one of the greatest recent achievements in human history."[5] And yet, virtually all of this "progress" stems from globalization—from manufacturing in China and elsewhere to the outsourcing of IT services to a wide range of countries in the global south, most notably India. If you believe that living on $1.90 a day is social progress, then it is time to declare victory. But if you take a good, hard look at the daily lives of the poor and the work

Figure 2.4 Global Distribution of Poverty

A Concentrated Problem

Although the percentage of people living under extreme poverty has fallen sharply, more than 700 million people remain in such dire straits.

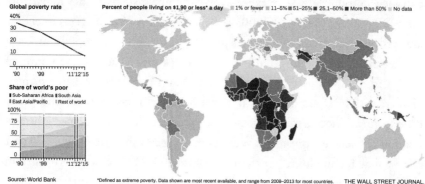

Source: World Bank   *Defined as extreme poverty. Data shown are most recent available, and range from 2008–2013 for most countries.   THE WALL STREET JOURNAL.

of social entrepreneurs who seek to empower them, you will see another reality entirely—a reality made up of huge unmet human needs and opportunities to improve life choices of the poor through market-based solutions to poverty.

Problems and Opportunities at the BOP

As an overview of significant possible market opportunities for social ventures, it is useful to try to understand the key problems of those who make up the population of the BOP market. Two efforts at the United Nations—the Millennium Development Goals (MDGs) and the Sustainable Development Goals (SDGs)—provide insight into these problems and opportunities.

The MDGs: Improving Life Choices

In *Development as Freedom*, Nobel Prize–winning economist Amartya Sen argues eloquently that what the poor really want is *improving life choices*.[6] His thinking and that of other economists were influential in developing the UN's 2000 MDGs. By 2015, these goals sought to[7]

1. eradicate extreme poverty;

2. achieve universal education;

3. promote gender equality and empower women;

4. reduce child mortality;

5. improve maternal health;

6. combat HIV/AIDS, malaria, and other diseases;

7. ensure environmental sustainability; and

8. develop a global partnership for development.

By 2015, each of these goals had come closer to being realized. For one, the number of people living in extreme poverty (defined in the MDGs as living on less than $1.25 a day) was cut in half. And between 2000 and 2015, the proportion of undernourished people, the number of children attending primary school, maternal and childhood mortality rates, and the rate of new HIV infections all saw marked improvements. National, international, and multilateral agencies, as well as the work of foundations and on-the-ground innovators like social entrepreneurs, all contributed to progress in these areas.

While there is much to celebrate in the MDG report of 2015, in the final analysis, social progress cannot be measured by counting the number of people above a socially defined subsistence level of income. Its essence must be reflected in transformative change that truly improves life choices.

The SDGs

The 2016 SDGs of the United Nations sought to capture what had been learned from the MDGs and to go further—to reflect the increasing scale and complexity of the work to be done in a world that had grown by more than a billion people since the MDGs were created. The SDGs posed seventeen new goals, which, like the MDGs, indicate market opportunities for social ventures.

Goal 1: End poverty in all its forms, everywhere.

Unlike the original MDGs, goal 1 acknowledges the systemic nature of poverty and its relationship to malnutrition, access to education and basic services, social discrimination, and barriers to participation in decision making. In each of these instances, poverty is both a cause and an outcome of systemic factors.[8]

Goal 2: End hunger in all its forms everywhere.

Here the SDGs underscore the interdependence between people-centered rural development in agriculture, forestry, and fisheries and the need to protect fragile environmental ecosystems. The SDGs place a greater emphasis on the influence of environmental degradation and climate change on urban migration and risks to food security.[9]

**Goal 3:   Ensure healthy lives and promote well-being
               for all at all ages.**

By integrating elements from the MDGs on child mortality, maternal health, and combating disease, goal 3 takes a more systemic and comprehensive stance relative to the challenges of ensuring healthy lives and promoting well-being for all ages.[10]

**Goal 4:   Ensure inclusive and quality education for all and promote
               lifelong learning.**

Goal 4 recognizes the inextricable link between education, quality of life, and economic development. In so doing it encourages a more systemic perspective on development than the MDGs, which counted kids in primary school as a proxy for success.[11]

Goal 5:   Achieve gender equality and empower all women and girls.

Goal 5 frames the issue of gender equality in a more holistic manner than the related MDG. It extends well beyond equal access to primary education to aspirations for gender equality in healthcare, decent work, and representation in economic and political decision making as foundations for a more peaceful, prosperous, and sustainable world. It posits a systemic link between gender equality and social transformation.[12]

Goal 6:   Ensure access to water and sanitation for all.

Despite progress from 2000 to 2015—most notably through the work of bottom-up innovators—the systemic challenges of addressing access to safe water and sanitation have become more onerous due to growing water scarcity and human wastewater discharge into rivers and seas, as well as more severe droughts and floods, and other natural disasters attributed to climate change. This goal acknowledges the embedded nature of water and sanitation challenges in a more complex ecological context.[13]

**Goal 7:   Ensure access to affordable, reliable, sustainable,
               and modern energy for all.**

Given the pivotal role access to affordable clean energy plays in meeting the global challenges of job creation, ensuring food security, increasing incomes, and mitigating climate change risks, it is surprising that goal 7 was not central to the original MDGs.[14]

Goal 8:   Promote inclusive and sustainable economic growth, employment, and decent work for all.

Around the world, the inability to create quality jobs in proportion to the size and growth of populations has led to erosion of the social contract and, in many instances, political instability. Many social entrepreneurs and impact investors count the number of jobs created as an "outcome"—a measure of success. But having a meager job does not guarantee an escape from poverty. With half the world's population still living on the equivalent of less than two dollars a day, goal 8 calls for a retooling of economic and social policies aimed at poverty eradication. What is needed here is a combination of sound macropolicy and bottom-up innovation.[15]

Goal 9:   Build resilient infrastructure, promote sustainable industrialization, and foster innovation.

Up until now, virtually all of the bottom-up work of social entrepreneurs has assumed major civil engineering deficits to be a given. Goal 9 recognizes the vital importance of investments in infrastructure—transportation, irrigation, energy, and ICT—to productivity, achieving sustainable development, and empowering communities. Improvements in infrastructure and advancements in access to technology are critical complements to bottom-up innovation that the MDGs failed to acknowledge.

Goal 9 recognizes that technology and industrial scale innovation are critical to raising incomes and extending the horizons for social change beyond what bottom-up innovation alone can achieve. This perspective both reframes the possibilities for eradicating poverty and calls for public-private partnerships and cross-sector collaborations.[16]

Goal 10:   Reduce inequality within and among countries.

Goal 10 tackles rising inequality—an issue not previously addressed in the MDGs but one of growing concern in the global economy. Growth as measured in GDP is not sufficient to ameliorate poverty or provide access to quality healthcare and education services for disadvantaged and marginalized populations.[17]

Goal 11:   Make cities inclusive, safe, resilient, and sustainable.

Goal 11 acknowledges unprecedented urban migration and the challenges it poses for livable cities:[18]

- Half of humanity—3.5 billion people—lives in cities today; by 2030, this number will rise to 60 percent of the world's population.

- Ninety-five percent of urban expansion in the next decades will take place in the developing world.

- Eight hundred and twenty-eight million people live in slums today—and the number keeps rising.

Cities occupy just 3 percent of the earth's land, but account for 60–80 percent of energy consumption and 75 percent of carbon emissions.[19] In addition, rapid urbanization is exerting pressure on freshwater supplies, sewage, the living environment, and public health.

Despite these alarming statistics, high-density cities are still viewed as bringing efficiency gains and technological innovation while reducing resource and energy consumption. A combination of top-down and bottom-up innovation is needed to achieve SDG targets for affordable housing, sustainable environment, transport, inclusive planning, and natural disaster preparedness.[20]

Goal 12: Ensure sustainable consumption and production patterns.

The challenges here are many and ultimately require reframing the concept of economic value to account for externalities as well as to foster business engagement in new forms of collaboration with government and across value chains. In the words of the SDGs themselves, it means "doing more and better with less"—in essence, minimizing resource use and negative externalities while improving quality of life. This goal means approaching production and consumption systemically, involving stakeholders from direct consumers to policy makers, and raising consumer awareness around sustainable lifestyle choices.

Value chain innovation is a significant driver of entrepreneurial ventures at the Base of the Pyramid (and a consideration across virtually every element in the business planning process described in chapters 4 through 10). Given a booming population, an expanding life span, and the existential threats of climate change, issues related to economic development must be reframed to encompass sustainability if we are to act as stewards for the quality of life for future generations.[21]

Goal 13: Take urgent action to combat climate change and its impacts.

Goal 13 acknowledges the clear evidence of a causal link between greenhouse gas emissions from human activities and the urgent threats climate change poses to our collective lives. Its achievement requires solutions coordinated at international levels and effectively implemented locally. Affordable and scalable solutions are now available to enable leapfrogging to cleaner, more resilient economies. In spite of the apparent withdrawal of the United States at the time of this writing, the recently ratified Paris Agreement and the quickening pace of grassroots efforts to turn to renewable energy illustrate the critical importance of combining top-down and bottom-up innovation to mitigate the existential risks of climate change.[22]

Goal 14: Conserve and sustainably use the oceans, seas, and marine resources.

Goal 14, together with SDGs 12, 13, and 15, reflects the more comprehensive environmental ecosystem emphasis taken by the SDGs compared with the narrower and less systemic approach to sustainability in the 2000 MDGs. Goal 14 recognizes the interdependence of life on earth—three-fourths of which is covered by oceans. It targets temperature, chemistry, currents, ocean life, and other factors that drive global systems and "make the Earth habitable for humankind."[23]

Goal 15: Sustainably manage forests, combat desertification, halt and reverse land degradation, and halt biodiversity loss.

Managing and combating desertification have been elevated to a specific SDG because of the urgent risks posed by human activities. Goal 15 references the loss of thirteen million hectares of forests every year and arable land losses at thirty to thirty-five times historical rates. Globally, 74 percent of the poor are directly affected by land degradation, 2.6 billion people depend directly on agriculture, and 1.6 billion depend on forests for livelihoods.[24] Here, as with other SDGs, there is an emphasis on viewing poverty from a larger systems perspective.

Goal 16: Promote just, peaceful, and inclusive societies.

Anyone who has worked with social entrepreneurs at the Base of the Pyramid quickly learns to appreciate the pervasiveness of corruption and its impact on venture development. "Corruption, bribery, theft, and tax evasion cost about U.S. $1.26 trillion for developing countries per year."[25] Those charged with enforcement of contracts and rule of law—the judiciary and police—are themselves frequently active participants in corrupt practices. In a similar vein, in 2011, the unraveling of social order in conflict regions contributed to a 50 percent rate of children leaving school. Goal 16 posits that development and the rule of law are interrelated. Formal markets reduce transaction costs and can make corruption more transparent—potential benefits of market-based solutions to poverty.[26]

Goal 17: Revitalize the global partnership for sustainable development.

Goal 17 posits that a successful sustainable development agenda requires partnerships between governments, the private sector, and civil society. These inclusive partnerships are "built upon principles and values, a shared vision, and shared goals that place people and the planet at the center."[27]

Large-Scale Systems Thinking

As we have noted, the SDGs differ in important ways from the original MDGs. While the latter were narrowly defined and more easily measured, the SDGs are defined in a way that requires systems thinking, greater accountability for outcomes, and a deeper understanding of causality in the presence of counterfactual evidence. For example, the MDG of increasing incomes above $1.25 per day was met largely through manufacturing migrating to regions with cheap labor—often with deplorable working conditions and poor environmental standards. This example also illustrates why it is so important to carefully define goals to make sure that meeting them actually benefits the intended beneficiaries.

The SDGs acknowledge the complex web of interdependent actors that hold unjust and unsustainable equilibria in place. They call for greater local accountability and an emphasis on systems thinking to

- integrate people-centered development with an increased priority for protecting fragile ecosystems,

- acknowledge interdependence among various goals, and

- emphasize the financing of infrastructure that is critical to support innovation and inclusive growth (Note: Civil engineering deficits were largely ignored in the MDGs).

In several instances, the SDGs extend the narrower focus of earlier MDGs. For example, they

- emphasize health and well-being for all life stages, as opposed to the narrower MDG focus on maternal health and more readily measured child mortality;

- emphasize inclusive lifelong quality education—beyond the MDG focus on primary school education—as a driver of economic growth;

- extend the emphasis on gender equality to the contexts of healthcare, decent work, and political decision making as a critical antecedent to a more just and prosperous world; and

- elevate the growing issue of economic inequality as a politically destabilizing concern.

In addition, the SDGs define new priority areas:

- The need to develop resilient and sustainable cities in the context of mass urban migrations—a priority largely ignored in the MDGs

- The increasingly urgent need for a comprehensive emphasis on environmental sustainability in all its forms—from systems of production and consumption to conserving water, land, and air ecosystems

- The salience of justice, peace, and corruption as significant potential barriers to be overcome in any effort to support sustainable progress

Our world has changed significantly since the year 2000. The SDGs place a renewed emphasis on the need for collaboration between government, the private sector, and civil society. It is here—where top-down goals and the bottom-up aspirations of communities meet—that social entrepreneurs have the greatest potential to catalyze social progress. They bring a depth of empathy for human needs and an ability to build the regional networks of trust and reciprocity needed for system solutions to find fertile ground.

Market-Creation Requirements for Serving Marginalized Populations

We began this chapter with C. K. Prahalad's assertion that unmet human needs at the Base of the Pyramid are a profit opportunity for companies that can overcome two major challenges: (1) how to provide affordable, easy-to-use solutions for the significant problems of the poor, and (2) how to provide ease of access to such solutions. While this assertion has catalyzed a great deal of activity, it oversimplifies value equation requirements for serving the poor, the challenges of market creation, and the degree of innovation required in enterprise development. Affordability, ease of use, and access are necessary but insufficient conditions for serving the poor.

Value Creation

Martin and Osberg suggest two broad categories of change mechanisms for improving the value of products and services to marginalized populations.[28] The first of these is *value-increasing mechanisms*—mechanisms that increase the value of products or services with no increase in cost to beneficiaries. They illustrate this type of mechanism with three examples:

1. Leveraging information transparency standards (e.g., Fair Trade, Marine Stewardship Council[29])

2. Adding value to existing assets through new methodologies (e.g., One Acre Fund, ESOKO)

3. Developing measurement rubrics to reframe government concepts of value and accountability in such areas as clean air, education, and global supply chains

In addition to value-increasing mechanics, Martin and Osberg talk about *cost-lowering mechanisms*—essentially mechanisms that lower costs without decreasing benefits or the value of products and services. They identify four examples of this mechanism:

1. Substituting lower-cost labor. The example of Sankara throughout the book illustrates how training allows the substituting of lower-cost labor. Living Goods also provides an excellent example of leveraging lower-cost labor with enabling ICT.[30]

2. Lowering the total cost of product ownership or services. Medical Technology Transfer Systems is an example of how simplified product design can lower total costs of ownership. Its infant warmer, phototherapy, and other neonatal technologies offer hospitals and clinics in poor countries more reliable, easier-to-use devices with low operating costs.

3. Lowering capital costs (CAPEX) by borrowing technology from one context for use in another. An excellent example is International Development Enterprises India (IDEI) treadle pumps and low-cost drip irrigation solutions, in which the components of the pumps and irrigation solutions are used in other products.[31]

4. Developing platform technologies with inherent economies of scale. Both Kiva and Medic Mobile accomplished inherent economies of scale (very low marginal costs) with software that scales simply by adding users to the system.[32]

These value-increasing and cost-lowering examples extend Prahalad's earlier "affordable, easy to use, and ease of access" value equation for serving the poor. In particular, they suggest that there may be significant points of leverage for large-scale change through applying ICT in innovative ways—to improve global supply chains and increase their environmental sustainability.

These value equation examples suggest that serving unmet human needs at the BOP requires both technology and business model innovation. An empirical study of five off-grid energy companies by Jain and Koch found that serving those in extreme poverty requires companies to develop innovation capability in (1) indigenizing technology (e.g., pay-as-you-go solar lanterns), (2) microprovisioning (e.g., thirty-watt solar home systems), and (3) embedding (e.g., integrating assembly, customer finance, and after-sales solutions in local geographies).[33] In a similar vein, Desa and Koch posit that locally embedded social entrepreneurs may pursue more comprehensive and transformative missions.[34] Where entrepreneurs who enter BOP markets from the outside tend to emphasize breadth scaling—the goal of penetrating wider geographic markets with a specific product or service solution to a narrowly defined problem and customer need—locally embedded entrepreneurs may focus, instead, on depth scaling (providing more products and services customized to the same beneficiaries).

The wide range of value equation examples we've observed suggests that BOP innovation is reframing the conventional concepts of customer value, commonly stated as:

Value = Benefits/Cost, *where benefit can be stated in the form of an economic surplus*

In BOP contexts, the following statement more fully elaborates processes for designing, delivering, and embedding solutions with customers and partners across innovative value chains:

Value = (Benefits + Value Chain Innovation) / (Direct Cost + Costs of Access)

This equation reflects the importance of value creation efforts to address structural parameters, and affordability constraints that exist in engaging with and serving BOP markets.

Market Creation

To overcome physical infrastructure deficits, the absence of quality assurance norms or verifiable certification standards, and asymmetries in market intelligence due to the informal nature of markets, market creation in a BOP setting requires value chain innovation. In addition, the absence of transparent regulatory provisions, contract law, property rights, and institutional voids in banking contributes to the challenges of market creation.

In *The Base of the Pyramid Promise—Building Businesses for Impact and Scale*, Ted London summarizes the challenges in demand creation and supply enhancement at the BOP. The former entails competing against nonconsumption in previously underserved or unserved markets.[35] This requires awareness raising, trust building, and, in many instances, overcoming culturally ingrained behaviors. In addition, creating economic buyers may require customer financing or cross-subsidized pricing schemes. In some instances, market creation may also involve advocacy for smart government subsidies to stimulate demand or mitigate perverse incentives.

Supply enhancement takes many forms in BOP markets. Technology solutions need to be designed for settings with minimal infrastructure, including the lack of access to reliable energy and after-sales service capacities. Technologies must be durable and easy to use. Products also need to be affordable and provided in microunits for households with extremely limited and frequently irregular cash flows. On the flip side of supplier enhancement, the poor must also be considered as suppliers in need of better inputs to increase productivity and the value of their outputs in agriculture and other areas. They are also in need of aggregation mechanisms to increase bargaining power in distant markets.

To Recap

Our approach to developing successful social ventures evolved out of more than a decade of work in challenging market creation environments. It acknowledges gaps in formal market intelligence and the need to ground solutions in a deep appreciation of contexts that are distinct from the reality of better-defined markets. As a guide, it requires social entrepreneurs to assess competitive landscapes and the specific parameters that influence customer demand. It also addresses the critical challenges of educating the market and distribution, as well as the need to specify how value chains must be designed to serve the poorest of the poor. As we will describe in later chapters, challenging BOP environments also underscore the importance of talent development for executing business plans and strengthening accountability for outcomes. Subsequent chapters will also describe opportunities for innovation in the legal structure of social businesses and their financing. We turn next to chapter 3, where we will describe our framework and contrast our approach to other business plan development paradigms.

Background Resources

Desa, C., and J. Koch. "Scaling Social Impact: Building Sustainable Social Ventures at the Base of the Pyramid." *Journal of Social Entrepreneurship* 5, no. 2 (2014): 146–174.

Hammond, A., W. Kramer, J. Tran, R. Katz, and W. Courtland. *The Next 4 Billion: Market Size and Business Strategy at the Base of the Pyramid.* Washington, DC: World Resources Institute, 2007.

International Finance Corporation (IFC). "Global Consumption Data for Inclusive Business." 2010. www.ifc.org/inclusivebusiness.

Jain, Sanjay, and James Koch. "Articulated Embedding in the Development of Markets for Underserved Communities: The Case of Clean-Energy Provision to Off-Grid Publics." Academy of Management Annual Conference, Vancouver, BC, August 2015.

Koch, J., and A. Hammond. "Innovation Dynamics, Best Practice, and Trends in the Off-Grid Clean Energy Market." *Journal of Management for Global Sustainability* 1, 2 (2014): 31–49.

London, Ted. *The Base of the Pyramid Promise—Building Businesses for Impact and Scale.* Stanford, CA: Stanford University Press, 2016.

Martin, Roger, and Sally Osberg. *Getting Beyond Better—How Social Entrepreneurship Works.* Boston: Harvard Business Review Press, 2015.

Prahalad, C. K. *The Fortune at the Bottom of the Pyramid: Eradicating Poverty through Profits.* Philadelphia: Wharton School Publishing, 2010.

Sen, Amartya. *Development as Freedom.* New York: Anchor Books, Random House Publishing, 1999.

Chapter 3

Paradigms for Social Venture Business Plans

To address a problem or opportunity in a market, the most common approach entrepreneurs in places like Silicon Valley take is to first develop a business plan for attacking the problem with laser-like focus. But *simply* developing a business plan is not always so simple at the BOP.

Our earliest experience with social ventures trying to address problems in the Base of the Pyramid markets was with laureates of the San Jose Tech Museum of Innovation's "Technology Benefiting Humanity" Awards. Laureates told us that their biggest need was help—specifically help using their resources, financial and otherwise—in developing sustainable scenarios for addressing an unmet need or market opportunity. The problems they were addressing were often urgent, but their solutions were not connected to market channels or effectively supported by governments—elements that can be vital to a project's success. If they envisioned themselves as running entrepreneurial start-ups, they were often living hand to mouth, supported by grants, donations, and volunteers, with few prospects for becoming financially viable. Their presenting challenge—how to use money (investment) to become sustainable—guided our early engagement with social entrepreneurs and our focus on developing sustainable business plans.

In this chapter, we consider a number of business planning paradigms that have been successfully used by social entrepreneurs. There are many different paradigms to assist in developing a business plan. The paradigm used in part II of this book (the GSBI paradigm) will provide relevant information for whatever paradigm you choose. Some foundations and venture firms have particular frameworks they prefer entrepreneurs to use in funding presentations. If this is the case, or if you prefer another approach, use it. Again, the GSBI paradigm we develop in chapters 4 through 12 will provide critical information for developing a successful social venture regardless of the final presentation framework you adopt.

The Purpose of Business Planning

Many different paradigms can assist in developing a business plan. These approaches have served a variety of purposes:

- To gain venture capital funding

- To develop an operational business plan

- To generate a business model

- To help ventures formulate business strategies

In this section we look at which paradigms most closely align with each of these purposes.

1. Gaining Venture Capital Funding

Venture capitalist William Sahlman outlines one framework in his *Harvard Business Review* article, "How to Write a Great Business Plan." It includes just four elements:[1]

1. People

2. Opportunity

3. Context

4. Risks and rewards

This framework, although simple, captures a number of factors of particular interest to an investor. In Silicon Valley, it is often said that venture capitalists are concerned with three risks. The first is *technology risk*. Does the technology or solution work? The second is *market risk*, or whether proven channels exist to create market demand of sufficient size. And the third is *people risk*. Is a strong leadership team in place? In more or less "known" industries, venture capitalists draw on their in-depth knowledge, their assessment of management teams, and an assessment of the size of the opportunities to determine risks relative to potential returns. Strong sector-specific acumen enables them to home in on critical success factors. As "active investors" in familiar sectors, a proposal or business plan that follows the Sahlman framework, leaving out financials, metrics, and clearly defined operating processes is not likely to derail otherwise attractive commercial investment opportunities. In contrast, though, leaving these factors as a question mark is more likely to be a red flag in assessing opportunities in the uncharted markets of social mission ventures.

2. Developing an Operational Business Plan

A very complete guide for small business entrepreneurs is contained in DeThomas and Grensing-Pophal's *Writing a Convincing Business Plan*. This paradigm contains seven elements:[2]

1. Financing proposal
2. Business description
3. Market analysis
4. Operating plan
5. Organization plan
6. Financial plan
7. Financial model

For social ventures, there are two critically important elements missing from this framework: mission and metrics—especially measures of social outcomes and impact. While profit-motivated businesses focus on financial objectives in target markets, social ventures require deep empathy with the unmet needs of underserved populations in areas where rigorous market intelligence is limited or missing altogether. Their efforts require a focused mission and strategies grounded in a well-defined theory of change, and metrics for assessing social outcomes. These metrics extend beyond measures of financial performance and take precedence over profits. With these two additions—mission and social outcome metrics—this paradigm could be used for both fund raising and managing a social venture.

3. Business Model Generation

Taking a graphical approach provides a "shared language for describing, visualizing, accessing and changing business models."[3] The nine basic building blocks of Business Model Generation (Figure 3.1) provide a cognitive map or logic for how a company intends to create and capture value:[4]

1. Customer segments

2. Value propositions

3. Channels

4. Customer relationships

5. Revenue streams

6. Key resources

7. Key activities

8. Key partnerships

9. Cost structure

By placing sticky notes in two-dimensional outlines for each of these nine elements, entrepreneurs can organize their thoughts visually, graphically developing and iterating on a business model.

This paradigm has been tested by over 450 entrepreneurs in a variety of markets, and Osterwalder's and Pigneur's book *Business Model Generation* describes the paradigm and methodology through numerous examples. While Business Model Generation seems like an excellent approach to developing a visual representation of how an organization could work, it omits five important elements:

1. How the venture gets funded, both initially and over time

2. An analysis of external factors that might affect the success of a venture (e.g., macroeconomy, demographic and sociocultural factors, technology, and public policy)

3. Metrics, or how the venture is to be measured

4. An assessment of the alternatives/competition

5. How the venture is to be organized

Figure 3.1 Business Model Generation

BUSINESS MODEL CANVAS

Key Partnerships	Key Activities	Value Proposition	Customer Relationships	Customer Segments
	Key Resources		Channels	
Cost Structure		Revenue Streams		

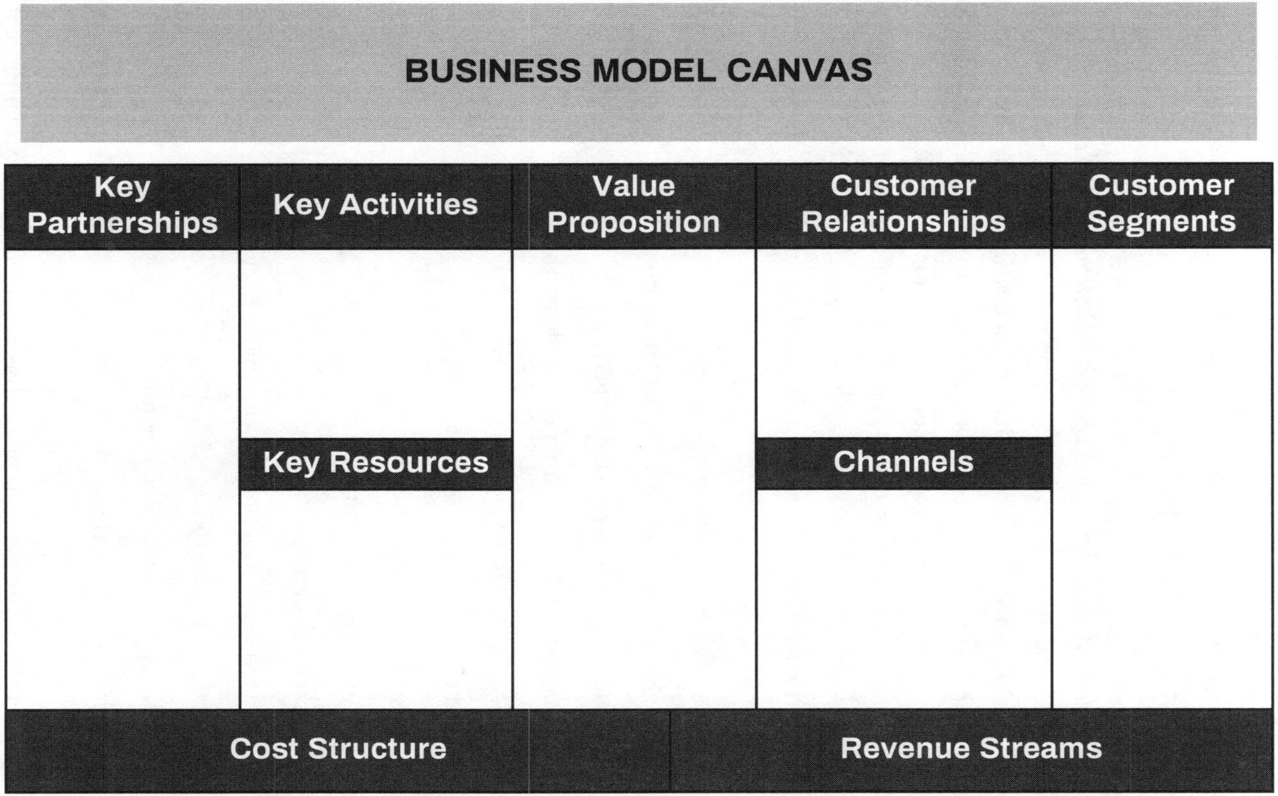

Source: Alexander Osterwalder and Yves Pigneur, Business Model Generation: A Handbook for Visionaries, Game Changers, and Challengers (New York: John Wiley & Sons, 2010).

Each of these considerations encompasses critically important and distinguishing characteristics of social businesses, as well as strategic decisions that can be critical to their success. Without good metrics and an explicit methodology for focusing on cash flow, Business Model Generation is a difficult paradigm to use in managing a venture.

4. Formulating Business Strategies (The Social Entrepreneur's Playbook)

The fourth paradigm—the Social Entrepreneur's Playbook—is based on a very practical book by Ian MacMillan and James Thompson. This paradigm was developed with an advisory group of almost three hundred social entrepreneurs and represents a very useful approach for conceptualizing a social venture. It presents a fourteen-step approach with accompanying templates to "pressure test, plan, launch, and scale a venture":[5]

1. Articulate your targeted problem and substantiate your proposed solution
2. Specify performance criteria
3. Define and segment your target population
4. Understand the beneficiary experience
5. Understand the most competitive alternative
6. Identify operations realities
7. Address the inevitable sociopolitics
8. Develop a concept statement
9. Frame and scope your venture
10. Specify deliverables
11. Establish assumptions and checkpoints
12. Launch the enterprise
13. Manage the upside and downside
14. Scale up the enterprise

Except for the missing elements of funding and metrics, the Social Entrepreneur's Playbook paradigm overcomes key omissions in the Business Model Generation paradigm. Unfortunately, it is missing any real discussion of metrics and funding—both of which are critical shortcomings.

Steps 13 and 14—manage the upside and downside, and scale up the enterprise—offer only general guidelines. Without an explicit financial plan or revenue and expense model (and carefully constructed metrics) it would be difficult to use the Playbook as a framework for developing and managing a social venture. As with the Business Model Generation, these missing elements are especially salient factors in social ventures. They provide explicit benchmarks for tracking results—both financial and social—and for making entrepreneurial adjustments that might increase the likelihood of developing a venture that becomes sustainable at scale.

The GSBI Paradigm: An Alternative for Building Better Social Ventures

The paradigm we use in this book was developed as a synthesis of several different frameworks, including the Barron's paradigm, the business plan frameworks used inside Hewlett-Packard and IBM, and the technology evaluation criteria used to judge the San Jose Tech Museum's Tech Awards, "Technology Benefiting Humanity." Our work assessing hundreds of Tech Laureate candidates led us to rediscover a Silicon Valley axiom: the idea that invention and innovation are not synonymous. Even in contexts where values and deep empathy for the poorest of the poor were the driving motivation for invention, the human benefits of technological advances could not be realized at scale without a plan for gathering and organizing resources to attack the problem—in effect, a business plan.

Our synthesized paradigm combines best practices from a variety of business planning frameworks with a touch of Silicon Valley acumen. It is based on more than a decade of work, testing and refining "what works" with more than 175 social entrepreneurs, nearly 100 Santa Clara University MBA students, and a similar number of Santa Clara University undergraduates. It consists of nine elements, all of which have evolved significantly through work with ventures across a variety of sectors. In fact, two of the elements in our paradigm—external environment analysis and metrics—were added at the suggestion of the first three GSBI cohorts involving forty social entrepreneurs.

Our paradigm is truly a synthesized approach for building better social ventures. It reflects the knowledge and collective intelligence of Silicon Valley mentors in the form of minimum critical specifications. Each of the elements in this paradigm (Figure 3.2) includes specific processes and recommended mechanisms for strengthening venture performance.

Figure 3.2 The GSBI Paradigm

Paradigm Element	Why Salient
1. Mission/Opportunity/Strategies	Focused theory of change
2. External environment	Local context and risks
3. Beneficiary needs ("market") analysis	Customer identification
4. Operations and key processes	Value chain innovation
5. Organization and human resources	Pivotal jobs and skills
6. Business model	Revenue and expense drivers
7. Metrics	Performance monitoring and measurement
8. Operating plan and budget	Cash flow and milestones
9. Financing	Capitalizing the venture

For the purposes of building a successful social venture, the GSBI paradigm is more comprehensive than other business planning frameworks. It addresses all of the elements in other frameworks in addition to metrics and venture financing—two considerations of particular salience to social ventures. Note that financing considerations play a pivotal role in the choice of legal structure. Here, social ventures have a range of options—from for-profit to limited profit (L3C), for-benefit (B-Corp), hybrid, and nonprofit forms, as well as co-ops. Each of these options comes with trade-offs for raising money and ongoing operations (eligibility for grants, equity investments, government contracts, etc.). By including financing as an element in our framework, we are acknowledging the need for business plans to specify the amount and timing of fund-raising required for a start-up to get to the cash flow it needs to break even. We are also acknowledging potential trade-offs between various sources of financing for early and subsequent growth stages. Including financing as an element in a comprehensive social venture business planning framework also facilitates an assessment of investment readiness.

The other element missing in alternative business plan paradigms is metrics. Given the emphasis on accountability for social outcomes and impact, this is a critical shortcoming. Our paradigm addresses social outcome and financial metrics, as well as metrics for monitoring internal processes and organizational effectiveness. Creating sustainable social impact in Base of the Pyramid contexts presents unique strategic and operating challenges. The GSBI paradigm places a particular focus on these challenges in the context of resource-constrained environments. In our model, metrics are seen as a mechanism for strengthening accountability and for supporting continuous innovation and entrepreneurial adaptation.

What Is Unique about Social Ventures?

Many years ago, Guclu, Dees, and Anderson described social entrepreneurs as innovative, opportunity-oriented, value-creating change agents who[6]

- adopt a mission to create and sustain social value—not just private value;

- recognize and relentlessly pursue new opportunities to serve that mission;

- engage in a process of continuous innovation, adaptation, and learning;

- act boldly without being limited by resources currently in hand; and

- exhibit a heightened sense of accountability to constituents served and for the outcomes created.

What also distinguishes the work of social entrepreneurs from that of their counterparts in purely commercial ventures is that they are often held accountable for social outcomes in the presence of high degrees of ambiguity. Their mission to disrupt an unjust or unsustainable condition can take many forms—from creating a scalable enterprise to cross-sector alliances for attacking social issues and public-private partnerships. The GSBI business planning paradigm evolved out of efforts to help the social entrepreneurs who lead such efforts integrate financial and other resources to develop financially sustainable and scalable social ventures. It has been tested and refined through work with social entrepreneurs across dozens of countries.

Social Venture Snapshots

Part II of this book describes our paradigm in detail, with examples and exercises for generating a social venture business plan or for analyzing how to strengthen an existing one. The examples we use are taken from exemplary social businesses: Grameen Shakti, Sankara, and a number of GSBI innovators. Profiles of the GSBI Innovator examples are included with each example. Each of these profiles uses our GSBI paradigm as a way of demonstrating how our framework applies in practice. A brief profile of Sankara and Grameen Shakti follows.

Social Venture Snapshot: Grameen Shakti

Grameen Shakti is a renewable energy social enterprise established in 1996 to promote, develop, and popularize renewable energy technologies in remote, rural areas of Bangladesh. It is part of the Grameen Bank family of companies, founded with the mission of alleviating poverty for the extremely poor through microcredit programs. Grameen Shakti is one of the largest and fastest-growing renewable energy companies in the world, training its engineers to be "social engineers"—pseudo evangelists who go door to door to demonstrate the effectiveness of renewable energy as well as to train local youth as technicians to ensure efficient and free after-sales service. The example carried through this book is based on Grameen Shakti's first ten years (1996–2006)—a period of time during which it developed and expanded its business.

Mission, Opportunity, Strategy

Grameen Shakti's mission is to bring affordable, renewable energy to rural communities in Bangladesh. In 1996, over one hundred million people in rural communities of Bangladesh were not connected to the power grid, and none of these potential beneficiaries used renewable energy for lighting or cooking. Instead, they used candles and oil or kerosene lamps for lighting, dry cell batteries for radios and cell phone recharging, 12V car batteries for televisions, and wood or coal for cooking. These lighting sources are insufficient for working at night, and combustible lighting and cooking fuel sources like coal and kerosene cause health problems.

Grameen has five key strategies: (1) acquire, assemble, sell, and service three product lines: solar home systems, cooking stoves, and biogas generation systems; (2) maximize impact on rural poverty through market penetration as opposed to an emphasis on profits—operationally, this may require a willingness to accept growth where marginal costs are greater than marginal revenues; (3) operate with a financially sustainable business model that does not negatively impact the environment; (4) return only investment capital (with no interest) to investors; (5) hire, train, and promote employees (including women) from/in Bangladesh, pay them competitive salaries, and provide safe working conditions.

External Environment

Most of Grameen Shakti's beneficiaries live in areas that are difficult to reach, isolated from each other by waterways or wetlands. Bangladesh's extreme climate also often includes monsoons and floods—conditions that also serve to make beneficiaries more difficult to reach, as well as potentially damaging solar lighting products. Environmental challenges aside, Grameen benefits from access to a young, energetic, and technically savvy workforce; the Grameen brand; and a supply of low-cost products from China.

Target Market

In 1996, approximately seventy-seven million people in Bangladesh (64 percent of the 120 million rural poor, and about fourteen million households) had no access to the power grid. This market can be segmented based on location/geography, annual income, occupation (farmer, fisherman, teacher, etc.), and needs (size of system).

Operations and Value Chain

Grameen Shakti's value chain consists of six key processes: (1) product definition, partner identification, acquisition, and pricing; (2) product supply; (3) distribution/delivery; (4) marketing, sales, and collection; (5) microfinancing; and (6) service/repair. For these processes, there are key partnerships with several suppliers, Grameen Bank (for branding and business processes), and, until 2010, local microentrepreneurs (for sales).

Organization and Human Resources

Grameen Shakti refers to itself as a "rural energy (social) business." Its legal structure is that of a nonprofit company with limited liability. It has a well-developed, strong organizational structure and provides training and competitive pay for all employees.

Business Model

Grameen Shakti derives revenue from (1) product sales, (2) interest on microloans, and (3) service contracts. Its main expenses include (1) product costs, (2) sales and marketing, and (3) costs of training and services. Since 2000, Grameen Shakti has been cash flow positive or breakeven. Figure 3.3 illustrates the Shakti business model using Osterwalder's Business Model Generation framework.

Metrics

Grameen Shakti uses nineteen metrics, divided into three groups: organization (e.g., offices, employees), business (e.g., installations and sales), and impact (e.g., carbon emission reductions).

Operating Plan and Budget

Grameen Shakti has an annual operating plan and budget for the company and for each branch office.

Financing

Since 1996, Grameen Shakti has had five rounds of financing totaling around $15 million, with about 60 percent coming from grants and 40 percent from loans.

Finally, as a comparison with the GSBI paradigm as described in this section, Figure 3.3 summarizes the Grameen Shakti business plan ("model") using the Business Model Generation paradigm format.

Figure 3.3   Grameen Shakti Business Model

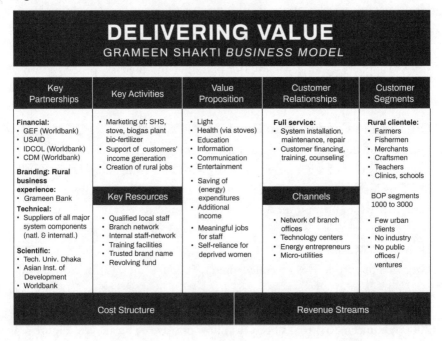

Social Venture Snapshot: Sankara Eye Care Institutions

Sankara Eye Care Institutions (SECI) is a "movement" founded by Dr. R. V. Ramani and Dr. Radha in 1977. It has grown to include fourteen specialty eye care hospitals across ten states in India—a cumulative total of more than one thousand beds dedicated to providing quality eye care to India's rural poor. Since the movement's beginning, the Sankara network has performed over one million sight-restoring surgeries and has become one of the largest providers of eye care in India. A highly qualified team of three hundred medical professionals combines empathy for patients with state-of-the-art medical technologies and practices in community eye care to provide top-tier eye care. Sankara is committed to providing clinical excellence while serving the poor with dignity and respect. Sankara has several key eye care programs in addition to its existing hospitals that serve the rural poor in India. Through these programs, Sankara offers total eye care, including preventive, curative, and rehabilitative medical care.

Mission, Opportunity, Strategy

Sankara's mission is to provide unmatched eye care through a strong service-oriented team. The Sankara opportunity is the large number of needlessly blind people in India. According to the World Health Organization, an estimated sixty-three million people in India are visually impaired, and approximately eight to twelve million are blind. Fifty-four percent of these cases of blindness are caused by cataract and uncorrected refractive errors—both of which are curable. The Sankara strategy is based on an integrated process of recruitment, treatment, and continuing care.

External Environment

The key external environmental factors affecting Sankara are a lack of skilled talent for providing professional eye care, geographic dispersion making it difficult to reach patients in need of cataract surgery, and lack of awareness and financial resources among potential patients.

Target Market

Sankara's target market consists of direct, indirect, and related beneficiaries. The direct beneficiaries (those that use Sankara's services) are the patients requiring eye care, including patients who receive eye screenings, eye exams, and medical procedures such as eye surgeries. The indirect beneficiaries are those that deliver the product/service (the medical staff), as well as the Sankara Academy of Vision, which trains the staff. Sankara's partners, which contribute funding to the organization, are also indirect beneficiaries. These include Sankara Eye Foundation (USA), Sankara Eye Foundation (Europe), and Mission for Vision Trust. Related beneficiaries include the female hospital staff and field workers (who are empowered via job opportunities), the families of individuals receiving eye care treatment (who may benefit from the patient's ability to return to work and earn an income), and the villages and communities in which Sankara conducts its eye camps. The economies of these communities benefit from the increase in earning power once the treated patients are able to return to work.

Operations and Value Chain

Sankara's value chain consists of ten key processes and a network of relationships that create value for the customer (paying and nonpaying patients of Sankara's eye hospitals). While support functions such as administration and HR are not normally included in the value chain, the recruitment and training of hospital staff is also a key process.

Organization and Human Resources

The Sri Kanchi Kamakoti Medical Trust, a registered public charitable trust in India, manages Sankara's eye hospitals. Overall, Sankara exhibits a functional structure, along with some minor elements of a divisional structure owing to its geographic spread in India. Because its form is simple and allows for centralized decision making, a functional structure is the ideal choice for Sankara's low-cost strategy. The board oversees a six-member leadership team. Each leader is assigned to a specific vertical such as paid hospitals, nonpaid hospitals, or medical administration. Each functional head at the unit (hospital) level reports to a dedicated president of the leadership team. Each unit head manages a functional team within the unit, such as medical administration, HR, or operations.

Business Model

Sankara is the leading provider of free eye surgeries in India, operating specialty eye care hospitals that offer comprehensive eye care services to two distinct markets: free services for the rural poor and affordable premium eye care for the urban middle class. Unlike government-run hospitals in India,

Sankara is able to provide high-quality affordable eye care keeping in mind patients' dignity while improving the overall welfare of its customers. Seventy percent of Sankara's income comes from the 20 percent of surgeries that are paid, with the remaining 30 percent made up of donations (15 percent), grants (10 percent), and interest on investments (5 percent). The key expenses are hospital staff and operations (85 percent), eye operations (10 percent), and administration (5 percent).

Metrics and Accountability
Sankara uses balanced scorecards to track and evaluate its various metrics. Automated daily reports are generated from the Hospital Information Management system highlighting the key performance indicators for the various daily activities for the different divisions.

Operating Plan and Budget
Sankara has reported profitable operations for the past ten years. Given its legal structure as a charitable trust, these profits are reinvested into the business to expand and grow operations. There is an annual budget and operating plan with goals for the year.

Financing
The sources of capital funding for new hospitals are primarily contributed (donated) through partners including Sankara Eye Foundation (USA and Europe) and Mission for Vision Trust. Recurring expenses are primarily covered by hospital collections via paying patients. The goal is to increase hospital collections in order to decrease the reliance on external donors and help each hospital become fully self-sufficient in five years.

Social Venture Snapshot: GSBI Innovators
As a third example, for each of the nine elements of the GSBI business planning paradigm, a different GSBI venture has been chosen. For each venture, the entire paradigm is summarized, with the specific element being illustrated presented in more detail. Thus, the entire paradigm is covered for a total of eleven organizations.

To Recap

In this chapter, we covered the main purposes of business planning as well as a number of different paradigms for social venture business planning. We then introduced our own paradigm, discussed elements that make social businesses different from traditional profit-seeking ventures, and introduced two of the organizations we will look at more closely as we work through the steps of developing a social venture business plan in part II. In the next chapter, we turn to the core element of any social venture: mission, opportunity, and strategies.

Background Resources

DeThomas, Arthur R., and Lin Grensing-Pophal. *Writing a Convincing Business Plan.* New York: Barron's Educational Services, 2001.

Guclu, Ayse, J. Gregory Dees, and Beth Battle Anderson. *The Process of Social Entrepreneurship: Creating Opportunities Worthy of Serious Pursuit.* Duke University Fuqua School of Business, Center for the Advancement of Social Entrepreneurship, 2002.

MacMillan, Ian, and James Thompson. *The Social Entrepreneur's Playbook.* Philadelphia: Wharton Digital Press, 2013.

Osterwalder, Alexander, and Yves Pigneur. *Business Model Generation: A Handbook for Visionaries, Game Changers, and Challengers.* New York: John Wiley and Sons, 2010.

Sahlman, William. "How to Write a Great Business Plan." *Harvard Business Review*, July–August, 1997, 99–108.

Part II

Managing a Sustainable/ Scalable Social Business

In part II, we will cover the seven basic elements that make up the GSBI business plan. Each of the next seven chapters starts with a delineation of the "basic knowledge" needed for completing the business plan element described in the chapter—and that the GSBI participants often needed mentors' help to formulate. Each chapter ends with a set of minimum critical specifications needed to complete the business plan element described in the chapter as well as a series of exercises aimed at helping practitioners develop that element.

Chapter 4

Mission, Opportunity, Strategies

In this chapter, we consider the first element of the business plan—a section you might call the "strategic plan" because it is used to define the mission (the social change your venture is striving to create), the opportunity (the size and nature of the desired social change), and strategies (the key activities that your venture will undertake to create the change). An overarching "theory of change" usually integrates these three elements.

Process

The "strategic plan" portion of the business plan consists of three main parts:

1. A mission statement, which is a short (fewer than ten words) sentence describing the social change to be made and the metric that will measure it

2. An opportunity statement, which describes the size and nature of the social change to be made, the local context in which this change is to take place, and how to identify (and count) the potential beneficiaries of the change

> **Basic Knowledge**
> A focused mission with a clearly defined theory of change that logically links strategies to a specific outcome measure strengthens discipline in both value creation *and* capital efficiency (cost/outcome).

3. A list of strategies (major programs or initiatives) to be undertaken to create the change

In this section, we will look closely at each of these parts, consider what they are (and sometimes are *not*), and provide a number of examples.

Mission Statement

At its most basic, a mission statement describes what is to be changed and for whom. A good mission statement can be expressed in fewer than ten words. For example: *eliminate needless cataract blindness in India,* or *provide electricity for households in Bangladesh.* Both of these are concise, clear, and to the point.

In addition to being short, a good mission statement is more concerned with *what* and *for whom* than *how.* Its main purpose is to focus and guide the organization. It is shared by all stakeholders, can be articulated by anyone, and motivates the actions of everyone in the enterprise. It can be achievable in a foreseeable amount of time and is measurable. A mission statement needs a single metric or measurable unit of benefit for "counting" successful outcomes directly attributable to the strategies that your enterprise uses to achieve the mission; for example, lowering the number of cases of cataract blindness to a certain number, or lighting a specific number of homes.

To be clear, a mission statement is not a vision, although it may be a more focused statement of the vision.

Vision statements tend to be broader and more ambitious. As high-level aspirations, they often are unlikely to be achieved, let alone measured. A mission statement—essentially composed of a verb, a noun, and a target—is, by comparison, much more focused. It specifies the customer population to be served and the ideal outcome or benefit. The difference between a vision statement and a mission statement is illustrated in the following example:

Vision: *Eliminate needless blindness*
Mission: *Eliminate needless cataract blindness in India*

Finally, a mission statement is not a statement of the entrepreneurs' values, nor is it the specific objectives or key innovations of the organization.

Values (e.g., we treat our employees well, or we believe in the dignity of those we serve) are attributes of the organization and its leaders that support the mission, and objectives can be derived from the *key strategies*.

Opportunity Statement

An opportunity statement is a statement of the total available market for the mission. It describes the size and attributes of the population or issue being addressed and the change that could result from the mission being successfully completed. The opportunity for change may be in the number of beneficiaries who could (measurably) be affected (nine million people in India with cataract blindness), or it may be in the measurable economic, environmental, or other outcomes that could result from the mission (e.g., 50 percent reduction in welfare payments to blind people).

The opportunity statement should also describe the key characteristics of the opportunity in terms of problem symptoms, beneficiary location, beneficiary characteristics, beneficiary ability/willingness to change and ability/willingness to pay for change, and the alternatives available. Essentially, the opportunity statement should include the beneficiary needs and attributes, particularly those that are necessary to understand in order to deliver a successful solution to the problem (i.e., to achieve the mission).

For example, 75 percent of needless cataract blindness in India occurs in rural areas, 60 percent of those in India with needless cataract blindness cannot afford to pay for treatment, and most of the 60 percent will not travel far to get treatment. In addition, they may not be comfortable in a hospital setting. The alternatives are nonconsumption (no surgery) or traditional surgery, which is very expensive and requires a sponsor for those who cannot pay themselves. It may also be helpful to illustrate the opportunity with a story about the problem area using a typical beneficiary—for instance, a person who ultimately received cataract surgery.

Key Strategies

The *key strategies* identify the key programs—activities, innovations, processes, and possibly skill or capability development initiatives—the enterprise must undertake to achieve the mission. Logic models (which make explicit a theory of change) can be useful for clarifying how an organization will achieve desired outcomes and social impact (Figure 4.1). They clarify the resources, activities, and capabilities needed to achieve social innovation outcomes and

Figure 4.1   A Logic Model for Access to Affordable Eye Care

Inputs	Activities	Outputs	Outcomes	Impact
Funding	Eye camps	Treatment of various eye diseases	Restoration of vision	Eliminate needless blindness
People (training doctors and nurses)	Eye screenings			
	Comprehensive eye care services and specialty services	Number of surgeries	Revenues for continued expansion	Allow individuals to live better, more productive lives
Hospitals, land, and facilities				
	School partnerships (Rainbow Program)			Women empowerment
Partnerships for camps				
	Programs like Maithri, Swagatham, etc.			Increase in jobs within the community
	Sankara Eye Bank			

impact at a cost that is affordable to underserved markets, and at a scale that is aligned with the size of the opportunity.

In the business planning process, logic models must be translated into specific strategies. Each of these strategies must have metrics that indicate the target impact of the strategy, the time frame in which the strategy is to be implemented, and the forecasted annual expenses and income for the strategy (if appropriate). Specific strategies must also take into account cause-and-effect linkages relative to activities, outputs, outcomes, and impacts, as well as the size of the opportunity.

A typical social venture generally has fewer than ten key strategies. Any more than that, and the mission is likely to be too broad or too complex and difficult to manage successfully. Generally, there need to be strategies for

- beneficiary (problem) identification and location;

- "convincing" the beneficiaries to consume or buy the product or service (marketing);

- developing or refining the product/service (research and development);

- creating the product/service (manufacturing);

- delivering or distributing the product/service (logistics);

- understanding the beneficiaries' ability to pay; and

- providing any needed financing, beneficiary follow-up (customer service/support), and measurement of outcomes or impact.

Included in one or more of the strategies may be elements of the business model specifying revenue and/or expense drivers, or even a short summary of the business model. For example, a mission statement to increase women's incomes might have "empower women to set up businesses to sell solar lighting systems" as a key strategy.

The following is an example of a set of key strategies:

1. **Use partners to create rural "camps" to locate blind people in rural areas and convince them that they can be cured.**

2. **Develop a hospital "mass surgery" process that**

   ∞ admits patients and determines their ability to pay,

   ∞ prepares patients for eye surgery,

   ∞ uses modern procedures and equipment with skilled eye surgeons to do high-volume surgery,

   ∞ teaches unskilled women to do admissions and patient preparation,

   ∞ provides surgeons with opportunities for skill renewal/ enhancement, and

   ∞ uses tiered or sliding pricing to charge those who can pay enough to allow "free" surgeries for all who cannot pay.

3. **Use a family-business approach to establish a strong culture, ensure control, build trust, and strengthen efficiency.**

4. **Motivate through mission, work environment, and "adequate wages" to improve employee performance and reduce turnover.**

Each of the key strategies must be focused, measurable, and achievable. It is also useful if the key strategies can be easily documented so that they can be replicated. The costs of the key strategies should decline with volume (economies of scale) and over time through economies of learning. The strategies must be more cost-effective than the alternatives and provide the intended beneficiaries with a more compelling reason to consume (use/buy).

Social Venture Snapshots

The rest of this chapter presents case examples of the missions, opportunities, and strategies for three organizations—Grameen Shakti, Sankara, and Fundacion Paraguaya Self-Sustaining Schools (SSAS). In each of these organizations, a concise mission statement provides the kind of focus that is needed to mobilize resources and effectively deploy them. For example, Sankara's single measure of success—number of successful sight-restoring surgeries—makes it possible to calculate cost per outcome as a measure of capital efficiency. With a careful reading of these examples it becomes evident that all three of these organizations have taken a systems approach to the opportunities they are addressing. Their business plans reflect an appreciation of the challenges of behavioral change and make effective use of logic models to specify activities or strategies that are linked to desired outcomes. These are critically important takeaways and they position each of these organizations for success in achieving its mission. In reading the following Social Venture Snapshots, reflect on the following questions:

1. What makes for an effective single measure of success?

2. What is the logic model for each of these ventures?

3. How do their strategies contribute to success in addressing opportunities?

In considering these questions and the takeaways from these three examples, you will be better prepared to tackle the exercises at the end of this chapter.

Social Venture Snapshot: Mission, Opportunity, and Strategies for Grameen Shakti

Mission

Bring affordable, renewable energy to rural communities in Bangladesh.

Opportunity

In 1996, over one hundred million people in rural communities in Bangladesh were not connected to the grid—and none of these potential beneficiaries used renewable energy for lighting or cooking. Most of these people live in areas that are difficult to reach and separated from each other by waterways or wetlands. They use candles and oil or kerosene lamps for lighting, dry cell batteries for radios and cell phone recharging, 12V car batteries for televisions, and wood or coal for cooking. Lighting sources are insufficient for working at night, and both lighting and cooking fuel sources cause health problems. Ninety percent of the rural population is considered poor, making less than $5 per day. Rural families spend about 7 percent ($0.35 per day) of their income on energy.

Strategies

1. Acquire, assemble, sell, and service three product lines: solar home systems, cooking stoves, and biogas generation systems.

2. Maximize impact on rural poverty through market penetration as opposed to an emphasis on profits. Operationally, this may require a willingness to accept growth where marginal costs are greater than marginal revenues (i.e., where sales of additional units have to be subsidized [via other income]).

3. Operate with a financially sustainable business model that does not negatively impact the environment.

4. Investors get only their investment amount in return (no dividends, no ownership).

5. Hire, train, and promote employees (including women) from/in Bangladesh. Pay competitive salaries and provide safe working conditions.

Social Venture Snapshot: Mission, Opportunity, and Strategies for Sankara
Mission

Provide affordable, high-quality, equitable eye care in India.

Measure of Success: For its mission, the single most logical measure of success for Sankara is the number of successful sight-restoring surgeries performed. To provide high-quality and unmatched eye care, Sankara would need to measure its success not just in the breadth of its market reach or the number of individuals it is able to serve but in the quality of service it provides to those individuals. Successful eye care will be measured by restored vision and quality of life improvement for those served. For instance, because of an improvement in their sight, Sankara patients are generally able to work and earn an income for their families, improving the overall quality of life for individuals and their families alike.

Opportunity

India is home to the largest population of curable blind worldwide. According to the World Health Organization, an estimated sixty-three million people in India are visually impaired, and approximately eight to twelve million are blind. Fifty-four percent of the blindness is caused by cataract and uncorrected refractive errors, both of which are curable.

Blindness and poverty are closely related. Adults and children living in poverty are more likely to suffer from malnutrition, poor water quality, and inadequate sanitation, making them much more susceptible to contracting and developing eye diseases. The majority of blind people in India live in remote rural areas where eye care facilities are less accessible. In the majority of instances, they are unable to travel to receive treatment. Government-run hospitals are often unclean, and the wait times are far too long. Moreover, the poor cannot afford to pay for treatment at most private hospitals. As a result, most of the rural poor in India resort to nonconsumption and do not receive treatment for curable eye ailments.

In addition to the rural poor, Sankara also has the opportunity to serve the urban middle class (a $3 billion market according to Sankara). This market is deemed its "paying customer" segment and is absolutely essential to operating the business. Sankara must maintain its paying-customer segment to subsidize the cost of the nonpaying customers.

Strategies
Financial: Cross-Subsidy/Hybrid-Revenue Model:
For Sankara to achieve its mission, it must maintain its key financial model ratio of 80/20. That is, income from the 20 percent of paying customers must cover the costs of the 80 percent of nonpaying customers. This metric is directly related to the output and outcome factors in its theory of change. Without maintaining this key financial ratio, both the elimination of needless blindness and the financial viability outcomes of Sankara's theory of change would be adversely affected. It would not be able to reach as many rural customers.

Partnership: Fund-Raising (Sankara Eye Foundation):
The key partnership with Sankara Eye Foundation initiates and drives community eye care activities by working directly with Sankara Eye Care Institutions in India. The foundation hosts events and works with major donors to generate a healthy source of contributed income for Sankara. Without this essential partnership, Sankara's inputs (number of hospitals and staffing) could potentially be threatened, and it would need to reduce the number and scale of activities undertaken.

Marketing: Targeting Two Key Markets:
Sankara operates "base" hospitals in urban areas and "community" hospitals in rural areas. Although Sankara provides the same care and quality of service to all of its consumers, it is targeting two separate markets (rural and urban) and two segments within each of these markets (paying and nonpaying). Because of this segmentation scheme, it is essential that it maintain a different marketing strategy based on the essential needs of each specific customer group. A universal marketing plan in no way would adequately address and reach the individuals in both rural and urban areas. Maintaining a dual segmentation marketing plan is essential for acquiring customers and maintaining an 80/20 financial model.

Customer Outreach: Outreach/Eye Camps:
The outreach camps are crucial in spreading awareness and reaching and gaining new rural customers. By going directly to the remote communities in need, these camps allow Sankara to provide quality care and a level of intimacy to consumers who may be unaware of the services it offers. Additionally, it provides an opportunity for the rural poor to have access to care and screenings they normally would have to travel significant distances to receive (which is unrealistic for

the vast majority). Outreach is an essential activity in Sankara's theory of change (and scaling) model.

Training: Sankara Academy of Vision: Sankara's educational training program attracts top talent throughout the country. By employing top talent in its hospitals, Sankara is able to maintain a strong staff that is passionate about the organization's mission of delivering quality service in a manner that can eliminate needless blindness for all. Another benefit in having a top-tier staff is that it attracts patients who are willing to pay. Continuing to value education and training is a critical success factor for retaining top talent and, in return, for maintaining its paying customer base.

Social Venture Snapshot: GSBI Innovator Fundacion Paraguaya Self-Sustaining Agriculture Schools (SSAS)

When Martin Burt attended the GSBI in 2005, his organization, the Fundacion Paraguaya SSAS—a school that educates and trains local youth to become successful farmers—was the first GSBI participant whose mission included the financial success of its clients, and was among the first GSBI participants to create a business plan that showed positive cash flow for the organization itself within two years, along with a plan for replication.

Mission

Provide practical and entrepreneurial education that enables graduates to achieve financial success.

In a video created for SSAS, Martin Burt argued that local farmers already knew how to farm, but what they did not know was how to make money farming. Burt pointed out that land reform, aid, and subsidies (the traditional government approaches to aiding poor farmers) had not worked and that local schools taught courses that were not connected to the life success of the students. The essence of the SSAS mission statement, a GSBI first, was to solve this problem by teaching children of local farmers how to make money farming while providing them a high school–level education that was relevant to success in farming. The main metric for the success of its mission was graduate income.

Opportunity

The opportunity was, in the first phase, to create the potential for sustainable farming income for a few thousand children of poor local farmers in Paraguay who were destined to become structurally unemployed, and in the second phase to replicate SSAS in other countries with hundreds of thousands of children of poor local farmers.

Strategies

The key strategies of the SSAS were the following:

1. Create a high school–level curriculum where the basic subjects (reading, writing, math, science) were all aimed at using the knowledge taught to create a successful local farmer.

2. Persuade the state to provide teachers for this school.

3. Use the school as an "example" or replicable model farm.

In addition, provide microfinancing access for the graduates' farming businesses and serve as a co-op marketing organization for their products, with both of these activities providing financing for the schools (hence the schools as well as the farmers become self-sustaining).

External Environment

SSAS's external environment was one of rural poverty with population decline as people moved to cities to find jobs, with failed government land reform and education ("debt-ridden schools"), and with no infrastructure capacity to support the growth and success of local farmers.

Market

The market for students was focused on children who came from chronically unemployed families and poor communities (direct beneficiaries). The "product" was the school and the agricultural products created and sold by the school. SSAS charged students a nominal tuition, and the students had to work on the school's farm for free. Microfinancing and products sold by the school's farm were at market prices. The school did the product placement and promotion using student-faculty teams. Indirect beneficiaries were the families of the students, and related beneficiaries were the communities in which the students lived.

Operations and Value Chain

The key processes of SSAS were (1) education (training), (2) agricultural production, (3) marketing of products produced by the school and its graduates, and (4) microfinancing. The value chain combined a high school–level of education with a farming supply chain.

Organization and Human Resources

Fundacion Paraguaya is a nonprofit. The organization has a CEO, three key directors (production chief, academic director, finance and administration director), a board of directors with farming experience, and three groups of employees: the agricultural high school (for 120 students per year), the junior achievement marketing organization, and the microfinance organization. There were 120 employees in 2005.

Business Model and Unit Economics

The key revenue drivers for the school were tuition (5 percent), a roadside store (10 percent), vegetable and fruit sales (20 percent), livestock sales (25 percent), and microfinancing and community education (40 percent). The main expense drivers were staff and facilities. The break-even revenue amount was $175,000.

Unit Economics: Although GSBI did not teach unit economics in 2005, using a unit of "1 student" and expenses of $175,000 (breakeven revenue number), the unit cost per student was $175,000/120 = $1,458 per student per year.

Metrics

Metrics for each SSAS were (1) number of students, (2) revenues, (3) expenses, and (4) annual incomes of graduates.

Operating Plan

In 2005, GSBI did not include creating an operating plan, but SSAS clearly had one.

Financing

The first SSAS was financed by Fundacion Paraguaya, with an estimated cost of $500,000 to set up the school, plus revenue subsidies of about $120,000 for the first two years. There was also contributed income in the form of salaries for teachers paid by the government.

To Recap

The "strategic plan" segment of a business plan is the place for social entrepreneurs to lay out an organizational mission (and a metric for measuring success), what they see as the main opportunity/problem to be solved, and specific of strategies for tackling those problems. The Minimum Critical Specifications Checklist covers the absolute baseline level of information this section should include. In the next chapter, we turn to the external environment.

Exercises

4.1 Mission Statement
Create a short (less than ten words) mission statement for your organization and select a single metric to measure the success of the venture in achieving this mission.

4.2 Opportunity
Provide a quantitative description of the opportunity for the venture and the key characteristics of the opportunity.

4.3 Key Strategies
List no more than ten key strategies (programs) used to create the change specified in the mission statement for the beneficiaries described in the opportunity. Taken together, these strategies should reflect your logic model or theory of change, i.e., the activities that will drive your success measure.

> **Minimum Critical Specifications Checklist**
>
> **Mission, Opportunity, and Strategies**
>
> - States mission in ten words or less
> - Specifies single measure of success
> - Defines opportunity and key strategies that will enable the venture to meet the opportunity
> - Reflects your logic model or theory of change

Background Resources

Dees, J. Gregory, Jed Emerson, and Peter Economy. *Strategic Tools for Social Entrepreneurs: Enhancing the Performance of Your Enterprising Nonprofit.* New York: John Wiley, 2002, chapter 1.

DeThomas, Arthur, and Stephanie Derammelaere. *How to Write a Convincing Business Plan.* 3rd ed. New York: Barron's Educational Services, 2008, chapters 4 and 5.

Prahalad, C. K. *The Fortune at the Bottom of the Pyramid: Eradicating Poverty through Profits.* Philadelphia: Wharton School Publishing, 2010, chapter 2.

Thompson, J., and I. MacMillan. "Making Social Ventures Work." *Harvard Business Review*, September 2010, 67–73.

Yunus, M., et al. "Building Social Business Models: Lessons from the Grameen Experience." *Long Range Planning* 43 (2012): 308–325.

Chapter 5

The External Environment

The external environment includes factors that affect a social venture but that it cannot control. If these factors pose a risk to the venture, they must be mitigated. Conversely, businesses can leverage some external factors if they are potentially helpful. While all businesses (not just social businesses) are affected (positively and/or negatively) by their external environments, a social business—particularly one operating in "underdeveloped/emerging" countries or in an impoverished area in a developed country like the United States—will face significant challenges from the external environment.

In less developed countries, situations like a lack of transportation or communications infrastructure, difficulty in creating and enforcing contracts, lack of banking or other financial systems, lack of ability to protect intellectual property, complicated tax or business regulation laws, governments or cultural groups that may be hostile or exceedingly bureaucratic, extreme climate or geography, and corruption can all pose a challenge to would-be social ventures. And as much as the external environment varies significantly among countries, there can also be substantial

> **Basic Knowledge**
> In severely resource-constrained environments, ventures must understand stakeholder interests and enlist partners to create shared value and leverage their strengths. Care in an environmental analysis can translate uncertainty into clearly identified risk mitigation and partner strategies.

variations within a country, such as in India. External environmental differences across geographic boundaries pose significant challenges in scaling a social business into more than one country, and often within a single country. In this chapter, we will work to identify the key elements of the external environment that affect the economic viability or change-making capacity of a social venture, as well as create a set of actions to mitigate negative elements and leverage positive ones.

Institutional Voids

A number of the criticisms of Prahalad's market-based approach for the BOP relate to the complexities of the external environment and market-related institutional voids. According to the transaction cost economics perspective, advanced economies (such as that of the United States) possess an elaborately developed institutional context that includes facets like well-defined property rights, rules of exchange, and the types of legal recourse that enable the emergence of well-functioning capital, labor, and product markets.[1] By contrast, these equivalent structures in emerging economies (such as that of India) are plagued by information and implementation problems, resulting in a host of market imperfections. A number of characteristics—from inadequate disclosure, to weak corporate governance, to the erratic enforcement of securities regulation—can characterize financial markets in these countries.[2]

In economic development literature, the term "institutional voids" refers to an absence of the requisite institutional arrangements and/or actors required to enable the smooth functioning of markets.[3] These voids raise transaction costs and, as a consequence, significantly hinder market-type activity. This stream of research, then, highlights how the lack of underlying institutional structures in these economies creates considerable challenges for the actors operating in such spaces.[4] Put differently, the imagery that this work conjures is one of barely functioning markets. De Soto evocatively captures this dynamic in describing how the absence of legal structures around property significantly hinders capitalism-related activity in emerging economies.[5]

Research in underserved communities has indicated that, given the uncertainty that weak institutions engender, developing relationships with local actors such as nongovernment organizations (NGOs) can offset the impact of such voids.[6] A more recent strand of scholarship on informal economies emphasizes the significant amount of business activity that occurs outside formal institutional boundaries but within the realm of informal institutions.[7] This suggests that markets exist where these two domains overlap.

C. K. Prahalad's original *Fortune at the Bottom of the Pyramid* thesis posited that there is a market waiting to be tapped.[8] While "institutional voids" research challenges this thesis, both perspectives share a few crucial similarities. Both reflect an outsider's perspective of the key features that characterize markets in these communities and provide prescriptions that reflect these worldviews. Their predominant focus is on the producer side (i.e., the firms and entrepreneurs that attempt to engage with these markets). Missing from these perspectives is a more in-depth understanding of the lives that individuals within these communities lead—and how exchange systems have evolved within these contexts. There is also little or no consideration of the nature of consumption (or consumers per se) in these situations. For these reasons, the external environment element of our business plan paradigm is extremely important for social ventures. The bottom-up perspective of these ventures provides a more detailed—and more grounded—appreciation of economic interactions and consumption experiences within these communities than top-down perspectives.

Process

Feedback from GSBI participants suggests that a social venture's external environment can have a significant effect on all elements of a business plan. Figure 5.1 illustrates how social ventures are embedded in external environments.

In settings of extreme poverty, institutional voids limit an organization's capacity to do business (transaction governance capacity). External environment analysis is essential for identifying assets and liabilities in external environments. The external environment can be analyzed in five dimensions or categories:

1. Economic environment (market-oriented ecosystem)
2. Legal/regulatory environment
3. ICT environment
4. Community/cultural environment
5. Natural environment (climate, geography)

Figure 5.1 Embedded Systems View Of External Environment

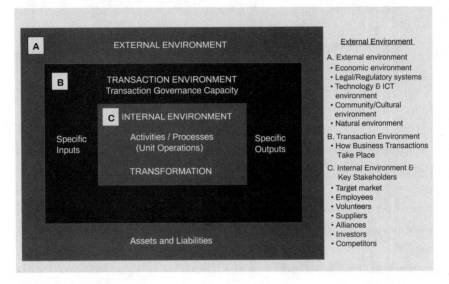

For each dimension of the external environment, a list of conditions that affect the social venture can be created, along with a list of the techniques/methods that can be used to mitigate negative or adverse factors—and to leverage positives or potential sources of momentum. In the following sections, we will take a closer look at each dimension of the external environment.

The Economic Environment

The economic environment consists of organizations, infrastructure, and ways of doing business. More specifically, organizations in the economic environment are potential suppliers, partners, competitors, customers, or other influencers. They can be small or medium enterprises, multinational corporations, governments or NGOs, political groups (e.g., political parties), trade groups or unions, microfirms (e.g., sole proprietorships, mom-and-pop stores), and even extralegal organizations (e.g., gangs, black market players).

Infrastructure includes physical elements such as roads, energy and telecommunication systems, and distribution networks for moving goods and services efficiently. Different ways of doing business include formal and informal mechanisms—things like organization and taxation, banking and unique financial transaction methods (e.g., microfinancing), accounting and financial reporting systems, payment conventions in one-to-one local cash or barter systems, and even bribes—all of which play an important role in the economic environment.

The Legal/Regulatory Systems

Regulatory and legal systems represent constraints within which your organization must operate. Oftentimes they may require a number of trade-offs. Prahalad posits that these kinds of considerations shape the "Transaction Governance Capacity (TGC) of an enterprise."[9]

TGC includes regulations for ownership and transfer of property, intellectual property rights and laws (if there are any), contracts or other methods of documenting business agreements and regulating business transactions, and processes (and institutions) for fairly implementing, enforcing, and changing laws and regulations that affect business conduct. For example, in Bangladesh, enforcing contracts and sales agreements is very difficult. If some of Grameen Shakti's solar home system customers felt that they did not need to pay because other customers were not paying, the Shakti team had to figure out how to make the act of not paying seem like a behavior that discredited the customer and undermined community norms essential to maintaining energy access for everyone. Similar group norm mechanisms in lending circles or self-help groups account for high microfinance repayment rates.

Technology and the ICT Environment

The information and communications technology (ICT) environment includes computer, network communication, and media technologies—everything from print media (e.g., newspapers) to radio, telephones (landline and cellular), networking (Internet), social media, television, and perhaps even movies. In developing markets, ICT environments may be underdeveloped or quite primitive. This can mean that the costs of search, information, and transactions are high compared with those of more developed markets.

The ICT environment affects communication with clients (customers, beneficiaries, and partners), marketing, business transaction processing, and supply chain management. For organizations that seek to scale, the back-office systems (accounting and financial reporting, payroll, employee records, etc.) are all very important elements of the ICT environment.

For those social ventures whose products and services involve the use of cell phones or personal computers for transactions, or are similarly reliant on a communications network, the ICT environment must be reliable. The good news here is that cell phone technology is leap frogging landlines and penetration has skyrocketed in many developing countries. Across some geographies, mobile banking is taking root and rapidly expanding. In these and other contexts, smartphone technology is also taking off. Still, the deployment of advanced communications technologies in developing economies lags behind the high-speed reality of developed countries. In many new markets, radio remains an important communications vehicle.

For social ventures, technology and ICT (especially cell phone ICT) represent substantial opportunities to reduce transaction costs, eliminate middlemen, reach markets, and simplify supply chains. For instance, cloud-based IT platforms have the potential to lower costs of transactions as well as build communities of customers and partners for a social venture. Technological advances such as solar systems or new medical devices can create opportunities for effective, low-cost solutions that social ventures can employ. As an example of the power of ITC to grow markets, the first GSBI social venture to effectively employ Web technology was online microfinance company Kiva. From fewer than 100 loans made in 2005, Kiva grew to over 33,000 loans in 40 countries with 148,000 lenders in just four years. As of this writing, Kiva has helped facilitate more than $1 billion in peer-to-peer lending.

The Community/Cultural Environment

The community/cultural environment consists of social norms and the belief systems of various groups (family, religious, ethnic, interest, and gender), formal institutions (e.g., schools), politics/political parties, and historically rooted practices or ways of doing business. In India, for example, more than 85 percent of jobs are in the informal economy, barter systems remain a prevalent form of exchange, and the elders in local governing councils, or panchayats, play a large role in determining how new market entrants are accepted across more than six hundred thousand villages. Community and cultural contexts must be taken into account in a social business, especially when the mission of the social business, such as the empowerment of women, may be adversely influenced by community norms such as discrimination or exploitation of women. In some instances, safety or the threat of physical violence in a community may prevent a social business from even starting, threaten its strategies, or cause it to have to relocate.

The community/cultural environment can be leveraged to benefit a social business. For example, several GSBI ventures used women's groups to provide services (e.g., cell phone rental, community health workers) or to distribute products (e.g., home solar-powered lamps). Moreover, elements in the community/cultural environment can be a resource by providing volunteers, employees, influential early adoption customers, and partners.

The Natural Environment

The elements of the natural environment often create the motivation for—or amplify the need for—a social business. Floods, hurricanes, air and water pollution, and earthquakes can all create problems that are best confronted by a social business.

Geographic elements of the natural environment can also influence the cost of doing business and methods of accessing beneficiaries. For example, rising sea levels attributed to climate change and frequent typhoons and flooding are major problems in Bangladesh that Grameen Shakti has had to mitigate by developing a resilient supply chain for scaling its solar home system venture. And GSBI venture Build Change created low-cost housing designs that reduce losses from earthquakes.

Social Venture Snapshots

The following Social Venture Snapshots look at an external environment analysis for each of three organizations—Grameen Shakti, Sankara, and GSBI Innovator Build Change. As you will see, each venture uses a slightly different version of the five-factor model suggested earlier. And while each approaches the challenges posed by the external environment differently, all three examples illustrate the potential for embedding solutions in local contexts through attention to driving and constraining forces.

The external environment analysis in each Social Venture Snapshot uses a matrix with four quadrants (Figure 5.2).

Figure 5.2   External Environment Analysis Matrix

Environmental Factors	Actions
Assets	Leverage
Impediments	Mitigate

Social Venture Snapshot: External Environment Analysis for Grameen Shakti (Solar Home Lighting Systems)

For Grameen Shakti, the current undesirable state for energy access is held in place by the logistical challenges of serving island communities, limited access to technical skills, and the inability of the poor to pay the upfront cost of energy investments. Shakti builds trust by leveraging the Grameen brand, building relationships with community leaders, and providing proof-of-concept evidence with early adopters. It partners with high-quality/low-cost manufacturers to supply solar technology, trains young people with technical degrees, provides access to customer finance, and embeds its operations through district branches that provide access to local service and repair.

As shown in Figure 5.3, Grameen Shakti faced several very difficult external environment impediments, such as weather, lack of roads and retail infrastructure, and lack of skilled employees. The Grameen Shakti business plan had to include actions to mitigate these impediments and to leverage assets of the external environment, such as young women who wanted to work.

Social Venture Snapshot: External Environment Analysis for Sankara

Sankara has developed a comprehensive organizational strategy for building a successful social venture. As Figures 5.4–5.7 indicate, this strategy mitigates salient risks in each facet of its operating environment. It leverages its mission through shared values with partner organizations and its strong leadership capacity. The detailed analysis in these figures provides clues for how Sankara has cracked the code for overcoming the challenges of providing access to quality eye care for the poor.

As you may recall, Sankara is an affordable eye care provider in India. Compared with Grameen Shakti, Sankara uses a number of different strategies for mitigating impediments and leveraging assets.

Figure 5.3 External Environment Analysis for Grameen Shakti (Solar Home Lighting Systems)

Environmental Factors	Actions
Assets	**Leverage**
Low-cost solar home systems (from Kyocera, Chinese, and other suppliers)	Use existing systems
Grameen brand	Use Grameen name to legitimize and help funding
Young people with technical degrees	Hire staff, bootstrap training
Community leaders generally have more money	Sell to leaders first and get endorsements
Young women who want to work	Train repair or sales staff
Impediments	**Mitigate**
Extremely poor customers	Offer microfinancing; sell solar lights as income and cash flow enhancing
Competition for skilled employees	Competitive pay, benefits, and promote from within
Cash economy, no IT support for transactions	Have lock boxes for money; develop manual journaling; develop rigorous auditing system
Informal markets instead of retail stores	Use markets for demos
Largely island communities, bad roads, and expensive transport	Local offices, bicycle, or jitney delivery
Expect solar to work forever	Provide full service and warranty plans
If one community does not pay, others may not pay as well	Gentle but firm insistence on payments, may need to involve wives
Difficult geography (islands)	Develop network of district offices
Heavy rain and monsoons	Include replacement warranty

Figure 5.4   The Economic Environment (Market-Oriented Ecosystem)

	Organization and Infrastructure	
External Environment Elements (EEE)	**Impediment (I) or Asset (A)**	**Sankara's Strategy for Leveraging Assets (L) or Mitigating Risk Factors (M)**
Suppliers	A: Low-cost suppliers of medicines and medical equipment	L: Cost is kept down through economies of scale
Partners	I: Limited resources for conducting screening camps	M: Local community sponsors collaborate to fund camps
	A: Partner Foundations (SEF USA and SEF UK) A: Mission for Vision Trust A: Others—Recurring grant providers	L: Donations for equipment, surgeries, new hospitals, and postoperative impact measurement L: Contributed Income • Govt. of India—for the Eye Bank • Sri Ratan Tata Trust for the Sankara Academy of Vision • District Blindness Control Society (DBCS) • Indian Council for Medical Research (ICMR)
Competitors	A: Aravind Eye Care A: Small eye clinics (private practitioners/sole proprietors) I: Vasan Eye Institute (100+ eye hospitals, part of Vasan Health Care network), Apollo Hospitals, Max Health Care, and other regional private hospitals	L: Follow similar, proven cross-subsidy business model L: Get referrals for surgeries and other procedures beyond the capabilities of these small enterprises M: Offer comparable value at better rates than large private eye hospitals
Customers	I: Blindness and poverty	M: Offer convenient on-site screening eye camps in remote villages followed by transportation of patients to the base hospital for free treatment

Figure 5.4 *(Continued)*

Organization and Infrastructure		
External Environment Elements (EEE)	**Impediment (I) or Asset (A)**	**Sankara's Strategy for Leveraging Assets (L) or Mitigating Risk Factors (M)**
Influencers	A: Aravind Eye Care popularized the subsidized, high-efficiency, low-cost model for delivery of healthcare	L: Adopt the same model and strive for self-sufficiency
Roads	A: Well-connected network of national and state highways	L: Establish a network of base hospitals in urban areas, free community hospitals in rural areas, and eye camps in remote rural villages

Figure 5.5 The Legal / Regulatory Environment

Social Structure and Constraints		
External Environment Elements (EEE)	**Impediment (I) or Asset (A)**	**Sankara's Strategy for Leveraging Assets (L) or Mitigating Risk Factors (M)**
Organization and tax laws	A: Sri Kanchi Kamakoti Medical Trust is a registered public charitable trust that manages the Sankara Eye Care Institutions	L: Exemption from payment of tax, donors pay tax-deductible donations. Focus on mission and reinvest surplus in growth
Regulations	A: Multiple surgeries can be performed in the same operating room I: Lack of efficient public healthcare initiative targeting rural poor	L: Attain high efficiency in the process by optimizing the time taken for each medical procedure M: Provide low-cost eye care to rural poor

(continued)

Figure 5.5 *(Continued)*

Social Structure and Constraints		
External Environment Elements (EEE)	Impediment (I) or Asset (A)	Sankara's Strategy for Leveraging Assets (L) or Mitigating Risk Factors (M)
Equivalent of HIPAA rights in India	I: The Government of India has created guidelines for Electronic Health Records (EHR) standards so that medical data becomes portable and easily transferable (India has no law on the lines of HIPAA, patient privacy provisions, or data protection)[1]	M: Promising Digital India[2] initiative by the Gov't of India's Department of Electronics and Information Technology that focuses on e-healthcare and its privacy needs
Health insurance	A: Purchasers of health insurance can avail an annual deduction from a taxable income for payment of health insurance premium[3]	L: Incorporate in business model to enhance patient experience/convenience

Figure 5.6 **The Information & Communication Technology Environment**

Computer, Network, and Media Technologies		
External Environment Elements (EEE)	Impediment (I) or Asset (A)	Sankara's Strategy for Leveraging Assets (L) or Mitigating Risk Factors (M)
Telephone	A: As a result of India's Universal Service Policy,[4] 98.3% of the villages have telephone services Mobile subscribers — 919.2 million *Penetration* — 76.0% Fixed subscribers — 32.2 million *Penetration* — 2.7%	L: Potentially leverage for communication with clients (customers, beneficiaries, and partners), marketing, business transaction processing, and supply chain management

Figure 5.6 *(Continued)*

| Computer, Network, and Media Technologies | | |
External Environment Elements (EEE)	Impediment (I) or Asset (A)	Sankara's Strategy for Leveraging Assets (L) or Mitigating Risk Factors (M)
Internet	I: Internet users (2011) — 125 million Internet subscribers — 22.9 million *Penetration* — 10% Number of PCs (e) — 60 million *Penetration* — 5% A: Use of smartphone retinoscope	M: *The Fletcher School-MasterCard Digital Evolution Index* places India as a "break out" country in terms of digital evolution, meaning the country has the potential to develop a strong digital economy[5] Future opportunity lies in being able to leverage digital evolution for patient online registration, appointment scheduling, online health records management, and other mobile, Web-based transactions (long-term opportunity) L: Screen on-site at the rural camps
Media technology (print media, radio, television, and movies)	I: Advertising of medical services by hospitals on TV and radio is considered unethical and is prohibited under the guidelines by the Indian Medical Association	M: Sankara adheres to very high ethical standards and follows the guidance of the Indian Medical Association. Uses other marketing strategies (print and social media)
Bankers	A: Central Bank of India, Canara Bank, and Axis Bank	L: Trusted partnerships, gives credibility to the organization

[1] http://en.wikipedia.org/wiki/Electronic_health_record#India, [2] http://deity.gov.in/sites/upload_files/dit/files/Digital%20India.pdf, [3] http://www.policyholder.gov.in/uploads/CEDocuments/Health%20Insurance%20Handbook.pdf, [4] http://www.budde.com.au/Research/India-Key-Statistics-Telecommunications-Market-and-Regulatory-Overview.html
[5] http://fletcher.tufts.edu/eBiz/Index#Insights

Figure 5.7 The Community/Cultural Environment

External Environment Elements (EEE)	Institutions, Beliefs, and Practices	
	Impediment (I) or Asset (A)	Sankara's Strategy for Leveraging Assets (L) or Mitigating Risk Factors (M)
Social bias	I: Mind-set from paying customers that "free or subsidized service may be associated with compromised quality"	M: Patient trust gained by value-based service and brand reputation as leading provider; focus on customer satisfaction; emphasize the social good provided by one paying surgery
	I: "If the others are not paying, why should I pay?"	M: Paying and nonpaying centers generally do not receive services under the same roof (separate hospitals)
	I: Educated rural women may not have the freedom to leave their communities in search of job opportunities	M: Rural women are empowered by the training provided for ophthalmological care and the job opportunities to work in camps/community hospitals
Community	A: Common practice of consulting a "family doctor" in India (equivalent to that of a primary care physician, but not necessarily connected to a hospital); often a private practitioner, who might provide referrals for specialists	L: Referral programs for eye care services through word-of-mouth marketing
Generational differences	A: Younger generation more in touch with digital/social media	L: Incorporate Web-based marketing approaches
		M: Improve quality of life by providing affordable eye care
Customers	I: Blindness, and a number of disabilities have associated social taboos; marginalized communities ignored	M: Vision screening for poor children in rural schools (Rainbow Program); integrated child development centers and orphanages (Maithri); outreach to other marginalized communities

Figure 5.7 *(Continued)*

External Environment Elements (EEE)	Institutions, Beliefs, and Practices	
	Impediment (I) or Asset (A)	Sankara's Strategy for Leveraging Assets (L) or Mitigating Risk Factors (M)
Volunteers	I: Lack of funding for programs and operations I: Lack of manpower to conduct the rural camps	M: Non-Resident Indians (NRIs) contribute to the SECI by volunteering for and donating to the SEF in U.S. M: Volunteers for the eye camps
Employees	I: Shortage of well-qualified and trained staff I: Huge healthcare job market with ever-growing demand	M: Sankara Academy of Vision provides in-house training for doctors M: Offer competitive salary and benefits to retain employees, focus on employee satisfaction and rewarding work culture

Social Venture Snapshot: External Environment Analysis for GSBI Innovator Build Change

As Figure 5.8 indicates, Build Change has taken stock of constraints in the external environments in which it operates to create locally suitable designs for low-cost earthquake-resistant housing, advocate for stronger government building codes, train local builders, and leverage partnerships together with its award recognition brand to educate and influence home owners.

Profile (GSBI 2007)

In 2007, Build Change created a successful model for building low-cost, earthquake-resistant housing for low-income populations in earthquake-prone locales. Its mission was simple: to reduce deaths, injuries, and economic losses due to housing collapses caused by earthquakes. It saw an opportunity in the one million people made homeless by earthquakes annually, and measures success in the number of earthquake-resistant houses built.

Mission, Opportunity, and Strategies

Mission	Reduce deaths, injuries, and economic losses due to housing collapses caused by earthquakes
Key metric	Number of earthquake-resistant houses built
Opportunity	One million homeless per year due to earthquakes for past seven years
Strategies	(1) Create design for low-cost, earthquake-resistant houses
	(2) Create bills of materials using local resources
	(3) Train local builders to construct houses

External Environment

The natural environment, particularly the geology of earthquakes, and the lack of building codes and technology in poor countries are the defining contextual elements for Build Change's mission. See Figure 5.8.

Market

One hundred thirty million people live in areas with constant threat of earthquakes. Government agencies have money to pay for earthquake-resistant housing, while potential home owners lack money and training but want to

Figure 5.8   External Environment Analysis for Build Change

Environmental Factors	Actions
Assets	**Leverage**
Government agencies for earthquake relief	Partnerships, awards
Community awareness of problem	Demonstrate success
Local community design preferences	Adapt standard design to local preferences
Impediments	**Mitigate**
Lack of building codes/regulations in poor countries	Develop/advocate standards
Lack of low-cost designs for earthquake-resistant homes	Develop/prove own designs
Lack of skilled professionals to build	Train builders
Severe damage caused by earthquakes	Target post-disaster locales

be involved in the building process. Direct beneficiaries are those who receive new housing, indirect beneficiaries are the communities in which they live, and the related beneficiaries are the governments, economies, and emergency relief organizations. Competitive advantages are the product (housing designs), process (local involvement), and lower cost.

Operations and Value Chain

Key processes: (1) create standard design(s) and adapt for local preferences and materials, (2) train local builders, (3) build and test houses, (4) gain support from locals (women) and implementing agencies, and (5) propose changes to local building codes.

Organization and Human Resources

Build Change is a U.S. nonprofit (501(c)(3))

Board of Directors (3): SE experience, Funding, Business experience + structural and geotechnical engineer, volunteer advisors

Founder and CEO (with building experience and civil engineering degree)

Director of Operations and Building

Local Staff per project

Business Model and Unit Economics

Key revenue drivers: 50 percent → 70 percent earned income (consulting and construction), 50 percent → 30 percent contributed income (grants and donations)
Key expense drivers: staff (70 percent), marketing (8 percent), materials (2 percent), facilities (10 percent), administration (10 percent)

Unit Economics: Unit = house. The goal is to drive the cost per house to less than $100 local materials + local labor.

Metrics

(1) Number of houses built, (2) cost per house, (3) revenue, (4) expenses (burn rate), (5) building codes adopted

Operating Plan

Within one year of leaving GSBI, Build Change adopted an operating plan that led to cash flow breakeven within two years and self-funding in five years.

Financing

Start-up funding in first and second years (negative cash flow) from grants and contributions.

To Recap

In many developing countries, external environment factors, which are outside the direct control of the social venture, can have a serious impact on a social venture's ability to confront challenges efficiently and effectively. Conducting an environmental analysis is important for identifying and mitigating potential impediments and for leveraging potential assets created by the external environment. The Minimum Critical Specifications Checklist outlines the most important points any external environment analysis should address. In the next chapter, we turn to the target market segment.

Exercise

5.1 External Environment Elements

As in the three Social Venture Snapshots, create a table (matrix or spreadsheet) that lists all the external environment elements (EEEs) that influence social venture success. To develop your list of EEEs, start with the five dimensions or categories in the "Process" section of this chapter. You need not be constrained by or include dimensions that do not apply. Identify whether each EEE is an impediment (problem) or asset (benefit) for the venture. For each impediment identify an ac-

Minimum Critical Specifications Checklist

External Environment

- Clarifies what holds current undesirable state in place

- Identifies pivotal ecosystem actors with influence on outcomes

- Specifies ideal partners for leveraging ventures strength

- Defines strategies for mitigating ecosystem risks

tion to mitigate the impediment, and for each asset identify an action to leverage the asset.

Background Resources

Coase, R. H. "The Problem of Social Cost." *Journal of Law and Economics* 3 (October 1960): 1–44.

Dees, J. Gregory, Jed Emerson, and Peter Economy. *Strategic Tools for Social Entrepreneurs: Enhancing the Performance of Your Enterprising Nonprofit.* New York: John Wiley, 2002, chapter 7.

De Soto, H. *Mystery of Capital: Why Capitalism Triumphs in the West and Fails Everywhere Else.* New York: Basic Books, 2003.

Khanna, T., and K. Palepu. "Is Group Affiliation Profitable in Emerging Markets? An Analysis of Diversified Indian Business Groups." *Journal of Finance* 55, no. 2 (2000): 867–891.

Khanna, T., and K. Palepu. "Why Focused Strategies May Be Wrong for Emerging Markets." *Harvard Business Review,* July-August 1997.

Mair, J., and I. Marti. "Entrepreneurship in and around Institutional Voids: A Case Study from Bangladesh." *Journal of Business Venturing* 24, no. 5 (2009): 419–435.

Prahalad, C. K. *The Fortune at the Bottom of the Pyramid: Eradicating Poverty through Profits.* Philadelphia: Wharton School Publishing, 2010, chapters 4, 5, and 6.

Webb, J. W., R. D. Ireland, and D. J. Ketchen. "Towards a Greater Understanding of Entrepreneurship and Strategy in the Informal Economy." *Strategic Entrepreneurship Journal* 8 (2014): 1–15.

Webb, J. W., G. M. Kistruck, R. D. Ireland, and D. J. Ketchen Jr. "The Entrepreneurship Process in Base of the Pyramid Markets: The Case of Multinational Enterprise/Nongovernment Organization Alliances." *Entrepreneurship Theory and Practice* 34, no. 3 (2010): 555–581.

Williamson, O. E. *The Economic Institutions of Capitalism.* New York: Simon & Schuster, 1985.

See also the World Bank's Doing Business website (www.doingbusiness.org) and search on country of interest and business topic of interest. This website is very useful in understanding key elements of the external environment (such as the ability to sign and enforce contracts) in each country.

Chapter 6

The Target Market Statement

The concept of a "target market" borrows from traditional business terminology. There, it means a certain group of would-be customers or consumers who are the "target" users of a good or service. For social ventures, though, it refers more to those individuals or groups that the organization is intended to serve—perhaps a subtle nuance. In this chapter, we look at the target market statement portion of the business plan.

Process

A target market statement identifies the precise group of beneficiaries you want to serve, describing, specifically, the size and characteristics of that group. For a social venture, the target market statement identifies the beneficiaries (customers) for whom the venture's products/services create value. There may be a distinction between those who will use the product or service (direct beneficiaries) and those who will pay for or benefit from creating or delivering the product or service (indirect beneficiaries). For example, early on, Grameen Shakti received grants to install specific numbers of household solar systems in particular geographic markets.

There are numerous other examples of third-party payers: organizations identifying sponsors for providing meals or education for children in the BOP (e.g., Save the Children), paying customers who cross-subsidize those who cannot pay, and network operators who pay for mobile banking infrastructure to increase the "stickiness" of cell phone users. Similarly, in two-sided platforms, suppliers of agricultural inputs pay for ICT platforms that provide small holders with market information paid for by advertising.

The target market statement should identify the attributes (needs) of your beneficiaries that make your product or service valuable to them. These attributes, if specific and descriptive, will identify a category of potential beneficiaries (customers) that view your product as compelling relative to their needs and alternatives for meeting their needs. The target market statement is made up of four parts:

1. A definition of the total available market—all the potential beneficiaries who could possibly use your product/service

2. A definition of the total addressable market—those beneficiaries you are currently targeting and could reach within a few years

3. A market segmentation table identifying beneficiary characteristics most relevant to decisions to use your product or service

4. A marketing plan that includes sales channels or how you will reach your intended beneficiaries

Basic Knowledge
BOP market intelligence is generally poor. Many ventures flounder by making gross extrapolations from macrodata. Need is not demand, and the poor are not an undifferentiated mass. The poor often exist in informal markets that are opaque to outsiders.

Segmentation is key to understanding human needs, cultural influences, how to adapt solutions to perceptions of value across geographies, and ability to pay. Investors favor "big" markets, but the 4 P's of go-to-market strategies must be adapted to heterogeneous contexts where market channels and last mile distribution are underdeveloped or major voids.

Step 1: Estimate the Total Available Market
To begin, estimate the size of the market—that is, how many people your enterprise could serve if it were completely successful. This estimation is usually a subset of the *opportunity* identified as part of *mission/opportunity/strategies*. You can use geographic boundaries (e.g., continent, nation, state) and

demographics (e.g., age, gender, social groups) to further segment this number. Specify the key needs/problems your strategies are intended to address (impact) in each segment. This is the *total addressable market*. In Figure 6.1, the *served/addressable market* includes both your *target market* and those that could be reached with your sales channels.

There are two approaches for estimating market size: top down and bottom up. In a top-down approach, data from summary sources (e.g., a census or other government survey) is used as the base. The market size estimate is then taken as a percentage of that base. For example, a service offering alternative energy might estimate that it can reach 75 percent of the one million homes currently without electricity. A bottom-up approach uses local data to aggregate the market size (e.g., there are one hundred thousand villages each with an average of four hundred homes, and if we reach 50 percent of the homes in

Two-Sided Platforms
Historically, users have almost always paid, albeit in many different ways, usually at time of purchase or subsequently through usage charges. But with newspapers, television, and finally the internet, technology has created the possibility that users may not pay for the services they received—payment instead being made by others such as advertisers. Two-sided platforms of this type are hybrid business models because they incorporate two value delivery systems, one for the user (such as a consumer that wants to search) and another for the customer who pays, such as a small firm that wants to place an advertisement where it can be seen by a particular kind of consumer.[1]

50 percent of the villages we will reach one million homes). Other possible data sources for market size include the World Bank, the International Monetary Fund, United Nations groups such as the World Health Organization, and market research firms such as International Data Corporation (IDC). An internet search on "emerging markets" will produce several additional sources of data to help estimate total available market for your venture.

Figure 6.1 Segmenting the Market

Total available market = How big is the universe

Served / Addressable market = How many can I reach with my current sales channel

Target market = Who will be the most likely buyers

Penetrated market = Existing user base

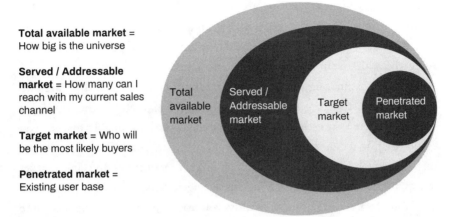

If your focus encompasses the U.S. domestic market, relevant statistics are available through SBA.gov, the U.S. Census Bureau (www.census.gov), and FedStats.gov.

Step 2: Define the Addressable Market

Identify the segments within the *total addressable market* you are currently targeting or could reach within a few years. This is the group of potential beneficiaries that could be reached with existing financial and human resources, or those that can realistically be marshaled. Identify why these potential beneficiaries will "consume" the product or service, rather than an alternative (including "nonconsumption"). This is the total addressable market positioning statement. Reasons to consume are closely related to your venture's value proposition—the pivotal dimension of your business model.

Step 3: Identify Market Segments

The target market is those customers (beneficiaries) that you are going to try to attract now. To do so, it helps to segment, or divide, the customers into different categories. Each category should be based on factors that will help your organization better understand specific characteristics of potential beneficiaries, how to reach them, and what kind of communication and messaging will convince them to use your organization's product or adopt its services. Demographic factors such as age, education level, income level, location, and size of family are relevant here, as are psychographic factors—things like group affiliation (e.g., industry or village organization), as well as cultural, religious, linguistic, and peer influence and personal aspirations. Altogether, this is your target market segmentation.

As with estimating the size of the total available market, there are two methods for estimating the size of your target market: (1) the top-down method, where you estimate what percentage of the available market you could reach in a defined time period (e.g., five years), and (2) the bottom-up method, which involves surveying units in a subset of the addressable market (e.g., two villages) and multiplying the average estimated market per unit in the subset by the total number of units you expect to reach in a defined time period.

Once you specify the existing market size and segments, you can begin developing a more in-depth characterization by differentiating attributes and needs of beneficiaries. One approach to developing a deeper understanding of these segments is to interview potential beneficiaries to more fully appreciate individual needs and the attributes that influence their day-to-day life choices. You may elect to focus your "marketing" efforts on a single segment or multiple segments. Segmentation may also lead to developing multiple marketing messages with different (or slightly different) products or services for each target market segment.

Market segmentation is important for many reasons:

- It identifies relevant characteristics of intended beneficiaries and helps determine their adoption and consumption patterns.

- It can be used for beneficiary analysis in product pricing, refining channel strategies, and building customer relationships through customer education, product or brand advertising, and other marketing processes.

- It can be used to enhance the effectiveness of communication and tailor marketing to the various groups or segments.

Figure 6.2 shows a number of different variables to use when categorizing and estimating the size of segments of your total market.

Figure 6.2 Variables for Market Segmentation

Type of Variable	Attributes
Descriptor variables	• Demographics • Socioeconomics
Psychological variables	• Attitudes • Interests • Culture • Opinions • Lifestyle • Personality • Aspirations
Product/Patronage characteristics (situation specificity)	• Purchase occasion • Use occasion • Usage rate • Brand loyalty • Benefits sought

Step 4: Develop a Marketing Plan

The final step in creating the *target market statement* is to develop a *marketing plan*. We will use a common framework for a marketing plan called the 4 P's: (1) product, (2) price, (3) placement, and (4) promotion.

Product, quite obviously, defines the product(s) or service(s) that you will deliver to your beneficiaries (clients, customers).

Price defines the amount (possibly nothing, or possibly different prices for different market segments) that you will charge for the product(s) or service(s). In a social business, there are five ways to create a price:

1. Subsidized (free): The costs will be borne by a third party on either a total volume or per unit basis.

2. Cost based: The price is based on either recovering the costs of each product or service (fully loaded cost basis) or recovering the marginal (incremental) costs of each product or service (marginal cost basis). Fully loaded cost basis is determined by dividing the total expenses of the organization for a time period by the number of units to be "sold" during that same period. Marginal cost basis is determined by dividing the (total) costs of goods sold (COGS) for all units sold in a time period by the number of units sold in that same period.

3. Market based: You set the price—below, the same as, or above the price of alternative products—based on what you think a beneficiary will pay for your product and its perceived value compared with alternatives.

4. Value based: You set the price based on a percentage of the monetary value of your product/service to the customer (e.g., the percentage of increased income or savings due to use of your product).

5. Ability to pay: You set the price of the product based on the ability to pay for each beneficiary category.

For many product(s) or service(s) in a social business, the price may not entirely cover the costs (expenses). However, the business model (chapter 9) you develop for your enterprise must still provide enough income to cover all your expenses.

Placement describes the methods (channels) used to deliver your product(s)/service(s) to the beneficiaries. Promotion describes what

Word of Mouth

Employing observations and in-depth interviews of a variety of buyers and sellers in rural and urban South India, Madhu Viswanathan documented how marketplaces in resource-poor contexts are typically rich in face-to-face interactions and exchanges that stand in contrast to the largely anonymous interactions typical of advanced economies.[2]

Word of mouth and one-to-one relationships between the individual and the neighborhood retail store owner take center stage in these situations. The nature of transactions is often fluid, with price and quantity being negotiated, installments not being paid, and prices being adjusted for personal circumstances to both the buyer's and seller's advantage. Functioning in "subsistence markets" requires developing trusting relationships and norms of reciprocity in exchange transactions that have a medium- to long-term perspective.[3]

is to be done to make sure the beneficiaries are aware of your product(s) and service(s). As the Word of Mouth sidebar indicates, marketing to the poor requires a deep appreciation of local context.

Social Venture Snapshots

The following Social Venture Snapshots look at *target market statements* for each of three organizations—Grameen Shakti, Sankara, and GSBI Innovator Digital Divide Data. We begin with Shakti. It provides an excellent example of a highly refined and detailed approach to market segmentation, with product offerings customized on the basis of income and ability to pay, as well as occupations, use cases, and geography. Interestingly, this more fine-grained approach to market segmentation has the positive effects of increasing product innovation, reducing the costs of ownership to target segments, and increasing market penetration.

Social Venture Snapshot: Marketing Plan for Grameen Shakti (Solar Home Lighting Systems) Beneficiary Analysis and Marketing

Direct, Indirect, and Related Beneficiaries (Solar Lighting Systems)

Direct: Rural poor-income earners and their families

Indirect: Grameen Trust and Foundation, United States Agency for International Development (USAID), and other funding sources, solar lighting system suppliers, and stove/biogas partners

Related: Families in rural communities, Bangladesh economy, and politicians seeking political stability

The "Total Addressable Market" Size for Direct Beneficiaries

In 1996 approximately seventy-seven million Bangladeshis (64 percent of the 120 million rural poor) were without access to the grid. This is about fourteen million families.

The Key Market Segmentation Bases for the Direct Beneficiaries (Geographic, Demographic, Product/Service Needs)

Segmented based on location/geography (sixty-four districts and forty thousand villages), annual income (50 percent 8K Taka–10K Taka, 40 percent 5K Taka–8K Taka, 10 percent <5K Taka), occupation (farmer, fisherman, teacher, etc.), and needs (10W home system: 1–2 5W lamps, 18Ah battery and 5/10 Amp charger; through 130 W "micro-utility" system [11 7W lamps, 100 Ah battery, 15 Amp charger, 17"–20" B/W TV]).

Competition, Differentiation/Compelling Reason to Consume

Candles and kerosene lamps and nonconsumption (no lights) are the main competition, along with solar system "giveaways." The main differentiation/reasons to consume are brighter lights (can work after dark, yielding 20–25 percent more income), great customer service, fewer health problems, and saves 324 Taka per month (kerosene plus battery recharging and replacement costs). Extra income plus cost savings pays for solar system in two to three years.

Go-to-Market Plan (4 P's) to Identify/Attract Direct Beneficiaries

Products: Ten solar systems (with solar panel, battery, charger, and lights) to match needs

Pricing: Solar home systems: 8.8K Taka ($128) to 64.5K Taka ($935), financed at 25 percent down and 4 percent interest over two years, or 15 percent down and 6 percent interest over three years

Placement: Developed own sales and service system

Promotion: Demos in markets and community leaders' homes, customer testimonials

Social Venture Snapshot: Target Market for Sankara

Sankara's target market analysis situates direct beneficiaries in a wider ecosystem of stakeholders. Each of these stakeholder groups benefits from engaging with Sankara in its mission of providing affordable, high-quality eye care to the poor. By segmenting its direct beneficiary target market along four dimensions, and by differentiating its service offerings and price relative to competitors, Sankara is able to increase its reach and impact. (Note: in your work on the exercises for this business element you should reflect on how effective market segmentation can foster innovation and enable you to increase market penetration.)

Direct, Indirect, and Related Beneficiaries

Sankara's target market consists of direct, indirect, and related beneficiaries. The direct beneficiaries (those that use Sankara's services) are the patients requiring eye care, including patients who receive eye screenings, eye exams, and medical procedures such as eye surgeries. The indirect beneficiaries are those that deliver the product/service (the medical staff) as well as the Sankara Academy of Vision, which trains the staff. Sankara's partners, which contribute funding to the organization, are also indirect beneficiaries. These include Sankara Eye Foundation (USA), Sankara Eye Foundation (Europe), and Mission for Vision Trust. Related beneficiaries include the female hospital staff and field workers (who are empowered via job opportunities), the families of individuals receiving eye care treatment (who may benefit from the patient's ability to return to work and earn income), and the villages and communities in which Sankara conducts its eye camps. The economies of these communities benefit from the increase in earning power once the treated patients are able to return to work.

Target Market Size and Key Market Segmentation Bases

An estimated thirty million people around the world suffer from blindness (mostly cataract blindness). This is the total available market for direct beneficiaries. As previously mentioned, within India, there are eight to twelve million needlessly blind. This is the addressable market for Sankara.

Sankara targets both the rural poor and the urban middle class in India. Given the cross-subsidy model, the middle class is key to Sankara's success. Best estimates indicate that the middle class in India comprises, at most, only 30 percent of the population. However, the middle class is the most rapidly growing segment of the population. While very limited data exists on the middle class in India, this population segment can be further divided into two income level groups, as noted in a 2007 McKinsey study:[4]

1) **Annual income of 200,000 to 500,000 Rupees (Rs):** Description of consumer: the lower end of the middle class. This segment primarily consists of young graduates, government workers, traders, and businesspeople. They generally own simple consumer goods such as a TV, refrigerator, mobile phone, and perhaps a mode of transportation. They do not have a lot of disposable income but strive to save for educational expenses and retirement.

2) **Annual income of 500,000 to 1 million Rs:** Description of consumer: the upper end of the middle class. This segment is successful in the workforce and primarily consists of senior government officials, high-level businesspeople, working professionals, and well-off farmers. They generally own many consumer goods beyond the basics, including air conditioning, cars, and electronics. They have disposable income to indulge in some splurges.

Sankara segments its customers in several distinct ways:

1) **Ability to pay:**

   ∞ Affordable premium eye care for urban middle class ($3 billion market, further described above)—20 percent of its customers

   ∞ Free eye care for rural poor—80 percent of its customers

2) **Geographic:**

   ∞ City hospitals (for urban customers)—20 percent of its customers

   ∞ Community hospitals (for rural, nonpaying customers)—80 percent of its customers

   ∞ Note: Sankara aims to target the needlessly blind who are within a 200 km radius of each of its hospitals

3) **Demographics:**

- ∞ Women

- ∞ Men

- ∞ Children

- ∞ Marginalized groups (e.g., transgender individuals)

4) **Types of eye care services:**

- ∞ Basic comprehensive care (eye screenings, fittings for lenses/glasses, etc.) versus specialty services (cataract surgery, glaucoma treatment, ocular oncology, etc.)

- ∞ Inpatient versus outpatient treatments

Sankara's competition and influencers are shown in Figure 6.3.

Marketing Plan (4 P's)

Sankara's marketing plan addresses the 4 P's (product, price, placement, and promotion).

Product: Sankara provides comprehensive and specialized eye care services, as illustrated in Figure 6.4.

Price: Sankara's pricing model differs based on the customer's ability to pay and the city within India where the services are being performed. Rural poor customers receive their treatment (along with lodging, transportation, and food) for free. City customers receive treatment at affordable prices. Sankara has committed that the cost of services will always be equal to or less than that of comparable hospitals. This is a key part of its strategy and ability to build trust within its communities. Figure 6.5 shows a sampling of prices for two common eye procedures at three Sankara hospital locations.

Placement (channels): Sankara currently has a network of fourteen city and rural community hospitals at which treatments and services are performed. In addition, eye camps in rural communities are a critical channel for conducting initial screenings of customers, who are then transported by

Figure 6.3   Sankara's Competition and Influencers

Competitor	Differentiation from Sankara	Compelling Reason to Consume
Aravind Eye Care Systems	65/35 ratio (paying vs. nonpaying customers) Quality of care (different level of service for paying vs. nonpaying customers) Geography (locations restricted to South India)	Affordable, quality eye care Trusted brand
Government health centers	Low quality of care	Free services
Private eye clinics	Higher prices No free services	Eye care expertise High-quality services
Multispecialty hospitals	Offer full medical services (beyond eye care)	Convenience

Figure 6.4   Sankara's Service Offerings

Comprehensive Eye Care Services	Specialty Services
• Cataract and IOL clinic • Corneal and external eye disease • Pediatric care • Glaucoma services • Vitreo retinal services • Occuloplasty and aesthetics • Low vision • LASIK • Contact lens clinic • Computer vision clinic • Ocular oncology	• Cataract • Glaucoma • Diabetic retinopathy • Ocular oncology • Cornea and refractive surgery • Pediatric ophthalmology • Eye banking

Sankara to one of its community hospitals for further treatment. The Rainbow Program provides an additional channel for delivering services to school-aged children. Teachers are trained to conduct initial eye screenings of their students, and then Sankara doctors conduct follow-up examinations and treatments as needed.

Figure 6.5 Sankara Competition Pricing

Hospital Location	Eye Exam Price (Rs)	Cataract Surgery Price (Rs)
Anand	200	11,950
Bangalore	300	21,000 — 30,000*
Coimbatore	100	12,000 — 34,000*

*Price range is dependent on type of lens chosen (locally made versus imported)

Promotion: Sankara is a well-known brand in India for providing high-quality affordable eye care. Much of its promotional activities are done via word of mouth. Promotional activities for the nonpaying segment are done via the eye camps and by spreading awareness in rural communities with the help of partners. For the paying segment, Sankara's promotional strategy has focused on spreading awareness within a five- to seven-kilometer radius of its city hospital locations. Promotional activities for the paying segment include billboards, flyers, and newspaper inserts in the target area, as well as screening events in apartment complexes, malls, and so on. Additional promotional programs include the following:

> *Corporate programs:* Sankara has corporate relationships with large and small companies in India, such as Philips India and Cognizant Technological Solutions. Sankara periodically conducts visual screenings of corporate employees on the company campuses. This strategy has been very effective on multiple levels—employees love the convenience, and it is a great way to increase awareness about Sankara's high-quality and affordable eye care services among the middle-class, urban corporate employees. Many of these employees and their families end up becoming lifelong Sankara patients.

> *Health insurance programs:* Sankara has tie-ups with health insurance companies such as United India Insurance and Star Health Insurance.

> *TPA programs:* Sankara has tie-ups with health insurance third-party administrators (TPAs) and offers cashless transactions, which is very convenient for patients.

> *Education/Conferences:* Sankara conducts periodic conferences where the latest eye care treatments and technology are dis-

cussed. External local doctors are invited to participate in these conferences, and many times they end up referring their patients with eye ailments to Sankara.

Social media marketing and online reputation manage-ment: Sankara has hired a third-party agency for social media marketing (keyword search ads) and for online reputation management such as closing the loop on any concerns posted online (e.g., long wait times).

It is important to note that Sankara does not implement TV or radio ads. In India, advertising of medical services by hospitals on TV and radio is considered unethical under the guidelines by the Indian Medical Association. However, this does not stop many private providers from continuing to advertise via this medium. Sankara always adheres to very high ethical standards and has chosen to follow the guidance of the Indian Medical Association.

Social Venture Snapshot: GSBI Innovator Digital Divide Data

Digital Divide Data (DDD) is one of the rare ventures to have participated in the GSBI on two occasions (in both 2004 and ten years later in 2014). The snapshot below is from 2004, when its business planning efforts were in an early stage of forming, with updates reflecting substantial progress by 2014. In 2008 DDD received the prestigious Skoll Award. It is a sustainable business recognized worldwide for the quality of its services, innovation, and social impact. The "Impact Sourcing" model established by DDD has been spread around the world by dozens of organizations.

Profile (GSBI 2004)

Digital Divide Data targets multiple countries with education/training sites that use students as staff in IT outsourcing, creating income for sites and jobs for the graduates.

Mission, Opportunity, and Strategies

Mission   Provide education/growth for students via high-
                           quality technology services to customers

Key metric	Average salaries for graduates
Opportunity	Hundreds of thousands of disadvantaged youth in developing world
Strategies	(1) Provide high school–level education and IT training
	(2) Offer low-cost, high-quality IT services to customers (e.g., data entry) using students as staff
	(3) Place graduates in IT jobs

External Environment

Lack of education/training and predominance of low-paying jobs in developing world; low confidence, self-esteem, and skills among disadvantaged youth (especially girls); high unemployment rates and low economic growth rates in targeted countries; opportunity for employment in outsourcing IT tasks (e.g., data entry) from developed world; access to IT technology and training courses.

Market

Total available market:

Direct beneficiaries: millions of disadvantaged, unemployed youth

Indirect beneficiaries: hundreds of companies needing outsourced IT services

Related beneficiaries: families of students, economies in target markets

Total addressable market: In 2004, target market was two countries (in 2015, four countries on three continents)

Target market segmentation: Digital Divide Data's market segmentation is shown in Figure 6.6

Competition: A few outsourcing companies (compete on price, quality), no IT training schools

Figure 6.6　Target Market Segmentation

Country	Population	Unemployment Rate	Student Gender/Age	# Students
Laos	6M	5.7%	Teenage girls	50
Cambodia	11M	7%	Teenage girls	100

Marketing Plan:

1. Product: high school–level education including IT training

2. Price: education/training is free, but students are staff for IT outsourcing business

3. Placement: create local schools as IT outsourcing businesses

4. Promotion: partners, outsourcing client references

Operations and Value Chain

The key processes for Digital Divide Data are (1) create education centers for IT outsourcing business, (2) recruit students, (3) train students, (4) recruit IT outsourcing clients, (5) complete outsourcing contracts with high-quality, (6) place student graduates (number of jobs).

The value chain serves to educate, train, and provide job placement for disadvantaged youth by providing high-quality IT outsourcing services using students as staff.

Organization and Human Resources

DDD has a U.S. nonprofit (501(c)(3)) for fund-raising and executive management, and local DDD centers are for-profit IT outsourcing businesses.

Board of Directors: in North America Chairman, BA Yale, MBA Stanford: CEO, BA Harvard, MBA MIT: CMO, BS Michigan, MA Tufts, MSc London School of Economics, employed by McKinsey: VP Business Development, BA Oberlin, MA Central European University; in each of Laos and Cambodia: General Manager and Operations Manager, locals

Business Model and Unit Economics

Key income drivers: grants (20 percent), outsourcing contracts (80 percent)

Key expense drivers: staff (50 percent), capital (30 percent), marketing/recruiting/job placement (20 percent)

Unit Economics: Unit = student; cost per student about $1,870

Metrics

(1) Number of students, (2) outsourcing revenue, (3) expenses, (4) net profit, (5) number of student jobs, and (6) average salary per student placed.

Operating Plan

Annual operating plans are created by each site.

Financing

Started in 2001 with donor financing; by 2004, 80 percent earned income financing and 20 percent donor financing.

To Recap

Markets at the Base of the Pyramid are not just like any other market. Informal markets—which can be less than intuitive to even the best-intentioned outsiders—make up a significant portion of BOP markets. To get the best sense of the needs of these kinds of markets, the kinds of cultural influences that are in play, and the ability of a given market to pay for goods and services, segmentation is a necessity. The Minimum Critical Specifications Checklist outlines the most important points any target market statement should include. In the next chapter, we turn to operations and value chain.

Exercises

6.1 Total Available Market

Create an estimate of the total available market that (1) divides the potential beneficiaries for your product into major categories (segments) using geography (or other major categorization); (2) determines the number of beneficiaries in each major segment; and, (3) specifies the key product/service needs of major segments. Cite the source (basis) for your estimation of market size.

6.2 Total Addressable (Target) Market Positioning Statement

Create a total addressable market positioning statement that identifies the characteristics and size of that segment of the total available market that you currently are targeting, and compares the venture's products/services with key alternatives, including nonconsumption.

> ## Minimum Critical Specifications Checklist
>
> ### The Target Market Statement
>
> - Specifies target market (direct beneficiaries, bases for segmentation, market size)
>
> - Clarifies who will pay (direct, indirect, or related beneficiaries)
>
> - Defines competition, differentiation, compelling reason to consume and influencers
>
> - Specifies marketing plan (4 P's) and how to engage direct beneficiaries
>
> - Provides evidence of a sufficient size of market to support a business

- Characteristics: Key characteristics that define potential beneficiaries for the products/services

- Size: Number of beneficiaries that currently use each alternative

- The positioning of the product/service compared with alternatives, including nonconsumption. You may wish to prepare a competitive alternative table that lists benefits/cost/beneficiary experience factors in the first column, advantages of your venture in the second column,

advantages of competitor 1 in the third column, and
advantages of competitor 2 in the fourth column

6.3   Market Segmentation Table

Create a market segmentation table identifying different addressable market subgroups, by distinctive attributes. For each segment, describe why the venture's offering will gain adoption.

6.4   Create a 4 P's Marketing Plan

P1.   **Product/Service:** Write a short description of each product or service the venture provides, including what it does and the benefits it provides the user ("the reason to buy").

P2.   **Price:** Specify a price for each product or service. Often pricing is set using a combination of two or more of these pricing methods—for example, a subsidized price based on a third-party buyer paying all or part of the cost-based pricing.

P3.   **Placement:** Describe how products/services are delivered to customers (your "channels"). Typical channels (in order of increasing costs) include use of an existing channel (coordination), use of an existing social group to create a new channel (collaboration), and creation of a completely new vertically integrated channel.

P4.   **Promotion:** Describe the methods you will use to inform beneficiaries about your products and/or services. Typical methods of promotion (in order of increasing costs) include word of mouth, partnering (the partner promotes), and advertising (print, radio, Web, TV).

Background Resources

Baden-Fuller, Charles, and Stefan Haefliger. "Business Models and Technological Innovation." *Long Range Planning* 46 (2013): 419–426.

Dees, J. Gregory, Jed Emerson, and Peter Economy. *Strategic Tools for Social Entrepreneurs: Enhancing the Performance of Your Enterprising Nonprofit.* New York: John Wiley, 2002, chapter 2.

DeThomas, Arthur, and Stephanie Derammelaere. *How to Write a Convincing Business Plan.* 3rd ed. New York: Barron's Educational Services, 2008, chapters 6 and 7.

Jain, S., and J. Koch. "Conceptualizing Markets for Underserved Communities: Trajectories Taken and the Road Ahead." In *Sustainability, Society, Business Ethics, and Entrepreneurship*, edited by A. Guerber and G. Markman. Singapore: World Scientific Publishers, forthcoming.

Rochet, J. C., and J. Tirole. "Two-Sided Markets: A Progress Report." *Rand Journal of Economics* 37, no. 3 (2006): 645–667.

Viswanathan, M. "Understanding Product and Market Interactions in Subsistence Marketplaces: A Study in South India." *Advances in International Management* 20 (2006): 21–57.

Viswanathan, M., and S. Sridharan. "Product Development for the BoP: Insights on Concept and Prototype Development from University-Based Student Projects in India." *Journal of Product Innovation Management* 29, no. 1 (2012): 52–69.

Chapter 7

Operations and Value Chain

The operations and value chain of a social venture describe the key processes that create value for its beneficiaries.

Within the boundaries of an organization, where inputs are transformed into outputs, both direct and indirect operating routines create value by contributing to the quality of outputs and organizational productivity, the motivation of people, and the organization's overall capacity to make change. These routines are shaped by the experience, values, and organizational philosophy of the founders. Their influence extends beyond rational mechanisms for the control and coordination of work to the shaping of organizational culture, the intrinsic or motivating nature of work, and organizational learning. These features often persist long after the founders depart and become institutionalized or taken for granted characteristics of "how things are done" within the organization.

In building better ventures, as a rule of thumb, there should be at least one core process for each *key strategy* (identified in chapter 4). If marketing is not explicitly a key strategy, there still needs to be at least one process for marketing (e.g., executing the *marketing plan* from chapter 6). The *organization plan* (chapter 8) should assign primary responsibility for each process to one individual (even if that processes is carried out by a partner). In small organizations, one individual may have responsibility for more than one process, but more than one person should never have responsibility for one process (even if multiple people carry out the process, only one should be "in charge"). When the venture creates its financial plan, each process should have a budget (specified financial allocations), including those processes that produce income for your organization.

Value chains encompass a range of actors—from customers to suppliers and channel partners, to community-based stakeholder groups and political entities. In some instances, value creation is reflected in the flow of products or services and monetized in the flow of money. In other instances, it is reflected in the flows of information, in-kind services, and formal or informal collaborations. Together with the *business model* (chapter 9), *operations and value chains* describe "how the business works" to create value for the beneficiaries—and to capture value to sustain and grow future organizational capacity.

The *operations and value chain* element of a business plan is the basis for creating the internal organization (workflow, job design, and accountability structure), external partnerships, and formal procedures or operating routines to implement the mission. It is the mechanism through which the organization creates the impact (value and desired change) called for in its mission statement.

- *Operations* are the key internal processes implemented to create value for beneficiaries and to capture sufficient resources to sustain and scale impact.

- *Value chains* show the relationships among these processes and key people or entities, both internally and externally.

Process

An organization's operations can be classified as primary (directly create value for the beneficiaries) and support (necessary to maintain and strengthen the primary processes). Examples of primary processes include the following:

- Developing new products (or product life cycle)

- Purchasing/ inventory management

Basic Knowledge

Operational excellence starts with repeatable processes. Specifying value chains enables ventures to identify internal capabilities and skills needed to achieve social impact and financial viability. Identifying and developing core competencies facilitates growth and differentiation. Value chains also specify where external partners are key to success and, where incentives are aligned, shared value can be created.

- Manufacturing products

- Distribution/delivery of products and services

- Locating beneficiaries

- Recruiting beneficiaries

- Quality control/assurance

- Arranging financing for beneficiaries

Support processes are those that are needed to fund or enable the primary processes. Examples include the following:

- Fund-raising and preparing reports for funders

- Hiring and training employees

- Setting prices and collecting fees

- Evaluating and rewarding employees

- Information technology, administrative and accounting services

Note that an organization probably will not have every single one of these primary and support processes, and may in fact have others that are not listed here. Most organizations can define their value creation with fewer than ten primary and support processes combined.

Many of the key innovations required for creating and delivering affordable, quality products or services for BOP or other underserved markets are process innovations—for example, using local raw materials such as rice husks or repurposed animal waste and locally developed skills to generate electricity through a gasification or bio-digester process.

A good way to identify key processes is to review chapter 4 and identify the specific tasks that need to be accomplished to implement each of your *strategies*. As you will recall, *strategies* for your social venture were specified on the bases of their relationship to the change/impact you seek to achieve through your *mission*.

For example, for the Sankara Eye Care System mission of "curing needless cataract blindness in India," a *key strategy* was to develop a "high volume surgery process." This strategy actually requires five primary processes:

P1. Identify and recruit patients (community outreach)

P2. Assess and admit patients to the hospital and decide on their "fee" (hospital admissions)

P3. Prepare them for surgery (presurgery care)

    a. Nonpaying patients

    b. Paying patients

P4. Perform surgery

P5. Perform postsurgery care and analysis

In addition, there is one important support process:

S1. Recruit and train employees

High-performing organizations are explicit about "variances" that affect quality or costs, as well as accountabilities for their control (see sidebar, "System Variances"). They are also mindful of the need to select the right people and create a positive, empowering organizational culture (a topic we address in chapter 8). The delineation of "key variances" for each process can help in developing effective process metrics (chapter 10).

Partnerships

In transaction economic theory, there are three primary organizational forms: integrated, hierarchical, and networked. In integrated forms, all of the factors required to create and deliver value are controlled by a single organization. This is referred to as a vertically integrated organization. Hierarchical forms exercise control through formal rules within hierarchically structured accountabilities and financial controls—archetype examples include franchise and holding company forms. Most organizations—and the vast majority of social businesses—are network forms. Network forms must depend on a number of other actors to create, deliver, and capture value. Figure 7.1 describes the nature of interdependencies and mechanisms such as memorandums of understanding (MOUs) or contracts for governing relationships where operations are not vertically integrated.

Partners may carry out some key processes, such as manufacturing or distribution and marketing (attracting customers or beneficiaries). In these instances, there should be a written agreement with each partner specifying what the partner will do for you and what you will do for the partner (e.g., payment processing, product design and manufacturing, providing metrics or assessing impact). Different types of partnerships involve different degrees of interdependence, and each can be characterized by the type of written agreement needed to formalize the value exchange relationship.

It is useful to create a table that shows key partnerships, the nature of relationship interdependencies, and the value being exchanged as part of the partnership. Figure 7.2 shows such a table for Grameen Shakti. In the example, two of the partnering relationships require more formalized or contractual agreements.

System Variances

Operations can be analyzed by examining key processes as though each of these steps is an operating unit subject to variances that drive organizational effectiveness and the quality of working life. Overall operating systems can be broken down into these unit operations.

High-performing systems identify variances that affect quality or cost as well as customer satisfaction, market penetration, and employee well-being, and specify mechanisms for their control. Specifying process variances—where they occur, where they are observed, and where they are controlled—is critical to effective systems design. Variance control should occur as close as possible to where the variance occurs, as opposed to being "passed down the line." This requires careful attention to job design and the empowerment of those who perform those jobs.

In social ventures, the values and mission of the enterprise can be powerful motivators, especially if combined with the selection of people for "fit" with mission and ability to learn, a high-performance culture, and an empowering work system. Controlling variances as close as possible to where they occur is a core tenet of socio-technical systems design thinking.

Figure 7.1 Partnership Types

Type of Partnership	What Is Exchanged	Written Agreement
Network	Information (e.g., client names)	Memorandum of Understanding (MOU)
Coordination	Common/shared processes for serving different beneficiary groups; or, separate but interdependent processes for serving the same beneficiaries	Memorandum of Understanding (MOU)
Cooperation	One partner "outsources" and pays another partner for products and services	Contract (service agreements that specify what, for how much, and by when)
Collaboration	Partners work together to implement processes (each partner pays its own expenses)	Contract (specifying complementary processes and how they are to be implemented to achieve impact)

Figure 7.2 Example: Grameen Shakti Partnernships

Partner	Type of Partnership	Value Exchanged
Grameen Telecom	Network	Knowledge of process for rural sales
Suppliers for solar home systems	Cooperation	Provides products and components in exchange for money
Grameen Bank	Collaboration	Office space in exchange for value to Grameen customers

Value Chain

The *value chain* identifies the flow of information, products, and possibly money among processes both within the enterprise and with partners or others in its enabling ecosystem. A value chain showing the flow of goods among partner organizations needed to create a final product/service for a beneficiary is often called a supply chain. Value chains and supply chains can be drawn as flow diagrams (see snapshots examples later in the chapter). If multiple value chain or supply chain partners are involved in implementing your mission, it is important to specify the monetary or other benefits they receive for each unit of value they provide in the value chain.

Social Venture Snapshot: Operations and Value Chain for Grameen Shakti (Solar Home Lighting Systems)

Grameen Shakti's value chain depicts a "whole product" solution—from solar home system design, to supplier selection, distribution, the microfinancing of sales, and after-market service. Success in achieving high growth rates and market penetration depends on Shakti's ability to replicate well-defined processes and systems of accountability across remote and difficult-to-reach geographic branches.

Omitting fund-raising, administration, and other support or "overhead" factors, the key operating processes that create product/service value for Grameen Shakti customers include the following:

1. Product definition, partner Solar Home System supplier selection, acquisition, and pricing

2. Product supply

3. Distribution/Delivery

4. Marketing, sales, and collection

5. Microfinancing

6. Service/Repair

These processes form a value chain as indicated in Figure 7.3 on page 116.

Social Venture Snapshot: Operations and Value Chain for Sankara

Because Sankara is a service organization, its value chain differs substantially from Grameen Shakti's. Its ability to achieve financial viability in centralized hospitals depends on repeatable processes specifically designed to deliver quality

Figure 7.3 Grameen Shakti: Value Chain Diagram

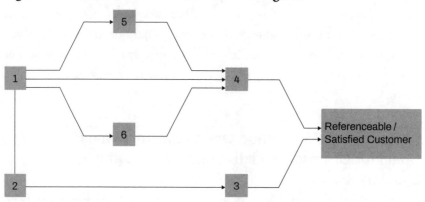

high-volume eye surgery and related services. These core capabilities are enabled by professionalized administrative and marketing support functions and complemented by volunteer networks. Sankara's approach to building a successful social venture reflects a resource-based approach to strategy—one that encompasses an academy for training future eye surgeons, an international network to access funding for expansion, and partnerships with local government and industry leaders.

Processes in the Value Chain

Sankara's value chain consists of a network of processes and relationships that create value for the customer (paying and nonpaying patients of Sankara's eye hospitals). While support functions such as administration and HR are usually not included in the value chain, we believe, in Sankara's case, that the recruitment and training of hospital staff is also a key process. Through its efforts to attract and retain talented staff, Sankara is able to ensure successful operation of its facilities, high-quality patient care, and economic betterment for the many women it employs. Sankara's value chain (Figure 7.4) consists of the following processes.

Customer Acquisition: Sankara must acquire customers for eye care treatment. These customers are segmented into two groups: paying and nonpaying customers, which are respectively served at the base (city) and community (rural) hospitals.

Community Outreach (rural eye camps): For the nonpaying customer segment, Sankara reaches people in rural communities via eye camps, where it spreads awareness about its offerings and conducts on-site screenings.

Marketing/Education (city customers): For the paying customer segment, Sankara conducts marketing efforts to spread awareness and gain customers for its base hospitals in major urban centers. These marketing efforts include traditional promotional methods like billboards, flyers, and newspaper inserts, as well as partnerships with corporations and health insurance companies, and external paid engagements for social media management and online reputation.

Transportation: For the nonpaying customer segment, Sankara transports patients from rural villages to its community hospitals via bus.

Eye Care Preparation and Treatment (free hospitals): Sankara provides comprehensive and specialty eye care services to nonpaying customers at community hospitals in rural locations.

Eye Care Preparation and Treatment (paying hospitals): Sankara provides comprehensive and specialty eye care services to paying customers at base hospitals in city locations.

Transportation: Sankara transports patients from free hospitals back to the villages after treatment is complete.

Postoperative Support (paying hospitals): Postoperative support is provided to paying patients at city hospitals after treatment is complete.

Postoperative Support (free hospitals): Postoperative support is provided to nonpaying patients in their respective villages.

Sight Restoration: Both the paying and nonpaying customers complete treatment at Sankara and depart with restored sight, poised to live healthier, more productive lives.

Sankara's network of processes and relationships involves working with local partners (steps 1–3 and 6–10), whereas the supply and maintenance of its technical operating infrastructure (steps 4 and 5) involves working with international suppliers of advanced medical technologies. Figure 7.4 depicts the Sankara value chain.

Figure 7.4 Sankara: Value Chain Diagram

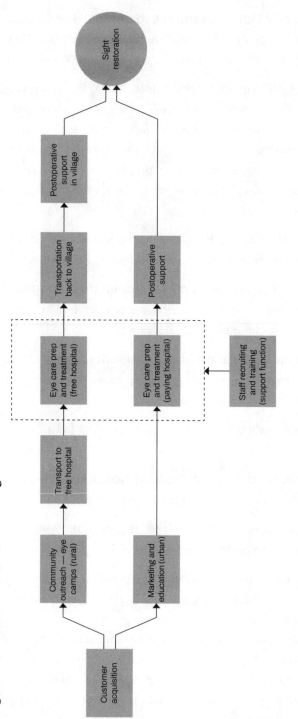

Key Internal Operating Processes That Create Product/Service Value

Primary processes that directly create value for the beneficiaries are the following:

- Identify and recruit patients

    ∞ Community hospital (nonpaying patients)—through community outreach efforts like camps and awareness programs

    ∞ Base/City hospital (paying patients)—through marketing

- Patient screening and diagnosis

- Patient treatment (clinical or specialty services)

- Post-treatment follow-up care and evaluation

Support processes that are needed to enable the primary processes include the following:

- Recruiting, education, training, and management of the medical and administrative staff

- Fund-raising through Sankara Eye Foundation (USA, UK) and Mission for Vision

- Acquiring more paying patients to maintain the 80-20 (unpaid vs. paid) ratio

- Construction of new hospitals and maintenance of existing hospitals

- IT, administrative, and accounting services

- Acquiring low-cost supplies and equipment (diagnostic and surgical)

Key Variances That Can Impact Cost or Social Value—Quality, Affordability to Customers, and Penetration

- Insufficient number of paying patients to maintain an 80-20 (unpaid vs. paid) ratio

- High setup and operating costs for the hospitals (in both rural and urban areas)

- Unavailability of sponsors for eye camps

- Reduced efficiency in treatment process

- Lack of community support for camps

- Lack of competitive pricing for services

- Lack of eligible personnel to undergo training

Key External Operating Partnerships

Without the following partnerships, Sankara would not be able to achieve its mission.

Sankara Eye Foundation, USA: SEF USA has more than two hundred volunteers working from different parts of America. Through various innovative and appealing programs and events, funds are being raised to support Sankara in conducting eye surgeries, procuring/modernizing equipment, and constructing new hospitals. SEF USA is a huge supporter of Sankara and a driving force of its Vision 20/20 goal. Over the past ten years, SEF USA has provided on average more than 50 percent of all donations that Sankara has received.

Sankara Eye Foundation, Europe: SAF aims to support the free eye surgeries at Sankara by raising funds through events, booths, and donors.

Mission for Vision Trust: The mission participates not only in the establishment of new hospitals but also in supporting the deficits in recurring expenditures. It also shares a common goal with Sankara: "No one should be needlessly blind." Stressing both community eye care service and overall quality of services provided, Mission for Vision has also put in place a regular ongoing audit on the postoperative patients. This helps in assessing the quality of care and the overall well-being of patients, and in evaluating the socioeconomic benefit that they have gained from better vision.

Gift of Vision Program (eye camps): Sankara reaches out to patients through its network of field workers, doctors, and paramedics. Screening is done on-site at eye camps in the village.

Screening programs: As part of the Rainbow School Screening Program, teacher volunteers are identified and trained to do preliminary eye screenings for students. Based on these screenings, the eye care team from Sankara visits the schools and screens the children for any diseases, and those found with eye problems are moved to the base hospital. Those requiring glasses are given spectacles free of charge.

Figure 7.5 Sankara's Key Partners

Partner	Type of Partnership	Value Exchanged
Sankara Eye Foundation — USA	Collaboration	*Fund-raising*: Funds for surgeries, equipment, and hospitals
Sankara Eye Foundation — Europe	Collaboration	*Capital*: Funds for new hospitals, running existing ones
Mission for Vision	Coordination	*Audit and Fund-raising*: Establishing new hospitals, supporting deficits in recurring expenditures, audit on the postoperative patients
Eye camps (Gift of Vision Program)	Coordination	*Coordination*: Raising awareness; screening and detection of defects/ailments; eye treatment
Student screening (Rainbow Program)	Coordination (training of ophthalmologists)	*Training*: Primary screening to detect early onset issues and treat before problems worsen
Sankara Academy of Vision	Collaboration (training of ophthalmologists)	*Training*: Training initiative enables socioeconomic empowerment of students from marginalized communities
Govt. of India and NGOs	Cooperation	*Grants*: Funds for surgeries, equipment, and hospitals

Sankara Academy of Vision: The Academy of Vision is recognized among the leading eye care organizations in the country. Through the academy, in 2013–2014 Sankara trained and developed 190 personnel to become ophthalmologists, optometrists, paramedics, technicians, eye care managers, and support personnel. Training through the academy also enables socioeconomic empowerment of students, with enrolled attendees coming from India, Nepal, Nigeria, Iran, and Azerbaijan. In a recent internal study, 85 percent of vision care technicians in the program were found to come from marginalized communities. Seventy-two percent of them reported more respect from their communities and families upon completion of the program at Sankara Academy of Vision. These individuals are now providing approximately 30 percent of their family's monthly income.

Government of India and NGOs: Key partnerships with the government of India and NGOs provide recurring grant funding to Sankara. NGO partners include Indian Council for Medical Research, Sri Ratan Tata Trust, and District Blindness Control Society. The government specifically supports the Eye Bank through its grants, and Sri Ratan Tata supports the Academy of Vision. The other NGOs provide grants for general use. Sankara's key partners are identified in Figure 7.5. Again, as noted in Figure 7.1, these partnerships may involve formal/informal MOUs or contractual agreements as mechanisms for ensuring accountability.

Social Venture Snapshot: GSBI Innovator Equal Access International

This snapshot for Equal Access International is from 2004 when Ronni Goldfarb attended the GSBI and was the first program attendee of a woman-led organization with its flagship initiative dedicated to the empowerment of women and girls. Her organization's mission was to create positive social change for millions of underserved people across the developing world by providing critically needed information and education. Equal Access is a classic example of a learning organization. By 2016 it was using multiple types of interactive media combined with diverse community engagement activities, with a broadcast reach to 200 million; 75 million regular listeners and viewers; and more than 118,000 people participating in community engagement activities across nine countries in Asia and Africa. Its successful growth could be traced to many factors—foremost among them its core expertise in creating innovative and culturally resonant educational media programming, its ability to adapt to new media platforms, and its ability to become a trusted brand for positive engaged lifestyles. For this snapshot, however, we will return to mentor notes from 2004.

Mission, Opportunity, and Strategies

Mission	To create positive social change for millions of underserved people across the world by providing critically needed information and education through innovative media, appropriate technology, and direct community engagement
Key Metric	Number of beneficiaries
Opportunity	Millions of people in least developed regions of the world lack the information and life skills to improve their lives and address challenges such as: HIV/AIDS, violence against women, livelihoods opportunities, and peacebuilding
	Development agencies, foundations, corporations, and investors have funding for breakthrough solutions that empower marginalized people and create positive social impact
Strategies	(1) Local staff in each country produce social and educational programming on key issues
	(2) Distribute needs driven programming at scale though satellite, FM radio, and ICTs, providing the tools and skills people need to improve their lives
	(3) Work with community beneficiaries and local organizations to implement on the ground activities that foster learning, empowerment, and positive social change

External Environment

- Widespread lack of information and education on health, life skills, education, and livelihoods in least developed countries

- Leverage existence of satellite, community FM radio, and emerging ICTs to provide needs driven information and education at scale

- Local communities know their information and educational needs

- Collaborate with local communities and leverage local partnerships to implement community engagement activities

Market

Initial target market was South and Southeast Asia, to reach underserved populations living on $1 day or less, where ICTs could provide critically needed information and education at scale. Selected countries and potential beneficiaries (Afghanistan: over 14 million, Nepal: over 9 million, India: over 300 million, Laos: over 700,000). Build capacity of local talent to develop content (products), distribute for free (pricing), coordinate with local organizations to promote and place. Product—information and educational content; Price—free; Placement—direct to communities and through local partnerships; Promotion—local media.

Operations and Value Chain

The key processes for Equal Access are: (1) development of social and educational media programming, (2) programming distribution, and (3) implementation of community engagement activities. Combined these three processes create social change. These are inter-related and tailored for each market with a value chain as shown in Figure 7.6.

Key partnerships in each market were needed for each process as shown in Figure 7.7.

Figure 7.6   Equal Access: Value Chain Diagram

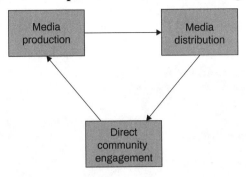

Figure 7.7   Equal Access Key Partnerships

Process Partner	Type of Partnership	Value Exchanged
Community engagement	Collaboration	Listening groups, facilitated learning, multimedia hubs, audience development and feedback
Media production	Coordination	Develop content in local language
Media distribution	Cooperation	Radio broadcasting (satellite and radio), internet data broadcasting

Organization and Human Resources

Equal Access is an international nonprofit (501(c)(3)) headquartered in the United States for executive management, business development, and other central services. Their locally-led branch country offices produce media programming and implement community engagement activities in each country where they operate.

Small board of directors:

CTO of Global Tele-systems Group, AOL Director of Product Strategy,

Equal Access President and CEO, and

Equal Access CFO

Small advisory board:

Intel Capital (VP of Business Development)

Monterey Institute of International Studies (Professor of Translation and Interpretation)

Organization:

President and CEO

Project director CFO

Country directors

15 local employees (country nationals)

Business Model and Unit Economics

Key income drivers: earned income from contracts to create content (60 percent → 80 percent), contributed income from grants (40 percent → 20 percent)

Key expense drivers: personnel (20–30 percent of revenue), local content development and distribution (70 percent of revenues)

Unit Economics: Unit = Beneficiary. 2004 cost/beneficiary = $0.25; 2008: $0.14; now: $0.01. Equal Access was first GSBI participant to use unit economics as a key metric.

Metrics

(1) revenues, (2) expenses and expenses as percentage of revenue, (3) number of beneficiaries, (4) cost/beneficiary, (5) changes in knowledge, attitudes, and practices

Operating Plan

For 2004–2005, Equal Access had an operating plan with quarterly milestones for seven key tactics.

Financing

Equal Access was initially funded with 60 percent grants versus 40 percent earned income, and in 2004 was financed with 75 percent earned income and 25 percent grants.

To Recap

For a social venture to achieve operational excellence, it needs to first develop repeatable processes. Value chains allow a venture to home in on the kinds of skills and capabilities that are needed to maximize social impact and become financially viable. They also help identify areas where it might be best to leverage the networks and capabilities of external partners. In the course of any partnership, it is crucial to create shared value. The Minimum Critical Specifications Checklist highlights the most important pieces this element of the business plan must contain. In the next chapter, we turn to organization and human resources (see Figure 7.8 for a prolog to chapter 8).

Figure 7.8 Value Creating Processes and Organization Capabilities
A Prolog to Chapter 8

In preparation for identifying the organization and human resource requirements for your venture in chapter 8, you may find it useful to summarize each value-creating step in your operations and the organizational capabilities (knowledge, skills, abilities) required for effective execution.

Operations (Value-Creating Processes) and Human Resources (Capabilities)

Step	Value-Creating Processes	Capabilities Needed
1		
2		
3		
4		
5		
6		
7		

Exercises

7.1 Identify Your Key Processes

List the (ten or fewer) key primary and support processes to implement your key strategies. For each process, specify the person responsible for the process.

7.2 Create a List of Your Operation's Partners

Create a table that lists your key partners, the operations they support, the type of partnership agreement you have (network, coordination, cooperation, or collaboration), and what value is exchanged (financial or otherwise) in the partnership.

7.3 Create a Value Chain Diagram

Minimum Critical Specifications Checklist

Operations and Value Chain

- Specifies value chain from product/service creation to delivery and after-market support

- Identifies potential process variances and socio-technical mechanism for their control

- Identifies partnerships for enhancing quality, cost reduction, and market penetration

- Clarifies how value chain supports scalability

The value chain diagram shows the relationships between processes—both internally and externally—in terms of the "flow" of value from one process to another and eventually to the beneficiaries. The arrows between the processes show how value flows to beneficiaries and how information and money flow to partners and back to the organization. Processes may be shown "parallel" to indicate that they occur roughly at the same time. Create your own value chain diagram. Figure 7.3 in this chapter provides an example from Grameen Shakti. Since there is not a single or commonly used format or style for a value chain diagram, you can use whatever format or style of diagram best conveys your value chain.

Background Resources

Dees, J. Gregory, Jed Emerson, and Peter Economy. *Strategic Tools for Social Entrepreneurs: Enhancing the Performance of Your Enterprising Nonprofit.* New York: John Wiley, 2002, chapter 3.

DeThomas, Arthur, and Stephanie Derammelaere. *How to Write a Convincing Business Plan.* 3rd ed. New York: Barron's Educational Services, 2008, chapter 8.

MacMillan, Ian C., and James D. Thompson. *The Social Entrepreneur's Playbook—Pressure Test, Plan, Launch and Scale Your Enterprise.* Philadelphia: Wharton Digital Press, 2013.

Microlinks. *Value Chain Development Wiki.* Washington, DC: USAID, 2009. http://apps.develebridge.net/amap/index. php/Value_Chain_Development].

Porter, M. E. "What Is Strategy?" *Harvard Business Review,* November–December 1996, 61–78.

Prahalad, C. K. *The Fortune at the Bottom of the Pyramid: Eradicating Poverty through Profits.* Philadelphia: Wharton School Publishing, 2010, part 4.

Wimmer, Nancy. *Green Energy for a Billion Poor.* Vatterstetten: MCRE Verlag, 2012, chapter 2.

Chapter 8

Organization and Human Resources

By identifying the key processes for your organization in chapter 7, you have created the "operations element" for your enterprise plan. You are now ready to create the organization and human resources element of the plan. This element includes the organization's legal form, the board structure and its composition, the key leaders who will make up your top management team, and a staffing plan. In a social business, a staffing plan may include volunteers in addition to paid employees. Note that there may be potential legal issues (e.g., liability) with having volunteers.

In social mission organizations, entrepreneurs face a number of unique challenges. For example, it is unlikely you can compete for talent at market rates, and it is likely that you will need to supplement paid employees with volunteers (particularly in the early stages). In addition, you will need to consider the likelihood of turnover in key positions, the eventual need for a successor to the founder/leader, the importance of choosing the right board, and the potential reality of needing to turn over control of the enterprise to a professional manager—a manager who must have a similar passion and share common values in order to succeed. As a result, the need for a good organization and human resource plan is at least as important—if not more important—for a social venture as it is for a profit-maximizing venture.

Process

In *How to Write a Great Business Plan*, William Sahlman posits that "without the right team, none of the other parts of the business plan really matter."[1]

The converse of his statement may also be a good guide: without a good business plan, it doesn't really matter who's on the team. Regardless of how you see it, odds are you will not get the right team in place without an organization plan. Although social ventures are driven by values, they still require a disciplined approach to organizational planning (see Figure 8.1). This plan should reflect a clear understanding of how your organization will operate, critical functions, key leadership roles, and how best to ensure that individuals with the right skills and "fit" with the organization's mission and culture staff a structure of accountability. Developing this organization plan requires four key steps to be followed:

Basic Knowledge

The best technology does not always win. Without the right team, none of the other elements of the business plan matter. Social businesses can leverage the following:

- Legal structures to attract different forms of capital (grants, equity, etc.)

- A compelling vision to attract talent and align behavior with an ethos of continuous learning

- Governing boards for effective oversight of strategic and operational plans and for access to networks or "bridging" social capital

1. Define the legal form of your organization.

2. Create the specifications for your board.

3. Define the key management roles (positions) for your enterprise.

4. Create a staffing plan that includes both employees and volunteers.

First, though, it is important to acknowledge the unique characteristics of social ventures and their founders. Founder values influence organization routines. They also help shape the kinds of norms that will attract people who "fit" a culture that strives for continuous improvement in serving society's needs. The creative tension that exists between the affirming human values of social venture founders and traditional approaches to organizational planning can stimulate the design of jobs and work systems that

Figure 8.1   Organization Plan: Balancing Conventional Models with Values

The values-based view of the organization must be balanced with the discipline of a conventional approach to designing organizations with the ability to execute strategy.

Organization Plan: Conventional Model	Values-Based View of Organization
Strategy: • What business are we in? • How will we compete?	**Fundamental values and beliefs:** • What are our basic values? • What do we believe in?
Functional strategies: • Marketing, manufacturing, finance, Human Resources, etc.	**Practices embody values:** • What policies and practices are consistent with our values?
Key success factors: • What are the critical tasks to execute strategy?	**Practices (routines) build core capabilities:** • What can we do to serve society's needs better?
Organizational alignment: • Systems, practices, staff, rewards	**Invent strategy that fits values:** • Capabilities serve unmet needs
Senior management's role: • Monitor alignment/compliance	**Senior management's role:** • "Manage" values and culture

are intrinsically motivating and attractive to both paid employees and volunteers.

As Figure 8.1 indicates, founder values influence a wide range of organizational processes and practices. Generally speaking, they seek to align structure, processes, and roles with the mission of stimulating positive social change. In this way, values foster new ways of doing things, such as the employment of marginalized individuals and other value chain innovations that embed social change in local contexts. Founder values need to be balanced with the discipline required to develop a formal organization, including specific decisions regarding formal structure, governance processes, leadership team composition, and staffing. These decisions will ultimately determine the ability to execute strategy.

Form of Organization

Depending on the country or countries in which the social venture will be doing business, there are several organizational options. Answering these questions will help you determine the best form of organization for your venture:

1. Are founders or employees to "own" or have shares in the venture, or are there to be no individual owners?

2. Are the founders to give up control of the organization (e.g., to majority shareholders)?

3. Does your mission encompass a return of surplus income to the owners as opposed to reinvesting the entire surplus in the enterprise?

4. What are the tax and regulatory reporting requirements that will affect your enterprise?

In most countries, the first decision in terms of organizational form is choosing between for-profit and nonprofit status. In general, if a business intends to have profits that are returned to the owners, or to increase the value of "ownership shares," then a for-profit model is required. Even with no intention to provide a financial return to the owners, an organization may choose a for-profit form either because country laws or regulations require it (e.g., this may be the case if your enterprise is selling goods and/or services) or because the founders feel that a for-profit form creates the right incentives and alignment between the motivations of employees and those who will provide capital.

For-Profit

Common reasons for picking a for-profit form of organization include (1) a desire to attract investors and employees who are motivated by the potential for increases in the value of their shares of ownership over time, (2) the desire to return all or part of enterprise profits to owner/investors, and (3) the desire for founders to retain control. In most regions, there are several alternative legal forms of for-profit organizations. For example, in the United States, these include sole proprietorships, general or limited partnerships, cooperatives, limited liability corporations (LLCs), and corporations (including B-Corp, and, in a few states, the social purpose corporation). Which one of these you pick determines what you do with your profits and who bears the risk of losses, how you are taxed, and how you are regulated. The LLC (profits may be paid out to owners) and C corporations (profits may be paid in dividends or kept in retained earnings) are used most frequently. A brief comparison of the organizational alternatives (in the United States) is given in DeThomas and

Derammelaere.[2] Note that the bases for choosing an organizational form may be very different in countries other than the United States. For specific legal advice on which form to pick, consult an attorney and/or a certified tax accountant.

In the United States, one form of corporate organization, called the benefit corporation, is being used by social ventures that want to operate like for-profit organizations, without a legal requirement that stockholder interests are put first. In most states, a benefit corporation must define a "social purpose"—not a profit-maximizing mission but a social benefit that includes some financial return (i.e., a profit) as part of the mission. A B-Corp can sell equity shares (to raise money), but, unlike a corporation, it can also accept grants or contributions (which, in the case of a B-Corp, are not tax deductible to the donors). Reporting requirements are often more stringent for a Benefit Corp than for other forms of corporation, and an annual Special Purpose Impact report is usually required.

Nonprofit and Hybrid

There are fewer nonprofit organizational forms. In the United States, the most common nonprofit organizational form is one with a 501(c)(3) tax status so that it can accept tax-deductible donations. Governments and government-sanctioned NGOs (e.g., school districts in the United States and BRAC—a Bangladesh development organization) are other forms of nonprofit organization. The reasons for choosing to operate as a nonprofit organization may vary across stages of the organizational life cycle. Contributed income may be essential for early stage proof-of-concept, training low-skill employees, or to fund capital expenditures. In later stages, contributed income may be needed to support ongoing operating expenses that exceed earned income potential, or to subsidize a subset of customers. A common rationale for electing to be a nonprofit is the desire not to be required to put stockholder interests first but for profits or operating surpluses to be reinvested in the business as a means of lowering the cost of services to customers or beneficiaries with limited capacity to pay. Rather than returning profits to the owners, this enables a nonprofit to penetrate its target market by increasing the ability to serve the poorest of the poor.

A mixed organizational form, called a "hybrid," combines characteristics of for-profit and nonprofit organizations through separate legal entities, independent but overlapping boards of directors, and possibly shared management. A hybrid form of organization should be chosen when there is clear separation between activities related to earned income (e.g., sales of products) and activities driven by contributed income (e.g., training). In general, hybrid organizations are more complex to manage and have higher total expenses than nonhybrid forms. A hybrid organization should be chosen only if there are clear advantages (e.g., increased income, greater capacity for growth, or lower operating expenses can be realized).

Cooperative

Finally, social ventures often use a cooperative form of organization. A cooperative (also known as a co-op) is "an autonomous association of persons united voluntarily to meet their common economic, social, and cultural needs and aspirations through a jointly-owned and democratically-controlled enterprise."[3] A cooperative is often involved in the distribution of goods or the supplying of services, typically organized by consumers or farmers, and operated for the mutual benefit of its members. Cooperative businesses are typically more economically resilient than many other forms of enterprise, and have the advantage of allowing the organization to have the bargaining power of a corporation without all the legal requirements. Cooperatives may include

- nonprofit community organizations;

- businesses owned and managed by the people who use their services (a consumer cooperative);

- organizations managed by the people who work there (worker cooperatives);

- organizations managed by the people to whom they provide accommodation (housing cooperatives);

- hybrids such as worker cooperatives that are also consumer cooperatives or credit unions;

- multistakeholder cooperatives such as those that bring together civil society and local actors to deliver community needs; and

- second- and third-tier cooperatives whose members are other cooperatives.

Governance and Boards

Regardless of the organization's form, it is always helpful (and often legally required) to have a board of directors. Some organizations also choose to have advisory boards that provide unique expertise and broaden or deepen access to relevant resources or capabilities.

The board of directors provides governance for the enterprise. In most cases it hires the CEO, and it is often involved in hiring others in the top management team. It has a fiduciary responsibility to the business itself—the owners, investors, employees, and customers of the enterprise. This includes the responsibility to see that financial and other decisions comply with legal and ethical standards and are informed by the interests of these third parties. (Note that some forms of organizations are required to have a board of directors.)

The members of the board of directors have various roles and responsibilities (areas of expertise) and often serve on committees (e.g., audit or compensation) to carry out these roles. While the size of the board depends on many factors, for most social ventures, an odd number (to avoid tie votes) and a small number (seven or fewer) of board members is preferable. (Note: Boards with fund-raising responsibility may be considerably larger, but in such instances a smaller executive board is, effectively, the governing body.) Board membership should include the following areas of expertise: financing (e.g., donors, foundations, and/or investors), financial management, knowledge of beneficiaries, access or links to essential network partners, and relevant expertise for guiding the top executive. Figure 8.2 illustrates the important roles of boards.

Advisory boards are often used to help with specific operations, such as product or service development, financing, or distribution. If you already have a large board, or have many people you want to engage as possible advisors, the best approach is to move in the direction of creating a smaller board focused on your business model and its execution. This board may include one or more advisory board members with specialized knowledge in technology, fundraising, or other areas where your business requires expertise. Whereas a board of directors has legal responsibility for guidance, advisory boards do not, and therefore it may be easier to recruit certain people to an advisory board.

Key Employees (Management)

The key employees of an organization include everyone responsible for managing the key strategies (chapter 4) and processes (chapter 7) of the enterprise.

Figure 8.2 Effective Governance of a Social Venture

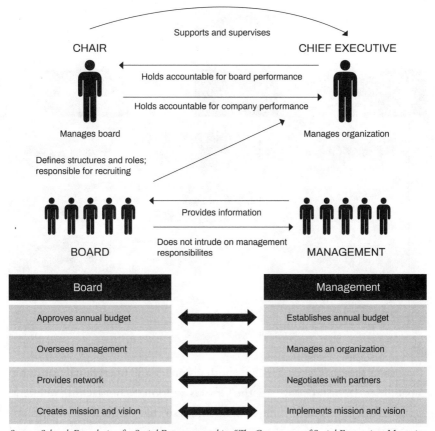

Source: Schwab Foundation for Social Entrepreneurship, "The Governance of Social Enterprises: Managing Your Organization for Success," World Economic Forum, June 2012, 16, http://www3.weforum.org/docs /WEF_Governance_Social_Enterprises_2106_light.pdf.

These key employees typically have management or leadership roles encompassing the following: CEO (or managing/executive director), product/service development, operations (manufacturing and distribution), finance, marketing and business development, sales (in nonprofits, this may primarily involve fund-raising), and human resources. In small organizations, there may be one key employee for more than one of these roles (e.g., a person who serves as both the chief finance officer and the controller, a chief operations officer who is also responsible for product sales and distribution, or a person responsible for both product and business development), but in no organization should there be multiple employees with the same role (see Figure 8.3).

Figure 8.3　Key Management Employees

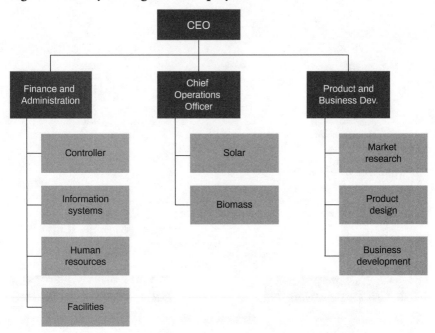

Leadership teams must include both visionary and operational leadership capabilities. In instances where the CEO is a visionary but lacking in operational acumen, it is important to define roles so that the individual with operational expertise always has the "final say" when it comes to operational decisions such as spending and cash flow management. Of three risk factors—technology risk, market risk, and leadership team risk—there is wide agreement among venture capitalists that the credibility, competencies, and effective functioning of leadership teams is the most important of these factors in firm performance.

Staffing Plan (Employees and Volunteers)

Since a social business may not have sufficient resources or cash flow to pay all employees, it may need to rely on volunteers for some important roles (be sure to check legal requirements that may prevent volunteers from assuming certain roles). Except for monetary compensation, all elements of the staffing plan for both paid employees and volunteer employees should be the same. The elements of the staffing plan include job descriptions (responsibilities, qualifications), reporting structures (and evaluation periods), workplace and time expectations, and compensation (both direct and indirect), as well as career development opportunities.

Volunteers are human resources—ones that are often critical to social mission ventures. They may outnumber paid staff and are often critical to the outcomes and impact of a venture. Through their contributed time, they may make products and services more affordable. They also may bring deep empathy for the poor, identify with the organization's mission and the populations it serves, and provide access to unique knowledge and skills. Miller Center for Social Entrepreneurship is an excellent example of the value of volunteers. The authors of this book played pivotal roles in the founding and development of the GSBI but were essentially Miller Center volunteers. The success of the GSBI was driven in large measure by carefully selected volunteer mentors with proven entrepreneurial acumen—an abundant resource in Silicon Valley and one that is widely regarded by GSBI alumni as the "secret sauce" of this internationally acclaimed program for accelerating social mission venture development around the world (see Figure 8.4.) This group has grown to more than two hundred actively engaged volunteers.

Company-paid support for volunteering is a widely growing best practice in corporate social responsibility (CSR) programs. In fact, many organizations regard volunteer programs as critical to their ability to attract and retain employees—particularly those seeking a higher level of meaning and purpose. Accenture, for example, was an early partner in creating access to technical expertise for ventures in Santa Clara University's GSBI, sending paid professional staff in 2006 to serve as consulting interns to three GSBI alumni ventures in India. Many other companies have become GSBI supporters along the way. Across the demographic continuum, a large pool of entrepreneurial volunteer talent exists to be tapped.

Organization Strengths, Weaknesses, Opportunities, and Threats

Many organizations find it useful to analyze their strengths, weaknesses, opportunities, and threats (SWOT) using the table as defined in Figure 8.5. A SWOT identifies key organizational strengths and opportunities for creating value, and key weaknesses and threats to this value creation. A SWOT, therefore, can be used by management in guiding staffing decisions and managing key employees.

Figure 8.4   Mentoring and the GSBI

*This document reflects early efforts to formally define the roles of mentor
volunteers in the GSBI. It illustrates the importance of job descriptions and
setting of clear expectations for employees and volunteers alike.*

Mentoring and the GSBI
Miller Center

Mission and Vision

The GSBI at Santa Clara University contributes to the sustainability
and scaling up of technology-based social benefit innovations identified
through prestigious recognition programs like the Tech Awards—
Technology Benefiting Humanity, and the World Bank's Development
Marketplace. It envisions a better world through the conscious striving
of social benefit entrepreneurs and the accelerated development and
diffusion of technologies that serve the urgent needs of humanity.

A Hands-On Learning Laboratory

This residential program combines the work of leading business school
faculty in entrepreneurship and organizational innovation with a network
of technologists and successful entrepreneurs from Silicon Valley who
serve as mentors to provide social entrepreneurs with the knowledge
and skills that they need to serve a larger number of beneficiaries in
an economically sustainable way. Attendance is limited to highly
select projects following a rigorous screening process. GSBI portfolio
organizations form a dynamic learning community for accelerating social
change through the development of business plans for proof-of-concept
projects that have already demonstrated an impact in achieving progress
in such areas as economic development, health, education, equality, and
the environment.

Mentor Roles

Mentors play a critical role in this transformational learning experience.
During the two-week period of the residential program, they will meet

with individual program participants at Santa Clara University on six or more occasions to review work in progress on business plans. They serve as coaches on such topics as marketing and market creation, business models, organizational development, and on strategies for achieving sustainability at scale. To help bridge the conceptual leaps—for example, from charity or welfare models to sustainability through earned revenues—mentors work with developing country social entrepreneurs prior to their arrival to complete online exercises designed to stimulate thinking about the importance of a compelling value proposition and understanding earned income strategies for achieving sustainability. Through the GSBI's distance learning platform, mentors also provide their social entrepreneur advisees with follow-up coaching as they work to refine and implement their business plans back home.

Figure 8.5   Organization and Human Resources SWOT Analysis

Strengths	Weaknesses
Organization/Human Resources elements that help the organization sustain/scale (e.g., experience of key people)	Organization/Human Resources factors that will hinder sustaining/scaling (e.g., lack of finance officer)

Opportunities	Threats
Organization/Human Resources factors that could improve sustainability or scalability (e.g., switch to hybrid organization, hire marketing director, use advertising partnerships)	Organization/Human Resources factors that could cause organization to fail (e.g., loss of key people, lack of expertise in key element of value chain)

Social Venture Snapshot: Organization and Human Resources Planning for Grameen Shakti

Grameen Shakti's board, chaired by Nobel Prize winner Muhammad Yunus, has particularly strong financial acumen. This reflects Shakti's roots in Grameen Bank, its commitment to customer financing, and its belief in the potential for energy access—as a productive asset—to lift people out of poverty. Shakti uses a divisional structure with operating units organized around geographic divisions, each with districts responsible for maintaining "sustainability (revenue/expense) ratios." The district engineers who head these branches play a pivotal role in establishing community trust and in Shakti's ability to grow in a sustainable manner. Its decentralized divisions are supported by centralized staff departments in human resources, IT and management information systems (MIS), accounting, procurement, inventory management, and technology. In addition, Shakti maintains a strong internal audit function that plays both an independent compliance role and a developmental role to spread best practices across divisions.

Legal Form and Structure

Although Grameen Shakti refers to itself as a "rural energy (social) business," its legal form of organization was chartered as Grameen Shakti Ltd., a non-profit company of limited liability. As Grameen Shakti grew, it was organized into Grameen Shakti Social Business (GSSB), which was owned by Grameen Shakti Ltd.

Key Employees and Their Roles

In addition to the managing director, each major function shown in the organization chart in Figure 8.6 has a general manager.

Early Board Members and Their Roles

Muhammad Yunus, chairman of the board

Director, represents Grameen Trust (financing)

Director, represents C.M.E.S (financing)

Director, represents Grameen Shikkha (women's training)

Director, represents Grameen Bank (financing)

Director, represents Grameen Knitwear (management of similar company)

Director and managing director of Grameen Shakti (represents the organization)

The SWOT analysis in Figure 8.7 provides a summary of the organizational strengths and weaknesses of Grameen Shakti as well as the opportunities it can leverage and the threats it may need to contend with.

Figure 8.6   Grameen Shakti Organization Chart

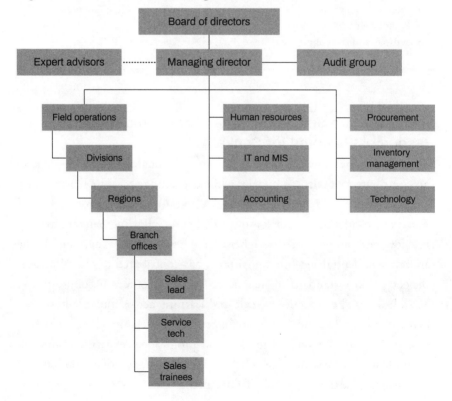

Figure 8.7 Grameen Shakti Organization and Human Resources SWOT Analysis (circa 2008)

Organizational Strengths	Organizational Weaknesses
• Strong board of directors • Good organizational structure • Well-defined jobs • Excellent training for staff • Opportunities for advancement • Opportunities for women • Adequate compensation • SMS-based sales information system • Comprehensive audit process	• Some staff have to work in remote, potentially dangerous areas • Competition for key employees • Some staff may not be trustworthy
Organizational Opportunities	**Organizational Threats**
• Promote from within • Profit sharing • Separate and thorough audits	• Loss of support from Grameen organization • New entrants • Accelerating change in technology

Social Venture Snapshot: Organization and Human Resources Planning for Sankara

Sankara illustrates how decisions about organizational design and leadership can contribute to low-cost strategies while deepening access to expertise and resources. In this instance the choice of a nonprofit legal form has enabled Sankara to fund a major portion of capital costs, allowing Sankara to keep costs low, and has permitted a higher rate of new hospital expansion. At the same time, a centralized functional form has contributed to organizational efficiency, helped standardize practices in human resources, accounting, and IT, and captured economies of scale and learning across multiple hospitals. Board composition and senior management leadership reflect a strong emphasis on tapping vertical market and professional expertise. Sankara's organizational structure acknowledges the importance of accountability for managing partnerships and effective marketing—key factors in its market penetration goals.

Legal Form and Structure

The Sri Kanchi Kamakoti Medical Trust manages Sankara eye hospitals. It is formally registered as an Indian Charitable Trust, which is "an obligation annexed to the ownership of property, and arising out of a confidence reposed in and accepted by the owner, or declared and accepted by him, for the benefit of another, or of another and the owner."

Per Section 2(15) of the India Income Tax Act, 1961, activities including "relief of the poor, education, medical relief, preserving monuments and environment and the advancement of any other object of general public utility" are recognized as charitable purposes. Per Section 2(15), along with Sections 11 and 12, of the India Income Tax Act, 1961, "trusts set up for social causes and approved by the Income Tax Department, get not only exemption from payment of tax but also the donors to such trusts can deduct the amount of donation to the trust from their taxable income."

Since Sankara's key strategy is to provide affordable (mostly free) and accessible eye care to its beneficiaries, its legal form (public charitable trust) is a fitting choice—one that enables the organization to fully focus on its mission while allowing it to raise funds/seek donations, reinvest any earnings back into the business, and utilize its resources efficiently for scaling activities. Its cross-subsidy business model further complements the legal form, helping the organization become self-sufficient and less dependent on donations. The added advantage of Sankara's legal form is the tax exemption for both the organization and its donors.

Organizational Structure

Overall, Sankara exhibits a functional structure, along with some minor elements of a divisional structure, owing to its geographic spread in India. A functional structure is the most ideal choice for Sankara's low-cost strategy, as it is simple in form and allows centralized decision making.

The board oversees a six-member leadership team. Each leader is assigned to a specific vertical, namely:

1. Paid hospitals (branded as "Vision Sankara")

2. Nonpaid hospitals (branded as "Sankara Eye Hospitals")

3. Human resources

4. Medical administration

5. Finance

6. Special projects (such as fund-raising events)

Each functional head at the unit (hospital) level reports to a dedicated person on the six-member executive leadership team, or Office of the President. Each unit head manages a functional team within the unit, such as medical administration, HR, or operations. Sankara's utilizing a mostly functional structure has the following advantages:

- It enables teams to focus on and accomplish functional goals (HR goals, operational goals, etc.).

- It allows for simplified mechanisms for control.

- It includes clear definition of responsibilities.

Although the structure is functional overall, the divisional nature is exhibited where the various functions are grouped into a unit (hospital). The units are geographically spread around the country, with each unit focused on a specific city (target market). Each hospital is also individually measured for its performance in terms of social impact and financial sustainability. Sankara's organizational structure is depicted in Figure 8.8.

Knowledge and Talent Requirements Critical for Executing Strategy

Sankara has a number of critical knowledge and talent requirements for executing against its mission and strategy, including medical expertise (ophthalmology), operational expertise, partnership development and management, marketing expertise, and human resources expertise.

Medical expertise is certainly one of the most important talent requirements for Sankara. Its core business revolves around its ability to provide comprehensive high-quality eye care treatment to patients with various needs. Knowledgeable and experienced medical staff, including ophthalmologists, optometrists, surgeons, doctors, and nurses, are critical to Sankara's reputation and continued success.

Operational excellence is a key talent requirement, as Sankara's scalability and sustainability are dependent on its ability to screen and treat patients in an efficient way through streamlined processes and procedures. Having

Figure 8.8 Sankara's Organizational (Reporting) Structure

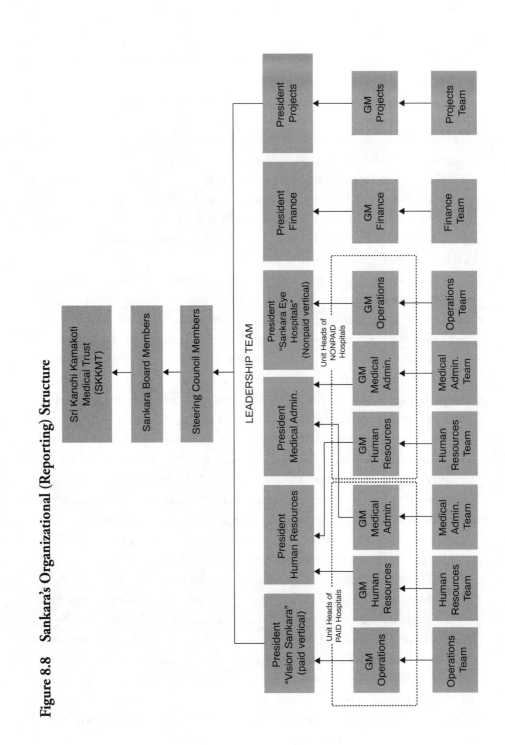

effective training programs for its medical staff is also key to achieving operational excellence in each Sankara hospital.

Partner management is another key knowledge area. Sankara partners with a number of entities that serve critical roles in its operations, such as providing funding/grants, helping with community outreach (like the eye camps cosponsored with Gift of Vision), assisting in screening students at schools (through the Rainbow Program), and training its medical staff (through partnership with the Academy of Vision). Given the importance of Sankara's many partners in its success, having talented staff dedicated to partner relations is crucial to ensuring the relationships are strong, mutually beneficial, and aligned to the same overall goals.

Marketing expertise is another key area of knowledge for Sankara. The biggest obstacle between them and achieving scalability and sustainability is its ability to continue growing its paying customer segment, which will offset a growing nonpaying customer segment. Without a strong marketing department to drive customer acquisition (both paying and nonpaying), Sankara will struggle to continue to expand and become financially self-sufficient. For the paying segment, marketing that effectively emphasizes quality of care is most important, whereas for the nonpaying segment, marketing in the form of general education and awareness of eye treatment is the goal.

Human resources is a final critical knowledge area for Sankara. Sankara believes its most valuable assets are its people, and that valuable people create a valuable organization. The productivity and performance of its staff directly impacts its success as an organization. Therefore, it is critical that the human resources function is focused on continually attracting, developing, and retaining talented team members who are aligned with Sankara's mission.

Based on these talent requirements, pivotal jobs for Sankara include the leadership team (to champion and drive the social mission of the company as well as its individual functions), hospital/medical staff, field workers (for eye camps and other outreach activities), head of operations, head of partner relations, head of marketing, and head of human resources. These roles drive the affordability of Sankara's services and penetration into new markets. For example, operational excellence and well-trained medical staff allow Sankara to achieve the economies of scale that drive down costs, thereby increasing affordability. Marketing staff and field workers strive to acquire new customers through traditional marketing channels as well as through outreach programs to increase penetration in both the paying and the nonpaying segments. In addition, human resources plays an important role in ensuring the proper staff are hired for both skills and ability to grow with Sankara's mission as well as fit with the organization's culture and long-term retention.

Board Member Roles and Expertise

Sankara has an eight-member board, chaired by Dr. S. V. Balasubramaniam. Its board members include individuals with expertise in finance and accounting; medicine, including auditory and laparoscopic surgery, oncology, and ophthalmology; hospital administration; fund-raising; land and capital; and support and community advocacy.

No key individual is in charge of making connections with partners and the board may be a bit large and somewhat overemphasize technical/medical expertise, an issue addressed in composition of steering council.

In addition to the board members, Sankara has a five-member steering council. Each steering council member brings an important area of expertise to Sankara, including (1) finance, (2) internal audit, (3) media and communications, (4) IT, and (5) ophthalmology. The specific skills of the steering council

Figure 8.9 Sankara Organization and Human Resources SWOT Analysis

Organizational Strengths	Organizational Weaknesses
• Employees hired from communities where hospitals are built, creating economic betterment • Excellent training for clinical and administrative staff • Empowerment opportunities for marginalized women • Automated performance management system • Competitive benefits for employees • Rewarding work culture	• Suboptimal board member expertise • Even number of board members • Cross-cultural management — replication of model in each new state is unique and challenging (per client interview) • Cross-functional integration is a challenge in functional structures • Dissatisfaction of corporate employees due to workload and stress level (per client interview)
Organizational Opportunities	Organizational Threats
• Collaboration/knowledge-sharing opportunities with similar organizations • Further penetration in new markets (still immense unmet demand)	• Competition for paying patients and employee talent from Vasan Eye Care, other eye and multispecialty hospitals • Succession planning — gaps in key roles (per client interview)

complement the wider expertise of the board. Additionally, the steering council reviews the board's performance on a quarterly basis, providing another check and balance.

Figure 8.9 provides a summary of Sankara's organizational strengths and weaknesses as well as the opportunities it can leverage and the potential threats to its organization.

Social Venture Snapshot: GSBI Innovator Industree Crafts

Neelam Chibber, managing director of Industree Crafts, participated in the GSBI in 2008. Her organization tackles the root causes of poverty holistically through an efficiently organized, ownership-based creative manufacturing ecosystem. Its vertically integrated solution combines retail sales and production companies to provide artisans with the design expertise and market intelligence needed to develop products that appeal to modern markets. By integrating artisan skills into the creative industries sector in the formal economy, the organization has succeeded in tripling artisan incomes.

Mission, Opportunity, and Strategies

Mission   Connect retail demand with artisan products created by poor women in India

Key metric   Artisan net income

Opportunity   Income for thousands of rural Indian women artisans averages about $1 per day

Strategies   (1) Create artisan production company

(2) Organize production by product theme and smooth demand

(3) Provide training and management support to artisans

(4) Produce high-quality products

(5) Market directly to urban consumers in India

(6) Provide product feedback to artisans

External Environment

Low income potential in rural environments leads youth to move to cities where unemployment is high. Skilled rural artisans are unorganized and unaware of market demand, technology, and best practices. Artisans have an overreliance on middle men (creates asymmetric market intelligence).

Market

Direct: thousands of rural artisans

Indirect: urban consumers $22.5 billion rupee market (2008), 9 percent annual growth rate

Related: families and local economy of rural artisans

Industree differentiates itself from the competition by being integrated end to end and by matching product design, manufacturing, and distribution to market demand.

Operations and Value Chain

Key processes are (1) artisan organization and training, (2) product definition, (3) product production, (4) product marketing and sales, and (5) consumer feedback.

In addition to its own stores, Industree partners with the government to provide professional management and infrastructure. Industree also partners with Fabindia on marketing.

Organization and Human Resources

Industree Crafts is organized as three companies: Industree Retail, Industree Production Aggregator, and Industree Production (artisan community–owned enterprises), which are related as shown in Figure 8.10.

All three companies have a common board and senior management.

Board: Mr. Kishore Biyani, Future Group (India Leading Retailer); Mr. Shankar Datta, executive of IRMA and BASIX, India's most prestigious Micro-Finance Institution (MFI) and rural livelihoods programs, and Neelam Chibber, Managing Director

Figure 8.10 Industree Crafts Corporate Structure

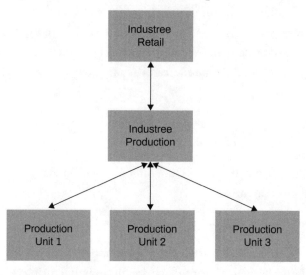

Figure 8.11 Industree Crafts Organization and Human Resources SWOT Analysis

Organizational Strengths	Organizational Weaknesses
• Employee skills • Employee business training • Empowerment opportunities for marginalized women • Ownership by employees	• Multiple organizations require more management, talent, and communication
Organizational Opportunities	Organizational Threats
• Further expansion of retail organization • Further development of employee ownership	• Loss of founder and key employees

Management team: Managing Director, Neelam Chibber, Industrial Designer; RS Rekhi, Operations MBA, and former IRMA employee, Gita Ram, Investor

An organization SWOT for Industree Crafts is shown in Figure 8.11.

Business Model and Unit Economics

Key income drivers: product sales (60 percent), contributed: grants (20 percent), fund-raising (20 percent)

Key expense drivers: product infrastructure (16 percent), production staff (16 percent), working capital (24 percent), training and capacity building (24 percent), and business planning (20 percent)

Unit Economics: Unit = artisan, investment of $2.5 million produces $18 million artisan net income for 10,000 artisans. Cost per artisan is $250; net income per artisan is $1,800.

Metrics

(1) revenue, (2) revenue per artisan, (3) expenses, (4) net income/artisan, and (5) number of artisans.

Operating Plan

In 2008, Industree had an annual operating plan developed in collaboration with GSBI mentors.

Financing

The $2.5 million investment in Industree came from debt (40 percent), artisan equity (40 percent), and a grant (20 percent).

To Recap

Without the right team in place—or a good business plan—it does not much matter how good your technology or product or service is. In terms of organization and human resources, social businesses do well when they choose the right legal and organizational structure for their particular circumstances and funding needs. They can also benefit from being mission oriented. Having a compelling vision can attract not only paid talent that is aligned with the mission of the organization but also volunteers—crucial for many social ventures that cannot necessarily afford all the help that they need. And finally, having the right governing and advisory boards in place can augment organizational expertise and provide access to helpful networks and critical resources. The Minimum Critical Specifications Checklist outlines the main boxes to tick for this element of the business plan. In chapter 9, we turn to the business model.

Exercises

8.1 Define the Form of the Organization

Specify the legal form of the organization for the enterprise.

8.2 Board Structure

Specify the number of board members and the role of each (responsibilities for each member). Specify the names and qualifications (or potential names and desired qualifications) of each board position. If there is an advisory board(s), identify the functions it (they) will perform. Specify the names and/or the key skills of advisory board members.

8.3 Management (Key Employees)

Create an organization chart (or table) showing the key employees, their roles, and their qualifications.

Minimum Critical Specifications Checklist

Organization and Human Resources Plan

- Provides clear evidence of senior leadership strengths

- Specifies board expertise and how it will contribute to success

- Provides strategic rationale for choice of legal structure

- Specifies risk factors through an organization SWOT analysis identifying capability gaps

- Clarifies how organization culture will drive extraordinary results through ordinary people

8.4 Staffing Plan

Create an organization chart (or table) listing all employees and volunteers, their roles (job descriptions), desired qualifications, compensation, and the date they are to be hired (if not already in the enterprise).

Note: The "Deliverables Table with Required Capabilities" referenced at the end of chapter 7, "Operations and Value Chain," can be used as a basis for determining key employee and volunteer positions, their roles, qualifications, and compensation requirements.

8.5 Organization/HR SWOT

Create a SWOT table for your (actual or proposed) organization.

Background Resources

Dees, J. Gregory, Jed Emerson, and Peter Economy. *Strategic Tools for Social Entrepreneurs: Enhancing the Performance of Your Enterprising Nonprofit.* New York: John Wiley, 2002, chapters 4, 5, and 11.

DeThomas, Arthur, and Stephanie Derammelaere. *How to Write a Convincing Business Plan.* 3rd ed. New York: Barron's Educational Services, 2008, chapter 9.

Income Tax Department. "India Income Tax Act 1961." http://www.incometaxindia.gov.in /pages/acts/income-tax-act.aspx.

Prahalad, C. K. *The Fortune at the Bottom of the Pyramid: Eradicating Poverty through Profits.* Philadelphia: Wharton School Publishing, 2010, part 4.

Sahlman, William Andrews. *How to Write a Great Business Plan.* No. E70 90. Boston: Harvard Business School Press, 2008.

Schonig, M., A. Noble, A. Heinecke, A. Achleiter, and K. Meyer. *The Governance of Social Enterprises: Managing Your Organization for Success.* Schwab Foundation for Social Entrepreneurship, June 2012. http://www3.weforum.org/docs/WEF_Governance_Social _Enterprises_2106_light.pdf.

Young, Dennis R. "Social Enterprise in the United States: Alternate Identities and Forms." Prepared for the EMES Conference, The Social Enterprise: A Comparative Perspective, Trento, Italy, December 13–15, 2001. https://community-wealth.org/sites/clone .community-wealth.org/files/downloads/paper-young.pdf.

Chapter 9

Business Model

At its most basic, a business model should define what value your venture creates as well as how the venture gets money (income), spends money (expenses) to create that value, and captures a sufficient surplus to sustain venture viability and growth. Essentially, the business model for a social business describes the financing of your theory of change. It helps focus the organization on the effectiveness of key processes used to create value. It also focuses decision making on the importance of managing the cash or working capital needed to sustain business operations. Finally, the business model is critically important in raising funds for your organization.

Process: The Four Elements of a Business Model

This chapter adapts its definition of a business model for social businesses from one first described by

Basic Knowledge
The organization's theory of change and strategy must be translated into the resource requirements and expense drivers in business models. Understanding unit economics—the revenue and expenses associated with a unit of output or benefit—is fundamental to the viability of a business model. Market channels will be revenue drivers only if financial models include adequate margins up and down value chains. Cash flow and revenue growth rates exceeding expense growth are indicators of scalability.

R. G. Hamermesh and his colleagues in a Harvard Business School Report.[1] The adapted definition consists of the following four elements:

1. Value proposition: What value do you create and for whom?

2. Income (value) drivers: How do you obtain money to create value?

3. Expense (cost) drivers: How do you spend money to create value?

4. Critical success factors: What are the key assumptions needed for your business model to create value and be financially sustainable (cash flow positive)?

Value Propositions

Value propositions are brief descriptions of what the organization does, for whom, and the value it provides. They articulate why the target customer/ beneficiary will choose to buy or use the organization's product or service offering(s) rather than other alternatives. In underserved markets, where customer education is needed, "nonconsumption" may be an alternative. The value proposition should derive from the mission, opportunity, and key strategies (Exercises 4.1–4.3). In the value proposition, value creation, revenues, and mission are all envisioned as mutually aligned.

Whereas a mission statement describes a desired change in broad terms—say, in the well-being of individuals in a particular market (e.g., "eliminate needless blindness")—the value proposition describes what the organization actually does, for whom, and why it is the best option. For example, "We provide low-cost, safe cataract surgery in India at much lower cost (60 percent of patients are free) and with fewer adverse events than alternatives." Characteristics of a useful value proposition include the following:

- Resonant with targeted beneficiaries: beneficiaries recognize that this message is for them (face validity)

- Understandable by beneficiaries, as well as employees, investors, and donors

- Important: relevant to sociocultural and economic realities of the beneficiaries

- Credible: can be supported by evidence (proof of concept and benefit)

- Deliverable by the organization through repeatable processes and effective use by beneficiaries

- Differentiated: "competitors" cannot easily make the same claim

- Clear why it is better than alternatives (including nonconsumption)

- Sustainable advantage: "competitors" cannot catch up quickly

- Fewer than twenty-five words

Income (Revenue) Drivers

Income (revenue) drivers monetize (fund) the value proposition. They may be based on sales of products, licenses, or services (earned income), or income from capacity-building grants, donors, or subsidies (contributed income). Since earned income reduces a venture's dependence on contributions—grants, donations, or third-party "sponsors" that are not tied directly to the venture's operations—it is often easier to sustain income if at least a portion of the funds needed to operate or scale are from earned income. The emphasis on market-based solutions to alleviate poverty in the BOP literature assumes that social mission enterprises can become economically viable through earned income.[2]

To be clear, it is imperative that your venture's earned income be a by-product of producing the products and/or services for the beneficiaries. It should not be an additional defocusing initiative—an activity that might distract from the venture's primary purpose. In some instances, earned income may not come from the direct beneficiaries. Third-party beneficiaries (e.g., governments, NGOs, businesses, or advertisers) may pay for the products or services based on their effective delivery, or because they stand to benefit from the opening of a new market or channel for reaching underserved populations. For example, Kenyan venture Safaricom financed the cell tower infrastructure and vast network of agent-based kiosks needed to support the phenomenal growth of M-Pesa (mobile banking), because doing so meant that more people joined its network—resulting in over $200 million in Safaricom profits each year.[3] Similarly, in Esoko's intermediary business model, its revenues are driven by supplier advertising and paid programing—both of which enable Esoko to deliver on its value proposition of providing smallholder African farmers with access to higher-quality agricultural inputs, expanded market access, and better prices for their crops.

Figure 9.1 provides a list of potential income drivers. It is very common for social businesses to have both contributed and earned income. This is a "hybrid income model," which is different from a hybrid organization in the legal sense. Any form of social mission organization can have a hybrid income model—both earned and contributed income. For example, Grameen Shakti is a for-profit organization with both earned and contributed income. Generally speaking, earned income growth can become more predictable as operating routines and processes become formalized. With organizational growth, improving organizational capabilities contributes to greater efficiency.

For each income driver in your business model, you need to specify the source of the income and the basis for estimating amounts. The basis may be per time period (e.g., annually—for donations), per unit of benefit (e.g., for each product or service delivered), per use (e.g., of a license), or per transaction. For example, income from cataract surgeries depends on both the number of paying beneficiaries (the revenue source) and the amount paid for a unit of benefit such as a corrective surgery (the basis).

Finally, ventures need to manage income drivers to achieve specified target revenue amounts in defined time frames (from your budget, to be created in chapter 11) and should review income drivers at least annually for possible additions or exclusions.

Expense (Cost) Drivers

In addition to key income drivers, it is also essential to identify key expense (cost) drivers—those uses of funds needed to create the described benefits in the value proposition—including any fund-raising, sales, and administrative expenses necessary to create income streams. Expense drivers can be categorized by major programs (e.g., the strategies identified in Exercise 4.3) or by type as in line-item budgets (e.g., salaries and benefits, rent, and utilities), or both. For example, line-item expense drivers such as product development, marketing, sales or beneficiary recruiting, distribution, service, and overhead might be categorized by program.

Expense drivers, like income drivers, have a source (the category or line item) and a basis (per time period, per unit, per transaction, or per use). It is often useful to know whether the expense drivers are fixed (do not change with volume or time), variable (change with volume or time),

Figure 9.1   Examples of Income Drivers (Sources)

Contributed Income Drivers

- Donors make (regular) contributions to fund product/service delivery (e.g., annual fund drive or Web-based solicitation of contributions)
- Cause-related contributions that a third-party (generally a large corporation) contributes from its sales, profits, or marketing expenses
- Although grants are generally considered to be contributed income, or one time "investments" to build organizational capacity, in instances where they are tied to specific deliverables and long-standing partnerships, they may become sources of sustainable income as contracted product or service revenues
- Social media–enabled incomes such as Kickstarter or other crowd-funding campaigns

Sales of Products or Services

- A direct, indirect, or electronic sales channel for products or services
- Direct sales channels can facilitate income from additional products/services (e.g., a multi-product channel)

Third-Party Earned Income Drivers

- Indirect beneficiaries (those who benefit from the market creation or the impacts of the products or services) provide the income (e.g., a government agency or NGO pays to rebuild houses after an earthquake)
- Third parties with interest in reaching a market pay through an advertising platform for content and services provided to direct beneficiaries

Fee-Based / Licensing Income Drivers

- Fee per use or transaction
- License to use your intellectual property

Subscription Income Drivers

- Fees to join service
- Fee to receive service

Ability to Pay Income Drivers

- Those that can afford to pay subsidize service delivery for those that cannot
- Different prices (and possibly products/services) for different market segments

Franchising

- Enable other organizations to provide your services in different markets or regions
- Franchising involves getting paid to use or replicate exactly your product/service and the corresponding marketing and supply chain

Figure 9.1 *(Continued)*

Advertising

- Corporate sponsor pays you for advertising its products or services to your beneficiaries

---

Network Models

- "In-kind" and/or financial resources accessed through alliances with shared values affinity groups or social movement entities united by a common purpose

---

semivariable (a fixed component plus a variable component), or one-time (nonrecurring). For each expense driver, you should identify the stream (line-item type) of expense (e.g., employee salaries) and the basis (sum of salaries of each employee).

Expense drivers must be managed to specified target amounts and defined dates from your budget (to come in chapter 11). It is useful to review expense projections for possible savings more than once per year.

Critical Success Factors

A critical success factor (CSF) is an assumption, capability, or operational competency that must be true to reliably deliver the value proposition, meet financial projections, and achieve specific growth objectives in the number of beneficiaries served. For example, for beneficiaries to buy home solar lighting systems, they might need to be convinced to use microfinancing. The success of the business model in supporting the value proposition for the target market depends on the CSFs remaining true. CSFs are the primary concern of the top management team, and changes in any CSF may require adapting or modifying elements of the business model.

Unit Economics

Unit economics captures income-expense ratios per unit over a specified period of time (e.g., one year). For an organization to be financially sustainable, the unit economics must be greater than 1 (i.e., the income per unit must be greater than the expenses per unit). The "unit" itself should be the unit of impact, or primary measure of success, identified in the mission statement. It can be a product sold (e.g., solar home lighting system) or a customer/beneficiary (e.g., household) or an event (e.g., surgery).

A simple calculation of unit economics would take total income minus total expenses divided by the total number of units to arrive at average profit per unit (average unit economics). You can also calculate marginal income per incremental unit of impact minus marginal expense per incremental unit (marginal unit economics). Ventures can make similar calculations at each link in the supply chain to assess whether incentives are sufficient to motivate performance for each organization in the supply chain. In economic theory, effectively incentivizing suppliers or intervening levels in distribution channels reduces a social venture's risk. We turn next to three exemplary business model examples, beginning with Grameen Shakti.

Social Venture Snapshot: Grameen Shakti Business Model

Value Proposition and the Key Differentiators

Grameen Shakti provides solar home lighting systems. These systems provide brighter light and healthier lighting than kerosene or candles. They are also less costly than kerosene and increase household income by allowing for increased work hours. Unlike other solar lighting providers, Grameen Shakti provides a range of product offerings tailored to individual needs, plus microfinancing to cover upfront costs, and after-sales service.

Key Income Driver Categories

1. Product sales

2. Interest on microloans (in early years)

3. Service contracts

Key Expense Driver Categories

1. Costs of products sold (product purchase, inventory, delivery)

2. Sales and marketing

3. Microlending

4. Costs of service

5. Audit

6. Training

Cash Flow Calculations

The company reported cash flow breakeven as of 2000. As of 2007, although all branch offices were cash flow positive, branch office surpluses did not cover all company overhead costs. By 2010, increased sales volume, plus service contract revenues, led to the solar lighting operations being cash flow positive, including coverage of all overhead.

Critical Success Factors

1. Ability to find, train, and retain employees

2. Branch staff becomes embedded and accepted as part of community served

3. Good-quality products that last

4. Sales of service contracts after warranty expires (and loan is paid off)

5. Ability to adapt to natural disasters (rains and floods)

Unit Economics

Unit = Branch office

Computation: Operating sustainability ratio = Income/Expenses × 100*

* Ratio needs to be about 115 percent to cover company overheads. In 2007, the range for branches was 103.57–118.50 percent, with an average of 109 percent.

Social Venture Snapshot: Sankara Business Model

The following analysis of the Sankara Eye Care business model is based on research by Danielle Medeiros, Cathryn Meyer, and Visswapriya Prabakar, a team of Santa Clara University MBA students, with the support of Sankara Eye Care. For fiscal 2014, 82 percent of Sankara's 170,690 surgeries were performed for free, and Sankara achieved a "sustainability ratio" of 0.91 (i.e., 91 percent of its total expenses were covered by earned income). Through the combination of earned income and donations, its hybrid business model generated a 321.64 rupee surplus per surgery.

Value Proposition and Key Differentiators

Sankara is the leading provider of free eye surgeries in India, operating specialty eye care hospitals that offer comprehensive eye care services to two distinct markets: free services for the rural poor and affordable premium eye care for the urban middle class; unlike government-run hospitals in India, Sankara is able to provide high-quality affordable eye care, keeping in mind patients' dignity while improving the overall welfare of its customers.

Key Differentiators

1. Financial model of 20/80 cross-subsidy: 20 percent of Sankara's customers "pay" for the remaining 80 percent of customers that are nonpaying. (Note: Aravind Eye Care Systems, which also operates on a similar cross-subsidized model, uses a 40/60 ratio for paying vs. nonpaying.)

2. Quality of care: Sankara truly values and believes in the dignity of its nonpaying customers. Therefore, the services offered to nonpaying customers are of higher quality than those of other providers (e.g., Sankara provides beds rather than mats on the floor).

3. Trusted brand value: Sankara is the leading provider of free eye surgeries in India (140,804 vs. Aravind's 85,935 during fiscal year 2013–14).

Key Income Drivers

Based on the "Consolidated Income and Expenditure Account for the year ended 31st March 2014," Sankara's key income drivers (Figure 9.2) are the following:

- Hospital collections:

  (Reliance Ratio* = 69.3%)
  Source: Earned Base—Consultation and treatment fees

Figure 9.2   Sankara's Key Income Drivers

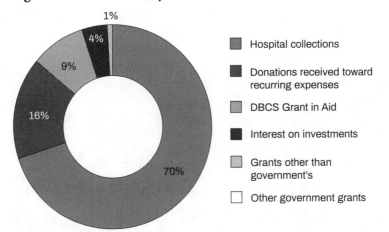

Source: Income statement and budget vs. actuals statement, Annual Report 2014.

- Donations:

  (Reliance Ratio* = 15.6%)
  Source: Contributed Base—Individual contributions
  (number of donors multiplied by average size of donation)

- District Blindness Control Society Grant:

  (Reliance Ratio* = 9.5%)
  Source: Contributed Base—Recurring grants

*Reliance Ratio = Single largest type of income/total income. For Sankara, earned income is 69.3 percent of total income.

Sankara's income drivers are summarized in Figure 9.2.

The recurring grant from the District Blindness Control Society (DBCS) contributes close to 10 percent of the total income. However, we learned in a client interview that there is considerable risk associated with this grant. Essentially a form of reimbursement from the government of India (Rs.1000 provided for every verified and successful eye surgery performed), it involves a laborious reporting and claim effort from Sankara's side. The risk lies in the fact that the government often randomly reassigns funds to other programs, leading to fluctuation in available grant money for Sankara, which in turn directly impacts the organization's income and financial sustainability.

Key Expense Drivers

Based on the "Consolidated Income and Expenditure Account for the year ended 31st March 2014," Sankara's key expense drivers (Figure 9.3) are the following:

- Establishment charges (47.6 percent)—includes employee salaries/wages and benefits

- Medicines and lenses (20.5 percent)

- Ward upkeep, repairs, and maintenance (9.8 percent)

  ∞ Ward upkeep (5.94 percent)
     Repairs and maintenance (3.86 percent)

- Food, transport, and camp expenses for nonpaying patients (8.8 percent)

  ∞ Cafeteria expenses (3.11 percent)
     Transportation expenses (4.53 percent)
     Camp expenses (1.19 percent)

- Administrative expenses—less than 5 percent of total expenditure

Figure 9.3   Sankara's Key Expense Drivers

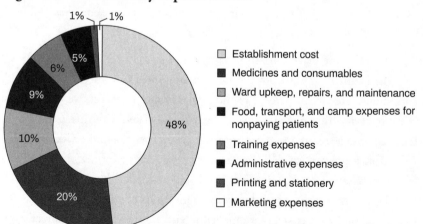

Source: Income statement and budget vs. actuals statement, Annual Report 2014.

One potential expense reduction that could both help improve Sankara's sustainability and decrease its reliance on donations/grants is the manufacturing of intraocular lenses. However, Sankara prefers to focus primarily on providing quality eye care, training, and capacity building, and has chosen to stay away from lens manufacturing (based on client interview). Moreover, dependence on in-house manufacturing would restrict Sankara's flexibility to scale to different states in India. Instead, Sankara maintains highly competitive rate contracts with its suppliers, made possible by its large volume demands.

Critical Success Factors

- Low-cost procedures for eye care system, materials, and supplies

- Successful training of all medical staff

- Maintain 80/20 model (nonpaying vs. paying customers)

- Camps remain effective way for locating beneficiaries (for free treatment)

- Reinvest surplus in staff training, improved processes, and new technology

- Motivate staff through work environment/culture and competitive compensation/benefits

- Use partnerships for funds generation, in-field screening, and raising awareness

Cash Flow Analysis

Sankara's sources and amounts of cash are larger than its current uses, leading to positive cash flow of 165,490,601 Rs at the end of fiscal year 2013–2014. Its primary sources of cash intake include funds from operations, donations, and loans, while its biggest uses of cash include salaries, benefits and other operating costs, fixed assets (hospitals and machinery), current assets (medical supplies, medicines, etc.), and investments. As Sankara looks to open an additional six hospitals by 2020 (a significant source of cash outflows), it must ensure that its sources of intake continue to increase at a rate to cover these expenditures. While the costs to open each hospital can vary based on geographic location, size of the facility, and market conditions, there are two types of funding needed for every new hospital: (1) capital funding, which covers land, infrastructure, equipment, and training, and (2) recurring funding, which covers ongoing operations and maintenance of each facility. The sources of capital funding for new hospitals are primarily contributed (donated) through partners including Sankara Eye Foundation (USA and Europe) and Mission for Vision Trust. Recurring funding is primarily covered by hospital collections via paying patients. The goal is to increase hospital collections in order to decrease the reliance on external donors and help each hospital become fully self-sufficient in five years.

Sankara has reported profitable operations for the past ten years, for which we have data (Figure 9.4). Given its legal structure as a charitable trust, these profits are reinvested into the business to expand and grow operations.

Figure 9.4   Sankara's Ten-Year Trend in Income and Expenses

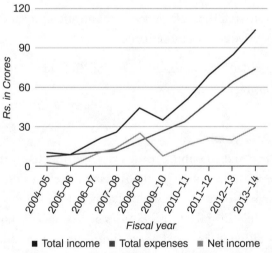

Source: *Financial performance snapshot, Annual Report 2014.*

- Total income, which consists primarily of earned income from patients, donations, and grants, has shown a positive average growth rate of 33.67 percent over the past ten years, with only one of those years (2005–2006 fiscal year) showing negative year-over-year income growth.

- Total expenses, which consists primarily of establishment (hospital) charges and medical products/medicines/lenses, has shown a positive average growth rate of 29.34 percent over the same period, with expense growth declining steadily since the 2011–2012 fiscal year.

- Sankara's income growth rates exceed its expense growth rates, leading to profitable operations. Optimizing this financial structure is critical to Sankara's ability to scale. Given the relatively small gap in the average growth rates of income versus expenses (33.67 percent vs. 29.34 percent), Sankara will need to continue to look for ways to increase income and decrease expenses to maintain profitable operations in the presence of its growth aspirations.

Additionally, although Sankara is currently operating in the black, the ultimate goal is to become fully sustainable based solely on earned income (without the reliance on donations). Sankara's facilities as a whole are currently 91 percent sustainable, meaning there is additional work to be done in terms of increasing hospital income (via paying patients) to reach 100 percent sustainability. Over the past ten years, the average year-over-year growth rate of hospital income was 34.9 percent, but this rate has been decreasing since 2011. This is concerning; if earned income via hospitals does not increase proportionally, Sankara will have no hope of sustaining its operations and scaling to twenty hospitals by 2020.

Ratio Analysis

Working Capital = Current Assets—Current Liabilities:
286,937,220 = Rs 513,704,942–226,767,722

Current Ratio = Current Assets/Current Liabilities: 2.26 = Rs 513,704,942 / 226,767,722

These ratios indicate good short-term (one-year) financial strength.

Unit Economics

We use an "eye surgery" as our main unit because collections from surgery are a key income driver (70 percent of total income). Sankara has unique unit economics due to its 80/20 model: treatment for the nonpaying customers (80 percent of the volume of total surgeries) is paid for by the paying customers (20 percent of the volume of total surgeries). Sankara needs to have high marginal revenue (income) per unit due to this model—paying customers need to cover the costs of nonpaying customers.

All data below is from the year 2013–2014.

Unit = 1 Eye Surgery:

- Number of free surgeries performed: 140,804
- Number of paying surgeries performed: 29,886
- Total surgeries performed: 170,690 units

Average Income, Expenses, Surplus (Deficit) per Unit:

- Income (Hospital): 667.7 million rupees (Rs)
  Revenue per unit = 667.7 million Rs / 170690 = 3911.77 Rs

- Expenses: 736.6 million Rs
  Expenses per unit = 736.6/170690 = 4315.42 Rs

- Deficit per unit = 3911.77–4315.42 = (403.65) Rs

- Unit economics = Income/Expenses = 3911.77 / 4315.42 = .91

Currently Sankara is 91 percent sustainable with earned (hospital) income. We have chosen not to include donations within this analysis because Sankara is focused on becoming 100 percent sustainable. On the other hand, if we include operational donations within this analysis, Sankara is operating at a surplus per unit.

- Donations (Operations only): 123.8 million Rs
  Donation revenue per unit = 123.8 million Rs/
  170690 = 725.29 Rs Surplus per unit = (403.65) + 725.29
  Rs = 321.64 Rs

Social Venture Snapshot: GSBI Innovator Kiva

Kiva is an international nonprofit organization that was founded in 2005, one year before cofounder Matt Flannery attended the GSBI. In Swahili, *kiva* means "unity." Its platform connects low-income people who are trying to create a better life for themselves, their families, and their communities through lenders funding loans. Kiva's platform technology and ability to leverage MFI partner infrastructure enables it to achieve economies of scale. Since attending the GSBI, Kiva has grown to provide 2.8 million borrowers with $1.12 billion dollars of loans from 1.7 million lenders, with a 96.9 percent repayment rate.

Kiva was GSBI's (and probably the world's) first online "crowd-lending" platform, and the first GSBI venture to use contributions by lenders as a primary income driver.

Mission, Opportunity, and Strategies

Mission — Connect lenders (in the United States) with small entrepreneurs in developing countries to help alleviate poverty

Key metric — Number ($ value) of loans

Opportunity — Eighty percent of the MFI market is unserved. Over five hundred million people are in need of MFI lending but only one hundred million are being served.

Strategies —
(1) Develop online platform where small entrepreneurs can request funding from lenders (in the United States)

(2) Develop network of MFI partners in developing countries that deliver loans to entrepreneurs and repayments to lenders

(3) Use online platform to report results to lenders

        (4) Facilitate lenders' use of repayments to make new loans

        (5) Ask lenders to pay fees to sustain Kiva

External Environment

Many potential lenders in the United States are willing to make small loans ($25–$100) to entrepreneurs in developing countries. Many more entrepreneurs want loans than can be supplied by current MFIs. Current MFIs are constrained by the ability to find money and qualify recipients. The internet is widely available in U.S. homes and widely accessible (through centers) in the developing world.

Market

Direct beneficiaries: five hundred million people in developing countries who need microloans; Indirect beneficiaries: millions of U.S. citizens with access to internet willing to make small loans; thousands of MFIs who need access to money to lend; Related beneficiaries: families of entrepreneurs and lenders, economies in developing countries; Competition: none in 2006; Future competitive advantages: first mover, lower costs of loans; Market plan received major promotional assistance from media coverage (*Businessweek*, BBC, *Wall Street Journal*, *The Oprah Winfrey Show*).

Operations and Value Chain

Key processes are (1) develop and maintain an easy-to-use online lending platform, (2) recruit entrepreneurs in developing countries, (3) recruit lenders in the United States, (4) develop network of MFI partners in developing countries, and (5) provide feedback and repayment to lenders.

    Partners: MFIs in developing countries; back-office services in the United States; PayPal for loans and repayments; Starbucks; originally MySpace, then Google to recruit lenders.

Organization and Human Resources

Kiva is a U.S. nonprofit (501(c)(3)) corporation.

Board of directors: 4

Four advisory boards: Microfinance, Website, Legal, Financial

CEO and seven staff in U.S. HQ.

Outsource: legal, finance, field audits. Thirty MFI partners in 2006.

Business Model and Unit Economics

Key income drivers: request lender fees of 2 percent (50 percent of income), 1–2 percent MFI partner fee (30 percent of income), and 2 percent interest on float (20 percent of income).

Key expense drivers: staff (80 percent), operations (20 percent).

Critical success factors: (1) lenders are willing to voluntarily pay fees, (2) local MFI partner organizations are honest in distributing loans, (3) local borrowers repay loans, (4) lender enthusiasm (amounts loaned, re-lend rates), (5) favorable regulatory status.

Unit Economics: Unit = dollars loaned; cost per $ loan = $0.05.

Metrics

(1) amount loaned, (2) loan repayment rate, (3) lending client retention rate, (4) revenue and profitability, (5) lender conversion and repeat loan rates.

Operating Plan

Kiva's first-year operating plan incurred significantly more expenses than planned because of the need to visit/audit all MFI partners.

Financing

Grants.

To Recap

If the mission is the aspirational spirit of a social venture, the business plan, in many ways, outlines the practical steps needed to realize it—it is where your mission, value proposition, value creation, and revenue all align. The answers to four key questions largely inform the business plan. What value do you create for whom? How do you get money to create value? How do you spend money to create value? And what key assumptions must you validate for your business model to create value and be financially sustainable? The Minimum Critical Specifications Checklist outlines the most important items to include in this element. In the next chapter, we turn to metrics and accountability.

Exercises

9.1 Create a value proposition and provide validating evidence for your value proposition (especially evidence based on your organization's experience in delivering this value proposition)

The easiest way to write a value proposition is to follow the two-sentence format below:

[Name of organization] provides [products/services], which are [statement of key differentiators], for [target beneficiaries], and thereby creates [statement of social value/impact], unlike [competition]. Over the past [xx] years, we have helped [xxxx] beneficiaries, creating [list of] benefits for each, compared with [the alternative].

However, as long as the value proposition and evidence statements are reasonably succinct (within plus or minus one hundred words combined) and contain information specifying the value you create, for whom, and how it is better than the alternative, you can use any sentence structure you like.

Minimum Critical Specifications Checklist

Business Model

- Defines a credible value proposition with compelling differentiators and a reason to pay

- Specifies income drivers and potential future revenue streams to strengthen scalability

- Specifies expense drivers with possible means of future cost reductions

- Provides credible financial data indicating path to positive cash flow and revenue growth rates greater than expense growth rates

- Clarifies unit economics (and if possible, the unit economics for each link in the supply chain)

9.2 Identify the key income drivers for your organization

List the major sources and basis (e.g.,_____paid surgeries at_____average revenue per surgery) for each of your planned income drivers. From these, create a "fishbone diagram" that shows the total income (in dollars or other currency) and the percentage of total income and/or amounts for each of the income drivers.

9.3 Identify the key expense drivers that will be required to obtain this income

List the categories and basis (e.g.,_____cost per surgery ×_____surgeries) for your key expense drivers. Use this list to create a "fishbone diagram" that shows the total expenses (in dollars or other currency) and the percent (or amounts) for each category.

9.4 List the critical success factors (or key assumptions) that will influence your income and expense drivers

List three to seven success factors, and for each, identify the results, actions, internal initiatives, or conditions in the external environment that you will need to monitor because of their potential influence on your income and expense drivers, and therefore your cash flow. These are success factor conditions that you need to manage, or at least track on a continuing basis.

9.5 Develop a unit economics analysis

Select the unit, and then compute either average or marginal income-expenses per unit.

Background Resources

Dees, J. Gregory, Jed Emerson, and Peter Economy. *Strategic Tools for Social Entrepreneurs: Enhancing the Performance of Your Enterprising Nonprofit.* New York: John Wiley, 2002, chapters 6 and 9.

DeThomas, Arthur, and Stephanie Derammelaere. *How to Write a Convincing Business Plan.* 3rd ed. New York: Barron's Educational Services, 2008, chapters 3, 10, and 11.

Hamermesh, Richard G., Paul W. Marshall, and Taz Pirohamed. "Note on Business Model Analysis for the Entrepreneur." Harvard Business School Report 9-802-048, January 22, 2002.

London, Ted, and Stuart L. Hart. *Next Generation Business Strategies for the Base of the Pyramid—New Approaches for Building Mutual Value*. Upper Saddle River, NJ: FT Press, 2011.

MacMillan, Ian C., and James D. Thompson. *The Social Entrepreneur's Playbook—Pressure Test, Plan, Launch, and Scale Your Enterprise*. Philadelphia: Wharton Digital Press, 2013.

Chapter 10

Metrics and Accountability

For a social entrepreneur, there are two main reasons to keep metrics for your enterprise. The first is to help manage your business: to measure progress in achieving the mission, to assess the efficiency and effectiveness of your operations (value chain) and organization, and to validate whether your business model is working as planned. The second reason relates to raising money. The individuals or organizations providing financing for your enterprise will want to know what return/impact their funds are enabling. In some countries, social businesses will also need metrics to comply with auditing and regulatory requirements.

In this chapter you will create a metrics dashboard using metrics in four categories, based on the framework (linear model) shown in Figure 10.1:

- Resource/input metrics, which capture financial and organizational resources

- Transformation metrics, which capture activities or key processes that drive desired outcomes

- Outcome metrics, which capture the results of activities or key processes

- Impact metrics, which capture the intended social changes resulting from outcomes

Involving the venture's management team and employees in developing the dashboard can contribute to accountability by increasing commitment to the use of metrics for assessing progress, efficiency, and effectiveness in ongoing operations. If the funding sources themselves are involved in creating metrics, then outcome or impact metrics can also be agreed on for measuring "social return on investment."

Process

The linear depiction of metrics in Figure 10.1 illustrates the relationship between operational measures of performance or results and your theory of change—or, the *social transformation* you seek to catalyze. For employees, this transformation extends to operational measures of excellence that will stimulate continuous learning and foster personal identity with a shared purpose.

Useful metrics for driving continuous improvement and the capacity for entrepreneurial adaptation share a set of common characteristics. These kinds of metrics

Basic Knowledge
Social ventures must be learning organizations that are operated like traditional businesses. A balanced scorecard for a social business includes metrics for

- financial resources,

- organizational resources,

- key processes or activities, and

- outcomes or impact.

Effective operating routines use these metrics to drive continuous improvement and adaptive capacity in the presence of constrained and contingent environments.

- can be linked directly to your mission, strategies, and key processes;

- are easy to quantify (or specify if qualitative in nature);

Figure 10.1 Creating a Metrics Dashboard

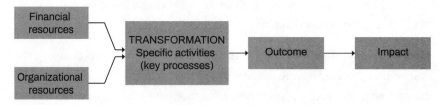

- are easy to collect and not an administrative burden;

- can be related to a specific time period for benchmarking; and

- are agreed upon (by employees and other stakeholders).

In selecting the metrics for your dashboard, you should consider each of the elements shown in Figure 10.1.

Financial Resource Metrics

Financial resources include both investment capital and financial resources generated from ongoing operations. The latter are obtained from profit/loss statements and balance sheets. They typically include income, operating and capital expenses, and cash balances, but they may also include assets (inventory, or accounts receivable or payable), gross margins on sales, and liabilities. Sometimes ratios (such as the current ratio—the ratio of current assets to current liabilities) are used, but this is more common in a profit-maximizing business than in a social business.

Organizational Resource Metrics

Organizational resource metrics attempt to measure the human resources involved in carrying out the organization's mission. Number and qualifications of employees and volunteers, number of unfilled positions (especially in the leadership team or other pivotal jobs), and employee and volunteer turnover are common organizational resource metrics. If partners are important for achieving organizational goals, then metrics often include measures of the number and performance or quality of partners. Organizational metrics are usually collected and monitored by management (or a human resources department in larger organizations).

Transformation (Activity/Process) Metrics

Transformation metrics can be used to assess operating routine efficiency and effectiveness across the value chain. Activity metrics may include number of beneficiaries served or hours of service provided, milestones like target dates for achieving specific objectives, productivity (output per unit of time or cost), and quality. It is useful for metrics to enable a comparison of actual results with objectives or benchmarks (e.g., baselines, previous time periods, or alternatives). Ideally, the collection and use of operating metrics should be incorporated into ongoing operations and be a basis for improving key processes.

Outcome Metrics

Outcome metrics, at their most basic, measure results. More specifically, they measure how well certain activities or processes transform specific resources into specific outputs and outcomes of benefit to your target customers. In systems terms, you can think of each of the activities or processes that compose your operation as a "unit operation," with standards or specific targets for quality and productivity. Together, these "unit operations" form a larger transformation process purposefully designed to produce outputs that will benefit those you serve—your target market (refer to Figure 10.1).

Number and quality of outputs are common output metrics. In some instances, these metrics may be used as a proxy for social benefit outcomes (e.g., number of solar home systems installed, number of successful sight-restoring surgeries). Transformation metrics for specific processes may also be used (e.g., time or costs associated with marketing, sales, or service; qualified lead-to-sales ratios). Whereas some of these metrics may be captured as the result of operations, others may need to be collected by a survey of beneficiaries. Survey questions should be carefully designed so that collection is not an imposition on beneficiaries or customers and that the questions do not bias the answers (e.g., "on a scale of 1–5, how did you like our service?" versus "how likely would you be to recommend our service to someone you know?"). In user surveys, it is best to stick to a small range of choices, such as easily interpreted five-point scales. Acumen's Lean Data Impact Measurement is a potentially useful approach for gathering output metrics as well.[1] The Lean Data approach, which can use a variety of survey methodologies, is designed to enable efficient data collection for client-centric metrics.

Impact (and Return on Investment) Metrics

Impact metrics measure the changes in economic or social well-being that result from the outcomes of the enterprise. These metrics are the most difficult to collect because they may need to be collected over time (e.g., changes in health or income). While "systems change" may be the overarching objective of a social mission enterprise, it is often difficult to determine whether the outcomes of your enterprise created a given impact (e.g., does the use of affordable computer-aided classes improve learning?). Impact metrics may also require "before-and-after" or control group comparisons. Randomized control trials that follow a protocol similar to that used by the Food and Drug Administration in assessing the impact of a new disease treatment are considered the gold standard for assessing impact. But these trials are often costly or impractical to conduct because of the difficulty of identifying a suitable control group. Therefore, for the dashboard you create in this chapter, the best impact metric may simply be a successful outcome (e.g., an unemployed person who is trained gets a job). Note that a "successful outcome" is very likely the single metric you created for your mission in chapter 4.

Measuring social return on investment (SROI) is generally complicated because of the effort required to measure impact in a way that can be directly linked to investment (for a good discussion of SROI methodology, see the monograph by Scholten et al.).[2] SROI metrics, therefore, tend to require special and often costly studies as opposed to measures that can be readily collected as part of ongoing operations. For your dashboard, cost per successful outcome is a simple return on investment measure you can use. To calculate for a given time period, divide the total capital and operating expenses needed to create successful outcomes by the number of successful outcomes. In the Social Venture Snapshots that follow, this is referred to as SROI Lite.

SROI Lite = Total investment/Number of successful outcomes = cost per successful outcome

Social Venture Snapshots

As an organization grows and/or changes, the set of metrics is likely to change as well. The following snapshots illustrate how the metrics guidelines in this chapter apply to three organizations. Note that each example uses a different set of metrics, but that the metrics can be categorized using the balanced scorecard categories defined in Figure 10.1 to create the metrics scorecard.

Social Venture Snapshot: Metrics Dashboard for Grameen Shakti
Financial Resources

1. Income

2. Expenses

3. Branch office operating sustainability ratio

4. Capital investment (total and per branch)

5. Breakeven sales

Organizational Resources

6. Number of branch offices

7. Number of staff (total, by job, by office and at headquarters, by gender)

8. Number of technicians trained

9. Retention

Process/Activity

10. Number of villages served

11. Number of customers and number of customers trained

12. Number of system owners

13. Number of maintenance agreements

14. Green jobs created

Outcome/Impact

15. Number of solar installations

16. Number of people impacted

17. Installed power capacity and energy generation per day

18. Increase in customer income

19. Carbon dioxide reductions

Alternative 1 Impact: SROI Lite (based on number of solar systems installed)

- Successful outcome: number of solar system installations (539,000 through 2005)

- Measure of investment: total capital invested, about $5 million (estimated through 2005, see Figure 12.3 in chapter 12)

- Investment per system installed = $5 million/ 539,000 = $9.27 per system

Dividing total investment capital raised ($5 million) by the 539,000 installed systems would give investment revenue per system installed. (An alternative SROI Lite would be the difference between the cost and revenues per unit installed—a measure of profit and/or subsidy per unit.)

Alternative 2 Impact: SROI Lite (based on number of beneficiaries in 2010)

- Successful outcome: a beneficiary using solar lighting

- Measure of investment: total capital invested = about $5 million (estimated)

- SROI Lite = $5 million/3.5 million = $1.43 invested per beneficiary

Social Venture Snapshot: Metrics Dashboard for Sankara

As with Grameen Shakti, the metrics dashboard for Sankara reflects a set of operational measures for monitoring critical financial and human inputs, as well as the effectiveness of internal processes for converting these inputs into desired outcomes. Its dashboard can be seen as a practical tool for managing and improving performance. Sustainability percent or ratio is a measure of the degree to which Sankara is sustainable from earned income, with the viability of Sankara's business model driven in large measure by its processes for maintaining high-volume surgery (see five process metrics below).

Financial Metrics

1. Annual earned income (via hospital collections) and year-over-year growth

   Company-wide and per hospital

2. Annual contributed income

   Sankara Eye Foundation

   Recurring grants from District Blindness Control Society, Govt. of India Company-wide and per hospital

3. Annual expenses and year-over-year growth

   Functional, program related (Gift of Vision, Rainbow, Eye Bank)

   Company-wide and per hospital

4. Sustainability % (ratio of income to expenses)

5. Comparison of actual expenses with monthly budget; year-over-year comparison

Organizational Resources (Physical and Human Assets)

6. Number of hospitals (city and rural)

7. Number of employees to staffing plan (doctors, optometrists, field workers)

8. Staff to patient ratio (ties directly to quality of care)

9. Staff satisfaction survey (periodic feedback given to supervisors, exit interviews if/when they leave Sankara)

10. Graduation rate from Academy of Vision

11. Employee male to female ratio (41 percent male and 59 percent female)

12. Employee turnover rate

Transformation (Process) Metrics

13. Number of surgeries per year (paid vs. unpaid) to maintain 80/20

14. Number of camps and productivity per camp (i.e., patients screened at a given site/month/year)

15. Yield per camp (outreach surgery cases)

16. Time per medical procedure

17. Patient wait time

Outcome Metrics

18. Number of successful sight-restoring surgeries

19. Overall customer experience (via survey)

20. Cost per surgery (to ensure the surplus from one paid surgery is enough to cover four free surgeries)

21. Number of villages/states reached across India

22. Number of schools screened

23. Recovery time after surgery

24. Postoperative satisfaction rate (internal and third-party evaluations)

    a. Paying patients—patient's responsibility to follow up one month after surgery (reason: urban population, higher awareness)

    b. Nonpaying patients—Sankara takes up responsibility to follow up with patient one month after surgery (reason: rural population, low awareness, limited resources).

    c. Six months after surgery—Mission for Vision randomly selects patients from a list of those receiving the operation to check the outcome of surgery. A questionnaire consisting of quality of life indicators is used for this purpose.[3]

Impact Metrics

25. Improvement in household income

26. Improvement in productivity at work (less time for a task)

27. Empowerment of rural women (74 percent of paramedics are women)

Social Venture Snapshot: GSBI Innovator Vision Spring (formerly Scojo)

When attending the GSBI in 2006, Vision Spring was known as Scojo and was in the fifth year of implementing its mission to provide affordable reading glasses and other eye care products in India and South America. In addition to its innovative approach for low-cost, last-mile distribution, Scojo was an early advocate for including metrics in the GSBI curriculum. It helped pioneer the use of balanced scorecard metrics for social ventures in the GSBI, and was the first to use employee and partner turnover metrics. Each of these metrics enabled Scojo to closely monitor two key business model success factors—its ability to retain the micro-entrepreneurs it had recruited and trained for its direct sales channel, and its ability to retain and grow the number of wholesale distributors. By 2017 its business model had evolved from a hub-and-spoke direct sales network of Vision Entrepreneurs to a B2B model with more than 95 percent of sales coming through partner organizations or wholesale distribution and more than four hundred distributor partners. Among its partners, BRAC had trained thirty-three thousand community health workers to sell reading glasses. The following data are from 2006 and include estimated or pro forma financials.

Mission, Opportunity, and Strategies

Mission   Vision Spring's original mission statement was to provide the poor with access to affordable reading glasses and other eye care products in India (and South America, from which it eventually withdrew).

Opportunity
Millions of people in India are unable to work because of poor eyesight (e.g., presbyopia). The key problem to be solved was providing access to low-cost reading glasses.

Strategies
(1) Create partnerships with low-cost manufacturers of reading glasses

(2) Develop a microfranchise distribution channel to deliver reading glasses to villages in India

(3) Empower the channel to succeed with a "business in a bag" solution kit

External Environment

Those with poor eyesight in rural areas of developing countries are unaware of the cause (presbyopia), and there is no access to affordable reading glasses, which can improve eyesight. There are low-cost manufacturers of reading glasses and potential customers can pay up to $3, but distribution channels do not exist for rural areas.

Market

Direct beneficiaries: over one billion people in rural areas (over two hundred million in India) need access to reading glasses to be able to work

Indirect beneficiaries: family and local employers

Related beneficiaries: rural economies

Competition: retail stores, free from charities

Competitive advantage: low-cost product, distribution channel

Operations and Value Chain

Key processes are (1) manufacturing partner selection and management, (2) microfranchise partners for distribution, (3) provide "business in a bag" to channel partners, and (4) set up "hub and spoke" distribution system with partners.

Organization and Human Resources

Vision Spring is a U.S. nonprofit operating globally.

Board of directors

Executive director

Director of programs

Partner franchises   Local subsidiaries

Business Model and Unit Economics

Key revenue drivers: operations (80 percent); contributions (20 percent)

Key expense drivers: staffing (35 percent); cost of products/franchise kits (30 percent); marketing (20 percent), general and administrative (15 percent)

Unit Economics: Unit = pair of reading glasses

2008: number of units: 862,980

Total revenue: $2,402,983 (per unit = $2.78)

COGS = $2,345,187 (per unit = $2.71)

Per unit gross margin = $.07

Over time Vision Spring developed a metric called Philanthropic Investment Per Pair (PIPP) because of its need to subsidize distribution through the development of a corporate infrastructure to serve its expanding network of partners and wholesale distributors. Vision Spring's use of PIPP reflects constructive tension between contributed and earned income. The lower the PIPP value, the more efficient its use of philanthropic dollars. A 2007 online case study from Global Innovation Exchange documents the evolution of Scojo/Vision Spring's business model and its use of metrics to facilitate its development as a learning organization.[4]

Metrics Financial:

1. Gross margin

2. Burn rate (expenses)

Units sold:

3. Number (per year, cumulative)

Turnover:

4. Employees

5. Partners

Economic impact:

6. Wages earned by reading glasses customers

Unit Economics:

7. PIPP (Philanthropic Investment Per Pair)

Operating Plan

No operating plan presented at GSBI, but an operating plan was developed in the following year.

Financing

Initial financing: $1.5 million grant pre GSBI

Subsequent financing: sought $400,000 per year for five years, primarily from grants or loans, for use in expanding distribution

To Recap

For a social enterprise, metrics are useful to both run your business more effectively and make a compelling case for funding. When building out your own metrics dashboard, it is important to include metrics around financial resources, organizational resources, key processes or activities, and ideally outcomes or impact. The Minimum Critical Specifications Checklist highlights the most important elements your metrics dashboard should include. The next chapter begins part III, where we shift focus from management of a sustainable social business to the two key aspects of execution: the operating plan and financing.

Exercise

10.1 Create a metrics dashboard with no more than fifteen metrics (total) divided into these five groups:

1. Financial resources

2. Organizational resources

3. Transformation (process/activity)

4. Outcomes

5. Impact (return on investment)

Background Resources

Acumen Foundation. *The Lean Data Field Guide*. November 2015.

Dees, J. Gregory, Jed Emerson, and Peter Economy. *Strategic Tools for Social Entrepreneurs: Enhancing the Performance of Your Enterprising Nonprofit*. New York: John Wiley, 2002, chapter 8.

Ebrahim, A., and V. Rangan. "What Impact: A Framework for Measuring the Scale and Scope of Social Performance." *California Management Review* 56, no. 3 (2014): 118–141.

Kaplan, Robert. "Strategic Performance Measurement and Management in Nonprofit Organizations." *Nonprofit Management and Leadership* 11, no. 3 (Spring 2001): 353–370.

Sawhill, J., and D. Williamson. "Mission Impossible? Measuring Success in Nonprofit Organizations." *Nonprofit Management and Leadership* 11, no. 3 (2001): 371–386.

Scholten, Peter, Jeremy Nichols, Sara Olsen, and Bert Galimidi. *Social Return on Investment (A Guide to SROI Analysis)*. FM State of the Art Series, 2006.

Minimum Critical Specifications Checklist

Metrics and Accountability

- Metrics dashboards should include financial, organizational, and transformation or process metrics, as well as outcome and, ideally, impact metrics.

- Cost per outcome can serve as a proxy for capital efficiency or social return on investment, especially for public goods or where best available charitable option is a benchmark.

- Metrics are added or eliminated on the basis of only one criterion: contribution to managing the enterprise as a social business.

Part III

Execution

With the majority of business plan creation behind us, part III turns to those elements that are key to execution. The development of financing plans and fund-raising goals, and budgeting and the creation of an operating plan are the two most crucial reasons for having a business plan. Over the next two chapters, we will pay close attention to the kinds of challenges that are unique to social enterprises—those businesses that aim to do well and good at the same time.

Chapter 11

Operating Plan

An operating plan translates a business plan into concrete milestones of what needs to happen to achieve program or project specifications, what resources are required, when these milestones need to be hit (due dates), and, most importantly, who "owns" them. Operating plans also include a budget (income and expense targets) and a cash flow statement that shows the plan's financial viability. Each of these three elements—income targets, expense targets, and cash flow—will be for a specific time period. In this chapter we will use a quarterly basis for a year (four quarters), although you may use a more frequent basis (e.g., monthly) if you want shorter interval insight into the status of your plan.

The operating plan is an essential management tool used to focus the enterprise, match resources with specific plans, track progress and do "course corrections" if needed, and hold individuals accountable for their performance. An operating plan appears to be an essential element of scaling a social venture. Conversely, not having a good operating plan is a frequent reason for failing to scale/grow a social venture.

Basic Knowledge

Operating plans translate conceptual business plans into budgets for both day-to-day operations and strategic initiatives with milestones and specified accountabilities. Integrated operating plans are critical for budgeting and efficient resource utilization, managing cash flow, and achieving priority objectives.

Steps in Developing an Operating Plan

Figure 11.1 shows the key steps in a process you can use to develop your operating plan from the business plan you created throughout part II of this book. Keep in mind that this is an iterative process. An operating plan should be revised on the basis of actual results relative to plan milestones as well as changing conditions in operating environments. In general, an operating plan changes at least annually, and sometimes more frequently.

Strategic Initiatives and Measurable Outcomes

The process for creating an operating plan begins with reviewing strategic initiatives with the management team. For each strategic initiative, create a measurable outcome. The management team should review the status of these proposed outcomes at least annually to assess progress in achieving your mission. For each measurable outcome, create a target completion date and an "owner"—the person on the team responsible for a specific outcome. For example, an organization dealing in eye care might choose to implement a new process for recruiting rural patients with cataract blindness as a strategic initiative. In terms of measurable outcomes and ownership, the organization

Figure 11.1   Operational Planning and Budgeting Process

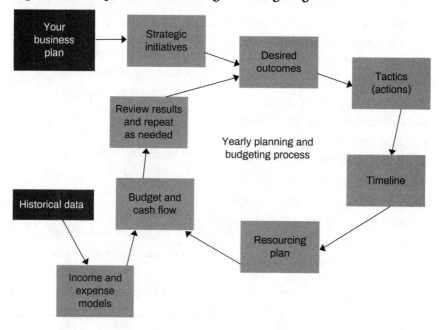

might task the recruiting manager (owner) to create collaborative partnerships with NGOs and to set up twenty eye camps (five per quarter).

Tactics

For each strategic initiative and associated outcome, the owner should create one or more tactics to achieve the outcome. Each tactic should also have resource requirements (staffing and other costs) for the year. Sticking with our eye care example, the recruiting manager, as a tactic, might propose contacting one NGO per week as a possible partner, and signing at least five per quarter. The manager might also propose that one staff member be added, including a budget for salary, office space, cell phone, and travel.

Timeline and Resource Requirements

A timeline is a chart or table that lists each tactic, in order of completion date. If a tactic has several completion dates, each one is listed. If one tactic depends on another being completed, this dependency should be shown. Each tactic/milestone should show the resource requirements for that tactic during the relevant planning period. The resource requirements should include the key expense drivers as well as other expenses specific to particular tactics or milestones.

There are several techniques (e.g., Gantt charts) and a few internet-based tools (e.g., BaseCamp) that you can use to build a timeline and resource requirements table. Figure 11.2 shows a simplified timeline table. Using the timeline table, you can then build a resource requirements table showing all the resources needed by type for all tactics, as illustrated in Figure 11.3.

Budget

From the resource requirements for strategic initiatives, the expenses and income associated with ongoing operations, and the plans for cash infusion

Figure 11.2 Timeline Table

Tactic	Owner	Q1 Due Date	Q2 Due Date	Q3 Due Date	Q4 Due Date
Contact NGOs	Ms. X	2 per week	2 per week	2 per week	2 per week
Sign NGO to base camp contract	Ms. X	5 by end of quarter	10 (5 new) by end of quarter	15 (5 new) by end of quarter	20 (5 new) by end of quarter

Figure 11.3   Resource Requirements Table

Tactic	Owner	Staffing	Salary $	Travel $	Office and Other Expense $
One line per tactic + One for management FTE and other overhead					

from fund-raising, you can build a budget (Figure 11.4). There are several good budgeting tools for small enterprises (e.g., Mint, Quicken, or QuickBooks), some of which can also be used to create your financial reports (including actuals versus budget and cash flow). At a minimum, a simple table or spreadsheet is all you really need. Be sure to include the income from all income drivers, costs by category or type for each step or process in the value chain, and expenses associated with the resource requirements for your strategic

Figure 11.4   Four Quarter Operating Budget

	Q1	Q2	Q3	Q4
BALANCE FORWARD	$10,000	$51,100	$42,800	$699,400
Friends and Family	$100,000	$25,000	0	0
Investors	0	0	$800,000	0
Loan	0	$100,000	0	0
Product Revenue	0	0	$10,000	$500,000
TOTAL INCOME	$100,000	$125,000	$810,000	$500,000
Headcount	3	4	4	6
Headcount $	$56,000	$76,000	$76,000	$84,000
General/Admin.	$500	$2,500	$5,000	$5,000
Sales/Marketing	$2,400	$4,800	$2,400	$4,800
Program $	0	$50,000	$50,000	$175,000
TOTAL EXPENSES	$58,900	$133,300	$133,400	$268,800
NET	$51,100	$42,800	$719,400	$500,600

Figure 11.5 2014 Operating Plan Summary

Enterprise Name:

Date:

Strategic Initiative	Desired Outcome	Strategic Initiative Owner	Key Tactics/ Actions	Owner	Resources	Budget	Planned Start Date	Actual Start Date	Planned End Date	Actual End Date	Comments

Figure 11.6 Cash Flow Statement Template

	Quarter 1	Quarter 2	Quarter 3	Quarter 4
Starting cash				
+ Cash inflows (operating income plus financing received)				
- Cash outflows (operating expenses plus cost of fund-raising received)				
= Ending cash				

initiatives. The GSBI has also found it useful to use an operating plan summary table (Figure 11.5) to combine the strategic initiatives, desired outcome, tactics, timeline, resource requirements, and budget info into one table.

Cash Flow

From the budget, you can create a cash flow statement by time period (usually a month, a quarter, or a year) showing the starting cash position, the income drivers (sources times bases), expense drivers (categories times bases), and ending cash (which becomes starting cash for the next period). The cash flow statement is useful for making sure there is adequate cash on hand to fund the enterprise.

To create this statement, fill in a table with a column for each time period (e.g., quarterly for a year, or yearly for four years) and rows for starting cash position, cash inflow (from income drivers), cash outflow (from expense drivers), and ending cash position. Figure 11.6 shows a template for a cash flow statement, and Figure 11.7 shows a cash flow management example.

Figure 11.7   Cash Flow Management Example (4 years)

	2007	2008	2009	2010
STARTING CASH	$40,000	$37,533	$25,408	$17,938
CASH IN	$107,213	$332,500	$516,500	$744,000
Earned	$19,000	$232,500	$466,500	$744,000
Contributed	$88,213	$100,000	$50,000	
CASH OUT	$109,660	$344,645	$523,970	$655,895
Operation	$60,700	$206,045	$278,270	$307,895
Cost of Goods	$48,960	$138,600	$245,700	$348,000
ENDING CASH	$37,553	$25,408	$17,938	$106,043

Social Venture Snapshots

The available documentation for Grameen Shakti does not include an operating plan, although it is clear from the documentation that there must have been one. For that reason, this chapter includes only two Social Venture Snapshots: Sankara and GSBI Innovator Video Volunteers.

Social Venture Snapshot: Operating Plan for Sankara

A strategic initiative for Sankara is to increase paying customer acquisition. Figure 11.8 summarizes the desired outcomes for this strategy, and the tactics required to implement them. The outcomes and associated tactics have been prioritized, and the prioritization legend is as follows:

(1) Highest priority

(2) Medium priority

(3) Lowest priority

Figure 11.8 Operating Plan for Sankara

Priority	Outcome	Tactic	Owner	Completion Date
1	Offer financing (credit) to paying patients	Research and choose a financing institution to partner with	Head of Finance	June 1, 2015
		Determine different financing options	Head of Finance and Billing Dept.	July 1, 2015
		Set up financing plans in billing systems	Billing Coordinator/ System Admin	August 1, 2015
		Train billing staff on financing mechanics	Head of Billing Dept.	September 1, 2015
3	Implement tiered pricing strategy	Determine new price tiers for procedures in each city hospital	Heads of Marketing and Finance	July 1, 2015
		Set up new pricing structures in billing systems	Billing Coordinator/ System Admin	August 1, 2015
		Train billing staff on new pricing tiers	Head of Billing Dept.	September 1, 2015

Figure 11.8 *(Continued)*

Priority	Outcome	Tactic	Owner	Completion Date
2	Vision wellness for students	*Schools:* Establish a partnership with the School Health Annual Report Program (SHARP) to shortlist the schools to reach out to in each city where Sankara has a hospital *Higher education institutions:* Create a list of institutions to reach out to in each city where Sankara has a hospital	Head of Business Development/ Partnerships	June 1, 2015
		Reach out to each and evaluate interest for on-site screening camp; if interested, create a contract for a screening camp and payment terms for participating schools/institutions (first batch - 5)	Business Development/ Partnerships Manager	July 1, 2015
		Screen students and identify those that need procedures in the hospital (1 camp)	Camp Coordinators, Outreach team of doctors and optometrists	August 1, 2015
		Add new patients to hospital database and maintain relationships through annual follow-ups	System Admin and Outreach team	September 1, 2015
		Assess the program's yield per school camp and update goals/ modify pricing for the following year	Head of Outreach and President of "Vision Sankara"	December 1, 2015

(continued)

Figure 11.8 *(Continued)*

Priority	Outcome	Tactic	Owner	Completion Date
3	Vision wellness for seniors	Create a list of retirement home communities to reach out to in the cities where Sankara has hospitals	Head of Business Development/ Partnerships	June 1, 2015
		Reach out to each and evaluate the needs of the occupants; establish paying capacities, insurance availability, etc; decide if convenient on-site screening camp can be held	Business Development/ Partnerships Manager	July 1, 2015
		Screen patients and identify those that need procedures in the hospital	Camp Coordinators, Outreach team of doctors and optometrists	August 1, 2015
		Add new patients to hospital database and maintain relationships through annual follow-ups	System Admin and Outreach team	September 1, 2015
2	Doctor referral program	Create a list of physicians to reach out to in the cities where Sankara has hospitals	Business Development/ Partnerships Manager	June 1, 2015
		Subdivide according to distance from hospital (5 km radius, 10 km radius, etc.)	Marketing/Sales	July 1, 2015

Figure 11.8 *(Continued)*

Priority	Outcome	Tactic	Owner	Completion Date
		Reach out to physicians through phone calls, visits, and email campaigns (multi-touch marketing)	Head of Business Development/ Partnerships	August 1, 2015
		Provide a point of contact for communication in order to form a trusted relationship	Business Development/ Partnerships Manager	September 1, 2015
		Set up an internal Referring Physician Database and maintain marketing communications by sending them newsletters, etc.	System Admin/ Marketing Manager	Ongoing
		Maintain periodic contact to get feedback and maintain relationship	Business Development/ Partnerships Manager	Ongoing
2	Patient referral program	Develop process/ database for maintaining referrals; develop coupons and flyers for customers	Head of Marketing	May 2015
		Train employees on referral process	HR/Admin Team	June 2015
		Implement referral program	HR/Admin Team	July 2015
1	Educational tools	Develop Web-based tools/lecture materials	Head of PR/ Medical Staff/ Customer Relations	May 2015

(continued)

Figure 11.8 *(Continued)*

Priority	Outcome	Tactic	Owner	Completion Date
		Train necessary staff involved in running lectures/maintaining online resources	PR/Medical Staff	June 2015
		Launch Web-based tools/develop lecture schedule/coupons	Head of PR/ Medical Staff/ Customer Relations	July 2015
1	Advertising campaign improvements	Develop new ad campaign with social benefit emphasis	PR Team/ Marketing Team	May 2015
		Roll out new ad campaign	Marketing/Sales	June 2015
		SEO	PR Team/ Marketing Team	July 2015

Social Venture Snapshot: GSBI Innovator Video Volunteers

Video Volunteers trains and equips local community video producers to provide a voice for the rural poor in India. In doing so, it strives to show India through the eyes of those living contemporary struggles. As a learning organization, its models for providing voice have tapped the potential of digital media and continued to evolve to strengthen the social capital of the poor through an emphasis on building the intellectual, creative, and leadership capacity of community media-makers, the ownership of content and solution-oriented stories, and community discussion of content for creating an operating plan. Since 2011, Video Volunteers has continued to grow to impact social justice in India through the videos created by its rural videographers. The Video Volunteers 2018 website describes its current initiative, India Unherd, as "a news agency for India's disenfranchised communities." In 2011, after completing the GSBI, Video Volunteers, with the help of four mentors, became the first GSBI venture to implement the process described in this chapter for creating an operating plan. The description of its *operating plan*, which follows, is based on a snapshot of this work created for GSBI 2012 by Eric Carlson and the Video Volunteers CEO, Jessica Mayberry.

Mission, Opportunity, and Strategies

Mission	Enable local community video producers to provide a voice for India's poor
Key metric	Number of videos in national media
Opportunity	625 million people in rural India are not covered in national media
Strategies	(1) Recruit, train, and equip locals in poor communities to be video producers
	(2) Manage community video producers to create stories about local problems
	(3) Edit video raw footage for use in TV and internet news
	(4) Use partners to place stories on cable TV and internet news sites
	(5) Use video stories to create community campaigns to solve problems (e.g., violence against women)
	(6) Create and distribute additional videos about impact of campaigns

External Environment

Local problems in most of India do not receive coverage by national media, and therefore 625 million people do not have a voice. National cable TV and internet broadcast coverage in India is extensive. Young people in local communities are eager to learn how to use video to document local problems. National news media need content, and it is too expensive for national media to have coverage in rural areas.

Market

Direct beneficiaries: people in rural areas in India who get training (hundreds) and a voice (millions) in national media

Indirect beneficiaries: news media that get content and create interest in rural communities

Related beneficiaries: communities that benefit from local stories

Competition: local stringers from national media (competitive advantages: cost and local knowledge)

Product: local video news stories from rural areas

Price: sold to national media for less than their own video creation costs

Placement: partners

Promotion: partners and via internet

Operations and Value Chain

Key processes are (1) recruit and train local video producers, (2) create raw footage and scripts for local news stories, (3) edit stories and scripts, (4) use partners to distribute edited stories to national media, (5) create community campaigns with stories, and (6) document impact with additional videos for distribution.

Key partners are (1) video suppliers for low-cost equipment and (2) NGOs, cable TV companies, and internet news sites for local stories.

Organization and Human Resources

Video Volunteers is a U.S. nonprofit (for fund-raising) and a media company in India.

CEO

    Head of training and production

        Local video trainers and managers

           Local video producers

Business Model and Unit Economics

Key income drivers: contributed: grants (50 percent → 20 percent); earned: NGO (50 percent → 30 percent), TV (0 percent → 50 percent)

Key expense drivers: training (33 percent), video production (33 percent), sales, general, and administrative (33 percent)

Unit Economics: Unit = videos placed. In 2011, the unit economics (cost per video placed) was $479.

Metrics

Key metrics are (1) number of community video producers, (2) number of videos placed, (3) millions of viewers for videos, (4) number of recorded instances of local action taken as result of videos, (5) revenue, and (6) expenses.

Operating Plan

As described earlier, Video Volunteers (VV) completed a nine-step process to create an operating plan.

Step 1: Confirm Mission and Key Strategies:

- Came back from GSBI to difficult situation (low morale); used a PowerPoint presentation to create excitement and ownership

- Went over to somebody's house—spent three days coming up with strategies

Step 2: Develop Strategic Initiatives:

- Distribute content to mainstream media

- Training and production

- Retention, recruitment, and impact

- Fund-raising and earned income

- Documentation, communications, and campaigns

Step 3: For each strategic initiative, define desired outcomes (with person(s) responsible dates)

Strategic Initiative 1: Distribute Content to Mainstream Media

Lead: Jessica

Team: Sarah (Head VVFS)

Tara (Design)

Intern (AIF intern for TV pilot and distribution)

Stalin (meeting MM, finalizing content for presentations to MM)

Measurable Outcome 1: Contracts worth $100,000 in place with station/s by EQ1

Measurable Outcome 2: 10 newspapers subscribing to VVFS by EQ1. Minimum ten media pickups per quarter, Q1.

Strategic Initiative 2: Fund-raising and Earned Income

Measurable Outcome 1: bring in $30,000 in contributed income per quarter

Measurable Outcome 2: bring in $20,000 in earned income per quarter

Lead: Jessica

Team: Naomi (Head Earned Income sub group)

Stalin (meeting funders and partners)

Research and Communications Intern (full time, to be recruited)

Sid (providing content to be used in donor/partner communication)

Step 4: Develop Tactics for Each Strategic Initiative:

- Set up a spreadsheet for each strategic initiative

Step 5: Develop a Timeline for Each Tactic:

- Set up a Word document for each tactic, updated every quarter with progress

Step 6: Create a Resourcing Plan:

- To start, did not limit resources in developing strategies/tactics

- Strategy leaders submitted resource requirements, which got incorporated into the budgeting spreadsheet

- Resource requirements could not be met immediately, so team had to make do with resources available

- Need to do job descriptions and fit available staff with strategic areas. Should "strategic areas" be the actual job description?

Step 7: Develop Income and Expense Models:

- Set up a budget spreadsheet, used to record targets and actuals by month

Step 8: Load Income and Expense Models into a Budgeting Tool:

- Use spreadsheet set up in Step 7

Step 9: Review and Repeat if Necessary: Guess what? Not every facet of the operating plan worked.

What worked:

> Strategies (except for income)
>
> Expense model (kept expenses in control)
>
> Learned how to talk about earned income and learned that first year would still require contributed income (so need not waste time with investors who are interested primarily in earned income)
>
> Learned how to understand market and the business principles of their market

What did not work:

> Income strategy (were not able to get large buyers)
>
> Decided to give content to one TV station, one website, one magazine—on a "per campaign" basis (did not set precedence of giving all content)
>
> Created a lot of interest from other media outlets
>
> Got income from large donor (did not solve long term income problem—still expect to eventually charge for content)

Financing
Grants and large donations.

To Recap
For a social venture, an operating plan is where the rubber meets the road—where the business plan is realized in hard numbers like due dates and budget specifications, and, most importantly, in who is responsible for what. The Minimum Critical Specifications Checklist lays out the bare minimum your operating plan should include. In chapter 12, we look at financing.

Exercises

11.1 Milestones (Timeline and Resource Requirements)
For the specific tactics for each strategy and associated outcome, create a timeline (schedule) and list the resource requirements (people and money).

11.2 Budget
Using the timeline and resource requirements for each tactic, create a budget as follows. First, for all the income-producing tactics, estimate the expected income (per quarter). If useful, itemize the income by category (donations, sales, fundraising). Second, for all tactics, combine the costs per quarter to create an expense budget per quarter. If useful, itemize the expenses by function or tactic (program budget). Your budget should then be able to be summarized in a table such as the Example Four Quarter Operating budget shown in Figure 11.4.

Minimum Critical Specifications Checklist

Operating Plan

- Strategic initiatives specify outcomes, milestones, resource requirements, and accountabilities.

- Budgets combine both ongoing revenue/expense targets and project-specific expense projections.

- The operating plan includes budget and cash flow statements.

11.3 Cash Flow

Using the budget, create a four-quarter cash flow statement consisting for four items for each quarter:

Starting cash position (= ending cash position from the previous quarter)
+ Income
−Expenses
= Ending cash position

Your simplified cash flow summary should look like the Cash Management Example above.

Background Resources

Dees, J. Gregory, Jed Emerson, and Peter Economy. *Enterprising Non-Profits: A Toolkit for Social Entrepreneurs.* New York: John Wiley, 2001, chapter 9.

DeThomas, Arthur, and Stephanie Derammelaere. *How to Write a Convincing Business Plan.* 3rd ed. New York: Barron's Educational Services, 2008, chapters 3, 10, and 11.

Chapter 12

Financing

To grow a social venture and its impact requires financing, often at multiple stages of growth. In recent years the amount of capital devoted to investing in social ventures has been increasing, with impact investors becoming better able to document both impact and financial returns. However, despite the increased understanding and investment knowledge among impact investors, there is not yet a clear delineation of the timing and uses for the different impact investment alternatives, often termed "asset classes."[1]

Chapter 12 reviews the main sources of financing for social ventures and describes four documents that will help you raise funds, regardless of the source. Finally, we cover due diligence and investment readiness.

> **Basic Knowledge**
> The choice of legal structure (e.g., for profit or not for profit) is a strategic decision with trade-offs that will determine the range of funding sources available and the nature of investor expectations. Funding sources and amounts vary at different stages of a venture's organizational life cycle. Success in accessing capital across life-cycle stages is dependent on the ability to achieve venture development milestones and the "investment readiness" criteria of alternative funding sources.

Funding Sources and Amounts

Most social ventures will seek funding from one or more of ten sources or "types." The following list shows these potential sources of funding in increasing order of (1) the difficulty of obtaining, (2) amounts that can be obtained, and (3) formal financial reporting accountabilities. Note that some ventures seek funding from multiple sources at the same time. In such cases it is very helpful to specify: the timing of each type of funding; the intended uses of each type of funding; and the priority for any repayments.

1. **Personal, Friends, Family, and Individuals:** Funding (usually cash) is provided by the entrepreneurs, their family and friends, and/or individual acquaintances who want to support the venture. Often the money is a gift or contribution. Sometimes the money is treated as a loan, in which case it should be documented along with payback terms, if any. Occasionally, the individuals receive stock (like an angel investor), and in this case there should be a professional valuation of the venture in order to create a fair valuation of the shares granted. Granting of shares, especially at different valuations, is highly discouraged because doing so drastically complicates fund-raising from other sources. This type of funding also includes online funding, such as Kickstarter.

2. **Grants:** Funding is provided by an organization, such as a foundation, governmental organization, NGO, corporation, or wealthy individual(s). Grants usually require completing a grant form or a response to a request for proposals.

3. **Soft Loans:** Funding is provided by an organization, such as those listed for grants, as well as banks or online lenders (e.g., Kiva.org), which will have "soft" or concessionary terms for repayment.

4. **Conventional Loans:** Conventional loans are provided by banks or other regulated financial organizations. These loans will have specific terms for repayment (generally tied to predictable cash flows). Conventional loans may have phased or structured exit (repayment) terms.

5. **Program-Related Investment:** Program-related investment usually takes the form of a loan, but occasionally comes as a grant for a specific program (e.g., adding a new product or service) in a social venture. The source of this type of funding is usually a foundation, government agency, or other interested party (e.g., an angel investor or a corporation).

6. **Demand Dividend:** A demand dividend investment is like a loan in the sense that the investor provides funds, but it is also like equity in the sense that the investor receives (is paid back by) dividends that can be "demanded" (based on an agreement at the time of funding) once the organization has positive cash flow. Sometimes the dividend is tied to revenue milestones, so occasionally this type of funding is called "revenue-based loan or debt."

7. **Convertible Debt:** Funding is provided from a grant-making organization, bank, venture capital firm, or high-net-worth individual with specific terms for debt or loan to equity conversion (e.g., a loan with interest at 6 percent for five years convertible to equity at a 25 percent discount to venture valuation).

8. **Angel Equity:** Funding is provided by wealthy individuals or groups of wealthy individuals with their own investment fund, in return for shares of the company (usually less than a controlling interest).

9. **Impact-First Equity:** Funding is provided by organizations such as those listed for grants, or by social venture capital firms that aggregate individual "impact-first" investments (the investors are primarily interested in the impact of the venture rather than in a financial return). In return for their investments, investors receive shares of portfolio companies (usually less than a controlling interest).

10. **Financial-First Equity:** Funding is provided by venture capital firms or corporations with funds, which are aggregated from individuals or other organizational investors, tied to shares of the company (usually a controlling interest). Note that if there are several rounds of equity financing, more than one class of stock, with different valuations, may be needed (e.g., one for each round of financing).

In comparing/selecting one or more alternative sources of financing, social ventures need to consider several variables:

1. What is the life-cycle stage (start-up, early results or proof of concept, beginning growth, rapid expansion, maturity)?

2. How much due diligence (effort) is required to obtain a term sheet (an outline of the terms of the financing agreement), and what will be the costs of managing reporting relationships with the financing source?

3. What are the funding sources' expected returns?

4. How long will the engagement (contract) with the funding source last, and what is the "exit strategy" (i.e., when does the engagement end)?

5. How much control/involvement with the enterprise does the financing source require?

6. Is the organization "investment ready"—can its valuation be calculated and does it have cash flow to support the investors' expected returns?

7. What organizational structure are you anticipating (e.g., to get equity financing in the United States requires a for-profit organization)?

A social venture seeking funding should also be aware of the funding preferences possible financing sources may have. Some sources focus on particular market sectors (e.g., energy), particular geographies or consumers (e.g., lower or middle income), how much funding is needed to purchase assets, and specific timing and percentage returns.[2]

In planning your funding strategy it may be useful to plan for "blended financing"—using more than one type of funding source for different stages of growth. Figure 12.1 may help in evaluating the desirability of funding types.

Once potential funding-type alternatives are selected, it helps to do some investigating. From your findings, create a list of possible sources to contact and from which to obtain sample "term sheets"—forms with details about the information and terms required for each source. Note that term sheets, which are agreed to by both the sources and the recipients of funding, specify all the details of the funding, including timing of payments, payment

Figure 12.1 Comparison of Social Venture Funding Sources

Source/Type	Appropriate Stage	Due Diligence and Effort to Manage	Expected Return	Duration and Exit	Expected Involvement
Personal, friends, and family	Start-up and early results, occasionally beginning growth	Low	Impact first, possibly financial	Flexible (patient capital), also flexible exit	Should be low, occasionally is high
Grants	Early results, beginning growth	High initially, then moderate	Impact, may expect some repayment of capital	Generally short term (grant is for a specific period), exit is time based	Should be low, occasionally is moderate
"Soft loans"	Early results, beginning growth, rapid expansion, maturity	High initially, then low	Impact, and payback of principal (at some time) and possibly below-market interest rate	Flexible (patient capital), exit is repayment of all or part	Low
Conventional loans	Beginning growth, rapid expansion, maturity	High initially, then low, will require assets as security and verification of financials	Payback of principal and market interest rate	Fixed time period, exit is payback	Low
Program-directed investment	Growth, rapid expansion	Moderate, will need status reports on program progress	May not require payback, or only repayment of principal	Fixed time period, exit is completion of program	Low
Demand dividend	Beginning growth, rapid expansion	High initially, then low once demand conditions and amounts are agreed to	Dividends paid in amounts and timing agreed on at time of financing	Agreed-on conditions and amounts of dividends, which are payback	Low/Moderate

Figure 12.1 *(Continued)*

Source/Type	Appropriate Stage	Due Diligence and Effort to Manage	Expected Return	Duration and Exit	Expected Involvement
Convertible debt	Beginning growth, rapid expansion, maturity	High initially, then moderate, will require organization to have *valuation* and proposed *capital structure*	Payback of principal plus below-market-rate interest and/or appreciation through conversion to equity	Flexible (patient capital), exit is payback or conversion to equity	Moderate
Angel equity	Start-up, early results, beginning growth	Moderate to high, will require *valuation* and *capital structure*	Appreciation through buyout or public offering	Flexible (patient capital), exit is payback, buyout, sale of company, or public offering	Low to moderate, may want to be on board or provide advice
Impact-first equity	Any	Moderate to high, will require valuation and capital structure	Impact, possibly below market rate of payback, exit through buyout or sale of company	Flexible (patient capital), exit is payback, buyout, sale of company, or public offering	Moderate to high — are owners of the company
Financial-first equity	Beginning growth, rapid expansion	High, will require valuation, capital structure, and complete verification (e.g., more than just financials)	Market rate of appreciation, exit through sale of company or public offering	Short to medium term, exit is through sale of company or public offering	High — are owners and expect financial returns

terms, amounts and equity (if any) exchanged, as well as timing of paybacks (as illustrated in Example 3, below).

To determine the amounts of financing needed, use the budget and cash flow statements from Chapter 11. The amount of funding needed in any year is determined by adding the following:

> **+ Any grant funding income you included in your budget—that is, income that was not earned (from sales) or contributed (by donors)**
>
> **+ Any cash flow shortfall (expenses in excess of income)**
>
> **+ A "contingency" (usually around 10 percent of the total) for unforeseen circumstances**
>
> **= Total amount of funding needed in a specific year**

When seeking funding, more than one year's worth of funding is usually requested.

Valuation

In equity funding, and occasionally in loan financing, it is necessary to create a company valuation (i.e., what the company is worth). There are many books and articles about valuation, and many investors have their own algorithms for establishing valuation.[3] In general, valuation can be based on one or a combination of the following:

- Replacement costs of assets (e.g., the costs of creating products and/or processes)

- Revenue (present value over several years—how much you would need to invest now at market rates to create the revenue stream)

- Earnings (present value over several years—how much you would need to invest now at market rates to create the earning stream)

- Opportunity costs (how much it would cost to create a revenue stream equal to that of the business)

Thus, an initial evaluation might be set at the (expected) cost of developing a venture's product/services. Later evaluation might be set based on the initial evaluation plus a multiple of the expected annual revenues or earnings.

Documents Used in Fund-Raising

From our experiences working with hundreds of ventures in the GSBI, we recommend that you create four documents to be used in fund-raising.

1. **Possible Sources:** Create a list of organizations that are to be contacted for funding, including the name of the person to be contacted, why this organization is an appropriate source of funding, and other ventures the funding organization has funded in the past.

2. **Elevator Pitch:** In contacting potential funding sources, partners, and others who may be interested in helping, it is valuable to have an elevator pitch. An "elevator pitch" is a two- to three-minute verbal summary of the following:

   ∞ Why the organization is the best at what it does (Why are you a better choice than the alternatives?)

   ∞ How the organization measures what it does (What metrics do you use to determine whether you are successful?)

The intended audience for an elevator pitch is someone who is potentially interested in helping the organization (financially) and therefore is interested in what the organization does but is generally unfamiliar with the organization and its intended beneficiaries.

3. **Business Plan Summary Presentation:** Once a funding source starts to show some interest, the next step is presenting the social venture and justifying your financing needs. For these meetings, it is useful to have a summary of the business plan, usually in a formal presentation format (e.g., in PowerPoint). There are many different outlines for business plans. A social venture will need a presentation tailored to the specific requirements for each potential funder, with requirements varying depending on the

funding source. So, before making a presentation, ask the funding source if it has an outline of the information it would like presented, and then create a presentation designed specifically for the source.

Some funding sources may require submitting a written business plan and/or financial statements and projections. The exercises in chapters 4–10 can be used as a starting point for this document.

4. **Investment Profile:** As a "handout" to go along with the elevator pitch or business plan summary presentation, it is useful to have an investment profile for your organization. The investment profile is a "leave behind" reference document for use following a business plan summary presentation. It may also serve as a document to be sent to potential funding sources before making a business plan summary presentation. Exercise 12.4 poses a set of questions that can be used to create an investment profile.

Due Diligence

Once funding sources have been identified and tentatively agreed to provide funding, a due diligence step is usually required before funding is actually granted. During due diligence, the funding source(s) will check whether the claims made in the business plan are accurate and may also examine claims of product acceptance and financial results. Figure 12.2, created recently for the GSBI, provides a prioritized (by importance) checklist for documents that can be used during due diligence for the three basic investment types (equity, loan, and grant). Note, however, that each funding source may have its own due diligence checklist.

Investment Readiness

In recent years, the GSBI has tried to help social ventures develop the ability to demonstrate "investment readiness," which means different capabilities at different stages. For early-stage ventures, for which grants, friends and family, soft loans, and possible angel investors are the appropriate sources of funding, investment readiness generally means that the product or services of the social venture can be demonstrated as viable, that the potential market can be quantified, and that there is some evidence of market acceptance. For an early growth venture, investment readiness (for loans, program related invest-

Figure 12.2 Due Diligence Checklist

■ Within 1 week ▨ Within 2-4 weeks ▧ Other

Document	Investment Type			Notes
	Equity	Loan	Grant	
A. Organizational Information (company and any subsidiaries)				
State government organizational filings (including articles of incorporation/ organization/formation, certificate of limited partnership, etc.) and all amendments.	×	×	×	
Internal constitutional documents (including bylaws, operating agreement, partnership agreement, etc.) and all amendments.	×	×	×	
Minutes of meetings of the board of directors, advisory board, board committees and shareholders, and all consents to actions without a meeting.	×			
Schedule of jurisdictions (states, countries) where the company is qualified to do business, has offices, holds property (including inventory), or conducts business.	×	×		
Most recently obtained good-standing certificates for jurisdictions (states, countries) where the company is qualified to do business.	×	×		
Federal and state tax exemption qualification (if applicable).	×	×	×	
B. Securities Issuances				
Sample copy of security certificates (stock, interests, others), warrants, and option agreements.	×			

(continued)

Figure 12.2 *(Continued)*

Document	Investment Type			Notes
	Equity	Loan	Grant	
Schedule of security holders, contact information, the number of securities held by each (including common and preferred stock, membership interests, partnership interests or equivalents), dates of issuance, consideration paid, and percent ownership (capitalization table).	×	×		
All outstanding options, warrants, or convertible securities, including convertible debt instruments (capitalization table).	×	×		
Any voting rights agreements, buy/sell agreements, stockholder agreements, warrant agreements, proxies, or right of first refusal agreements.	×	×		
Any debt arrangements, guarantees, or indemnification between officers, directors, or security holders of the company.	×	×		
Any other contracts, arrangements, or public/private documents or commitments relating to company securities.	×			

C. Financial Information

Document	Investment Type			Notes
Audited financial statements since inception (unaudited if audited are not available).	×	×	×	
Quarterly income statements, balance sheets, and cash flow statements for the last two years and the current year (to date).	×	×		
Description of accounting methods and practices, including any changes in the last three years.	×	×		
A three-year operating budget and financial projections.	×	×		

Figure 12.2 *(Continued)*

Document	Investment Type			Notes
	Equity	Loan	Grant	
A complete and current business plan, including material marketing or consulting studies or reports prepared by the company.	×	×		
Accounts receivable aging and accounts payable aging schedules for the last year.	×	×		
Product or service pricing plans and policies.	×	×		
Revenue, gross margin, and average selling price by product or service.	×	×		
Extraordinary income or expense details.	×	×		
Explanation of any material write-downs or write-offs.	×	×		
A summary of all bad debt experiences.	×	×		
Details of any outstanding contingent liabilities.	×	×		
Accountant report on the company's financial condition.	×	×		

D. Tax Information

Federal, state, local, and foreign tax returns for the last three years.	×			
Details of any tax audits.	×			
Evidence that current on sales tax, unemployment, social security, excise, and other tax payments.	×			

E. Contracts and Agreements

Schedule of all subsidiary, partnership, joint venture, or strategic alliance relationships and obligations, with copies of related agreements.	×	×		

(continued)

Figure 12.2 (Continued)

Document	Investment Type			Notes
	Equity	Loan	Grant	
License agreements (inbound and outbound).	×			
Purchase agreements.	×			
Schedule of all bank and nonbank lenders holding outstanding company indebtedness within the past two years, including a brief description of the material terms of the relationship and copies of related agreements, including credit agreements, debt instruments, security agreements, mortgages, installment sale agreements, and any liens, equipment leases, or financial performance guarantees.	×	×		
Schedule of insurance arrangements (and copies of related agreements) covering property, liabilities, and operations, including product liabilities and a description of any other relevant arrangements pertaining to the company's liability exposure, including special reserve funds and accounts.	×	×		
Schedule of major suppliers, vendors, and customers, with copies of material agreements with each.	×	×		
Any additional material agreements or contracts.	×			

F. Government Regulation

Document	Investment Type			Notes
Copies of all permits and licenses.	×	×		
Copies of reports made to government agencies.	×			
Details of inquiries made by local, state, or federal agencies.	×			

Figure 12.2 *(Continued)*

Document	Investment Type			Notes
	Equity	Loan	Grant	
G. Litigation				
Description of any current and known potential litigation, including potential damages.	×	×		
Settle documentation.	×			
Summaries of disputes with suppliers, competitors, or customers.	×			
H. Products and Services				
Schedule of all existing products or services and products or services that are under development, each showing offerings by product or service line, including market share where possible.	×			
Inventory analysis including turnover, obsolescence, and valuation policies.	×	×		
Backlog analysis by product line including analysis of seasonal issues.	×			
Schedule of major suppliers including dollar amount purchased per year, with copies of related agreements.	×			
I. Marketing				
List of competitors by market share.	×	×		
List of the company's twelve largest clients, including sales information and any unfilled orders for the last two years.	×	×		
Analysis of pricing strategy.	×	×		
Current advertising programs, marketing plans, budget and printed brochures and marketing materials.	×			

(continued)

Figure 12.2 *(Continued)*

Document	Investment Type			Notes
	Equity	Loan	Grant	
Sales commission structure.	×			
Sales projections by product line.	×	×		
Any pertinent marketing studies conducted by outside parties.	×	×		
J. Management and Personnel				
Management organizational chart and list of company directors, with bios of senior personnel.	×	×	×	
Schedule of compensation paid to officers, directors, and key employees, showing salary, bonuses, and noncash compensation (i.e., use of cars, property, etc.) with copies of related agreements.	×			
Employment and consulting agreements, confidentiality agreements, nondisclosure and noncompetition agreements, loan agreements, and documents relating to transactions with officers, directors, and key employees.	×	×		
K. Property and Equipment				
Schedule of all real property owned by the company, including details of any easements or other encumbrances, and copies of titles, mortgages, and deeds of trust.	×	×		
Schedule of company leases and subleases, including a description of company space expansion plans, with copies of related agreements.	×	×		
Patents, copyrights, trademarks, any trade secrets, any licenses to or from the company, and any other intangible assets developed/ owned/licensed by the company.	×	×		

Figure 12.2 *(Continued)*

Document	Investment Type			Notes
	Equity	Loan	Grant	
L. Impact and Mission				
Schedule of social, economic, environmental, or other impact objectives, with copies of related program, mission, impact, or sustainability policies and guidelines (as applicable).	×	×	×	
Describe the intended use of the funds, including whether any will be used (directly or indirectly) for lobbying or political purposes.			×	
Schedule of personal financial capital committed by founders and principal investors, including copies of related documents.	×	×	×	
Schedule of the nature and scale of expected impact (e.g. year 1, year 3, and long term) and the metrics used to evaluate/report impact, including reporting intervals and required documentation.	×	×	×	
Schedule of existing impact investments, including date of investment, material terms, and mission/program target of investor.	×	×	×	
"Other" – please provide any impact metrics specific to your enterprise not otherwise addressed above.	×	×	×	
M. Miscellaneous				
Detail of in-progress research and development efforts, including commercial analysis and documentation policies.	×			
Copies of past and present press releases, existing articles related to the company and its industry, company newsletters, and investor relations material.	×			

ment [PRI], or equity investors) means that the product or service can be replicated and that there has been a successful market trial of the venture's product or service. And for a venture seeking funding for rapid growth, investment readiness means that the venture's processes can be scaled to volume and that there is evidence of a significant market, where the product/ service can be delivered to market with positive cash flow.

Social Venture Snapshot: Grameen Shakti

What follows are examples of Grameen Shakti's funding sources and elevator pitch. As Figure 12.3 indicates, from 1996 to 2001, Shakti raised money

Figure 12.3 Summary of Funding Sources and Uses

Timing	Source	Type	Amount	Use	Return
1996–1997	Rockefeller Brothers	Grant	$75,000	Start-up	No
1996–1997	Stichting Gilles	Grant	$75,000	Start-up	No
1996–1997	Grameen Fund	Loan	6 million Taka (about $150,000)	Start-up	No interest, indefinite repayment
1996–1997	Grameen Trust	Grant	2.5 million Taka (about $61,000)	Grant to experiment with wind energy	No
1996–1997	Grameen companies	In-kind	Office space and other pro-bono services	Start-up	No
1998	IFC/GEF	Loan at 2.5%	$750,000	Install 32,400 solar systems	10 years, with 10% reduction for each year in which company was pretax positive cash flow (1st year was 2000)
2001	USAID	Revolving fund	$4 million	Growth— offices, staff, and inventory	Revenue returned to revolving fund

from multiple sources. In the early part of this period, funding came from grants, loans, and in-kind investments. This was followed in 2001 by support from USAID in the form of a $4 million revolving fund to provide customer financing and support growth in branch offices, staffing, and inventory. The total funding of $5 million raised by Shakti during 1996–2001 provided minimal financial returns to investors but yielded dramatic growth in social impact.

Elevator Pitch (ninety-second description of Grameen Shakti Solar Home Lighting Systems business)

Grameen Shakti provides eleven models of solar home (and solar mini-grid) lighting systems to over forty thousand rural villages in Bangladesh. These systems

- provide brighter lighting than alternatives (increasing working hours, which increases family income 15–25 percent and allows children to study two to three more hours per night),

- provide healthier lighting than kerosene or candles, and

- are less costly (over their lifetime) than kerosene lighting.

Unlike other solar lighting providers, Grameen Shakti provides a complete product offering, including the choice of multiple product configurations, plus microfinancing and product service. From its inception in 1996 through 2010, Grameen Shakti installed over 500,000 solar lighting systems benefiting over 3.5 million people and reducing carbon dioxide emissions by over 120 tons per year. In addition, Grameen Shakti achieved a cash flow breakeven operation while employing over 100,000 Bangladeshi men and women.

Social Venture Snapshot: Sankara Investment Profile

The Sankara investment profile provides an excellent example of a document that can be used with potential investors to summarize what is compelling about your venture and its financing plans. As a reference document it highlights the company's significant impact to date, a credible

Figure 12.4 Sankara Investment Profile

SANKARA
EYE CARE INSTITUTIONS, INDIA
EYE CARE BEYOND COMPARE

Eliminating curable blindness across India

Investment Required

Sankara is looking for $ 1.25 M in soft loans and $ 1.25 M in grants to fund our upcoming hospital in Rajasthan.

Description

Sankara currently operates 13 eye hospitals in India. Our mission is to eliminate curable blindness across India by scaling to 20 Sankara Community Eye Hospitals serving over a million rural poor every year.

Headquarters Coimbatore, India
Established 1977
Impact Areas India
Type Non-Profit
Sector Health
Staff Size 1,184
Annual Budget $ 12.4 M
Major Funders Sankara Eye Foundation, Mission for Vision Trust, Calvert Foundation
Stage Revenue

Management Team

CEO Dr R.V. Ramani

President Community Eye Care
Bharath Balasubramaniam

President Medical Administration and Training Dr Kaushik Murali

CONTACT US
+91 97 60 98 6845
BHARATH@SANKARAEYE.COM
WWW.SANKARAEYE.COM
FACEBOOK: /GIFTOFVISION
TWITTER @SANKARAEYE

Sankara Eye Care Institutions (SECI)

Target Market

India is home to the largest population of 'curable blind' worldwide. According to WHO (2010), an estimated 63 million people in India are visually impaired, and of these, approximately 8 -12 million are blind.

Value Proposition

Sankara operates super specialty eye care hospitals with most modern infrastructure and comprehensive range of eye care services. Sankara serves and provides value to two distinct markets:

Free eye care for the rural poor through outreach: Sankara caters to villages located within 200 km radius of the base hospital. The rural poor are screened by Sankara staff at the villages and those requiring surgery are taken to the hospital for treatment. The entire treatment including surgery, stay, food and transportation (to and from the village) is provided for free.

Affordable premium eye care for the urban middle class (a $ 3 billion market): Sankara's paying section offers highest quality eye care with highly experienced medical staff for the urban middle class – premium services at affordable prices.

Surplus from 1 paid surgery allows for 4 free surgeries for the rural poor, and ensures financial sustainability in its mission to eliminate curable blindness across India.

"Vision is the Gift of God and to be blind is unfair if it can be cured with quality eye care."
BHARATH BALASUBRAMANIAM,
PRESIDENT COMMUNITY EYE CARE

GSBI

SANKARA EYE EYE CARE INSTITUTIONS
WWW.SANKARAEYE.COM/ BHARATH@SANKARAEYE.COM

growth trajectory based on milestones achieved, the planned uses for investments needed, and distinguishing elements of its value proposition (see Figures 12.4 and 12.5).

Figure 12.5 Sankara Investment Profile

Eliminating curable blindness across India

Impact to Date

1.1 Million + free eye surgeries for the rural poor

3 Million + rural inhabitants screened for eye care

4.5 Million + children screened

100,000 + free eyeglasses to poor children

55% of surgeries on women

74% of the paramedics are women, recruited and trained from economically poor families

Milestones Achieved

2013 Performed one millionth free eye surgery at Coimbatore

2013 Opened two exclusively paid hospitals in Mumbai and Kanpur

2013 Performed 140,800 free eye surgeries and 29,800 paid surgeries.

2013 Received $700,000 in debt funding from Calvert Foundation

Growth Plan

2014 Inauguration of Kanpur Community Eye Hospital for the rural poor in October

2015-2016 Expansion to Rajasthan (Jodhpur), Madhya Pradesh (Indore), and Chattisgarh (Raipur)

Key Awards

2012 S.R. Jindal Award for Rural Development and Poverty Alleviation

2012 Dharamsey Nansey Oman Award for Outstanding High Quality High Volume Eye Care Service Delivery instituted by VISION2020: The Right to Sight – INDIA

2014 IMC Ramkrishna Bajaj National Quality Performance Excellence in Health Care

On March 4, 2013, Sankara doctors successfully removed the cataract from Shanthi's left eye, marking the millionth free surgery for Sankara. Shanti is back at her weaving loom supporting her disabled husband and four young children.

"When it is hard to find care and love amongst family and friends, Sankara has given me all that and much more, in fact a bright future for me and my family."

SHANTHI, *SANKARA PATIENT, AGE 35*

Social Venture Snapshot: GSBI Innovator Ziqitza Health Care Limited

Ziqitza Health Care Limited (ZHL) provides ambulance services in cities of over one million population in India. When it began in 2005, thirty-five of thirty-seven such cities had no ambulance service. ZHL received significant funding after the 2007 GSBI, which helped the venture grow rapidly to provide ambulance services in multiple cities. Please see the William Davidson Institute case study of the Acumen funding of Ziqitza for further details (case 1-428-788, May 2009).

Before Ziqitza, emergency transportation to hospitals was by rickshaws, private cars, or "van ambulances" with no equipment or trained technicians. Ziqitza offers a 24/7 call center, ambulances with technicians trained in basic and advanced life support, and an ambulance tracking system to navigate congested urban streets and efficiently utilize its emergency transport services. By January 2018, Ziqitza was operating in eighteen states, with three thousand ambulances, and had served more than eight million emergency clients. This snapshot is from the 2007 GSBI.

Mission, Opportunity, and Strategies

Mission	Provide the best emergency medical services (EMSs) in cities of over one million in population
Key metric	Number of persons transported
Opportunity	No organized EMSs in thirty-five of thirty-seven cities of over one million population, affecting over one hundred million people
Strategies	(1) Organize EMS teams
	(2) Acquire state-of-the-art equipped ambulances
	(3) Partner with EMS call services (e.g., 1298 emergency phone number)
	(4) Provide EMS using ability to pay business model

External Environment

Key factors in the external environment include the following:

- No ambulance services in thirty-five of thirty-seven cities of one million or greater populations

- 80,000 deaths and 1.2 million serious injuries from auto accidents each year

- India has the fastest-growing number of heart attacks per year in the world

- Heavy traffic in major cities

- Increasing healthcare center awareness of EMS

- Shortage of training for EMS personnel

- Widespread use of landlines and cell phones and availability of 911-like services in major cities

- Some resistance from local governments and some hospitals to EMS

- Need to educate market about EMS

Market

Direct beneficiaries: over one hundred million people who live in cities with over one million population; 72 percent have the ability to pay; 80,000 deaths and 1.2 million serious injuries from auto accidents each year; India has the fastest-growing number of heart attacks per year in the world

Indirect beneficiaries: families of those affected by serious auto accidents or heart attacks

Related beneficiaries: population health and economies in affected cities

Product: EMS ambulance services

Price: ability to pay as determined by hospital of choice: those transported to full-service hospitals pay full price, those transported to government hospitals pay a subsidized price (about 50 percent of full pay), and those who cannot pay are free

Placement: partner with hospitals and 911-like services

Promotion: advertising (media and on ambulances)

Competitive advantage: response time, price, quality of service

Operations and Value Chain

Key processes are (1) call service for emergency calls, (2) dispatch service for ambulances, (3) ambulance operations, (4) ambulance staff training, and (5) billing.

Key partners are emergency phone service companies (cooperation).

Organization and Human Resources
Organized as an LLC in India; key management positions held by five founders; twenty-five employees in 2007

Business Model and Unit Economics

Income drivers: ambulance sponsorships (20 percent), operations (80 percent)

Expense drivers: costs of services (25 percent), payroll (35 percent), facilities (40 percent)

Unit Economics: Unit = person transported. 2007/2008: 52,195 persons transported, $4.5 million in expenses = $82.38 per person

Metrics
Key metrics are (1) income, (2) expenses, (3) number of persons transported (percentage of emergencies), (4) number of ambulances in service, and (5) driver attrition.

Operating Plan
ZHL has a monthly operating plan, which was cash flow positive in April 2007.

Financing

Equity: initial funding (2005): $120,000 each from four founders: = $480,000

Grant: Ambulance Access for All (AAA) Foundation (2005): six ambulances at $45,000 each = $270,000

Five-year loan: $5.94 million (2006)

Equity: Acumen Fund (2006): $600,000

Equity: Acumen Fund (2007): $900,000

The due diligence process for the two equity investments made by Acumen Fund is documented in a case study done by the William Davidson Institute at the University of Michigan (case 1-428-788, May 2009). As part of the due diligence, in addition to the business plan, ZHL submitted four documents: (1) projected income statements, (2) balance sheets, (3) cash flows, and (4) operating metrics. As stated in the case study:[4]

> *The founders anticipated that ZHL's marketing campaign and quality service would lead to an increase in the number of trips a day per ambulance and a higher proportion of cardiac emergency calls. Additionally, the founders expected the percentage of advertising revenues to total revenues to fall over time, as EMS operations improved and market share increased. For a discount rate, the founders calculated a cost of equity of 15%. In a memo to Acumen Fund, the founders justified the 15% by the following excerpt from the Case Study:*
>
> > *The annual interest yield on government bonds for maturities between 5 to 10 years is in the range of 7.9% to 8.05%. We have assumed a risk premium of nearly 100% over the risk-free rate to adjust for the risk that an investor takes to invest in a business. In addition, the long-term return (~10 years) of equity listed on the NYSE (US) and BSE Sensex (India) is in the range of 15%. The return that we have assumed excluded dividend returns, which the company is confident to delivering over a period of time.*

Further, the case study states:[5]

> *To get the investment approved, "the recommenders" needed to provide the Investment Committee with a reasonable valuation of the company, a description of the different valuation methodologies used, a proposed term sheet, and a clear rationale for why the investment would fit into Acumen Fund's portfolio.*

Though ZHL did not have any debt at the end of its first year, the company expected to borrow funds in its second year to acquire more ambulances. When the debt was included, ZHL calculated a weighted average cost of capital (WACC) of 12 percent.

When using comparables, the founders valued their company assuming a P/E ratio of 15 as of March 2012. This ratio was considered to be conservative because the average P/E ratio of the Bombay Stock Exchange Sensex index (top thirty companies) was about 19. Unfortunately, there was no direct company comparison available in India to determine whether this P/E ratio was reasonable. The term sheet taken from the case study and shown in Figure 12.6 was created and signed by both parties.

Figure 12.6   ZHL Term Sheet

ZHL Term Sheet
For Issuance of and Subscription for Series A Preference Shares and Equity Shares

Nature of this document
This term sheet (the "Term Sheet") is non-binding and is subject to, among other things, fulfillment of the conditions set forth in the "Conditions Precedent" section below.

Issuer
Ziqitza Health Care Limited, a public limited company organized under the laws of India ("ZHL" or the "Company")

Investor
Acumen Fund, Inc., a not-for-profit corporation organized under the laws of New York, United States of America ("Acumen Fund")

Issue Amount
The value of the Offering will be INR 69 million (the "Issue Amount").

Date of Issue
The share issuance contemplated by this Term Sheet (the "Offering") is anticipated to occur on or before January 15, 2007.

Amount of Offering
The Offering will consist of [5,982,638] Series A senior cumulative compulsorily convertible participating preference shares (the "Series A Preference Shares") with a par value of INR 10 per share and a subscription price of INR 10 per share, and 10,000 equity shares with a subscription price of INR 917.36 per share (with a par value of INR 10 and a premium of INR 907.36 per share).

Figure 12.6 *(Continued)*

Existing Shareholding

The existing shareholding of the Company consists of the following:
- 50,000 equity shares issued and paid up at face value of INR 10 per share; and
- 175,647 equity shares issued and paid up at INR 100 (with a face value of INR 10 plus a premium of INR 90 per share), as further described in Appendix A attached hereto.

Valuation of the Company

INR <TBD> million prior to the investment contemplated by this Term Sheet and INR <TBD> million after the conversion of the investment contemplated by this Term Sheet

Use of Issue Amount

The Issue Amount will be utilized by the Company to:
- Acquire 31 Advanced Life Support Ambulances (including prefabrication work and medicinal equipment) and 1 call center at an aggregate estimated cost of INR 61.50 million; and
- Fund marketing expenses in the amount of INR 7.50 million.

Or in any manner that the Board deems appropriate subject to prior written approval (which shall not be unreasonably withheld) of Acumen Fund

Conditions Precedent

Acumen Fund's investment in the Company pursuant to this Term Sheet will be subject to customary conditions,
including, without limitation, the following:
- (a) The completion of legal due diligence by Acumen Fund and the resolution of any issues arising therefrom in a manner satisfactory to Acumen Fund;
- (b) The approval of such investment by the Investment Committee of Acumen Fund;
- (c) The execution of a Shareholders' Agreement by and among the existing shareholders of the Company and Acumen Fund (the "Shareholders' Agreement"); and
- (d) Government of India regulations and norms, as applicable.

(continued)

Figure 12.6 *(Continued)*

Preference

Dividends for Series A Preference Shares will be declared and paid, or sufficient monies set aside for such payment, before payment of dividends to any other shareholders or class of shareholder, including, without limitation, all equity shares. Series A Preference Shares will have a liquidation preference over all other shares of the Company, including, without limitation, all equity shares, with respect to payment or distribution of assets upon liquidation in the amount of the Liquidation Value per share. For the purposes hereof, "Liquidation Value" means the amount for which the relevant shares were issued plus accrued dividends plus declared but unpaid dividends.

Series A Preference Shares and Policy

A dividend of <TBD%> per annum, payable half-yearly in arrears on October 15 and April 15 of each year (each, a "Dividend Payment Date"), will be paid on the Series A Preference Shares. Dividends will accrue on shares of the Company from the date on which such shares were issued. Any dividends accrued but remaining unpaid on any Dividend Payment Date will be cumulated with, and become payable along with, dividends payable on subsequent Dividend Payment Dates.

Merger, Consolidation or Sale of Substantially All of the Assets of the Company

Unless waived by the holders of Series A Preference Shares, the following events will be deemed a liquidation of the Company for the purposes of determining such holders' liquidation preference:

(i) Any consolidation or merger of the Company with or into any other corporation or other entity, or any other corporate reorganization, in which the shareholders of the Company immediately prior to such consolidation, merger or reorganization, own less than fifty percent (50%) of the Company's voting power immediately after such consolidation, merger or reorganization, or any transaction or series of related transactions in which in excess of fifty percent (50%) of the Company's voting power is transferred or in which management control is transferred; and/or

Figure 12.6   *(Continued)*

(ii) Any sale, lease, or other disposition of all or substantially all of the property, assets, and/or business of the Company.

Conversion

At any time prior to the fourth anniversary of the date of issue thereof, Acumen Fund will have the right but not the obligation to convert all or part of its Series A Preference Shares into fully paid equity shares based on a conversion rate that would, if applied to all Series A Preference Shares issued pursuant to this Offering, result in Acumen Fund holding the number of equity shares equal to TBD of all equity shares in the Company. On the fourth anniversary of the date of issue thereof, any and all Series A Preference Shares not converted into equity shares by Acumen Fund will be compulsorily converted into the number of fully paid equity shares that would result in Acumen Fund holding the number of equity shares equal to <TBD%> of all equity shares in the Company.

Governance

Except as otherwise required by applicable law, the overall management and operational control of the Company shall be exercised exclusively by the Board of Directors or similar governing body of the Company (the "Board"). The maximum size of the Board will be seven (7) directors. Any increase in the number of directors on the Board will require the prior written approval (which shall not be unreasonably withheld) of Acumen Fund.

The shareholders agree that the Board will at all times include at least one (1) director appointed by Acumen Fund; such director shall be non-retiring.

Voting

Holders of equity shares will be entitled to one vote per equity share. Holders of Series A Preference Shares will be entitled to one vote for each equity share issuable upon conversion of its Series A Preference Shares. Holders of Series A Preference Shares will be entitled to vote on any matter which the holders of equity shares are entitled to vote and the holders of Series A Preference Shares and the holders of equity shares will vote as a single class.

(continued)

Figure 12.6 *(Continued)*

Except as otherwise required by applicable law or agreed by the shareholders of the Company, all decisions of the shareholders of the Company will require the affirmative vote of shareholders holding not less than 51% of the equity shares of the Company, including the equity shares issuable upon conversion of the Series A Preference Shares.

Voting for Certain Actions

An affirmative vote of the Investor will be required for the Company to:

(a) Liquidate, dissolve or wind up the affairs of the Company;

(b) Alter or change the rights of the Series A Preference Shares in any way;

(c) Increase or decrease the authorized number of equity shares or preference shares;

(d) Create any new class of shares;

(e) Redeem/buy back equity shares;

(f) Effect any merger, other corporate reorganization, sale of control, or any transaction in which all or substantially all of the assets of the Company are sold;

(g) Amend or waive any provision of the Company's Memorandum or Articles of Association;

(h) Appoint any statutory or internal auditor; or

(i) Make any decision or take any action that may adversely affect the rights or voting power of the Series A Preference Shares.

Affirmative Covenants

The Company will:

- Maintain at its registered office complete and accurate corporate, financial and tax books and records in accordance with Indian GAAP. The Company will provide Acumen Fund with documents that it may reasonably request in order for it to prepare its financial statements or tax filings with regulatory authorities;

- Provide access to its premises, books of account and other corporate, financial and tax books and records to each of its shareholders during normal business hours;

- Maintain adequate insurance, including, without limitation, customary directors' and officers' indemnification insurance;

Figure 12.6 *(Continued)*

- Comply with applicable law;
- Take actions to preserve (i) its corporate existence, (ii) its rights, franchises, and privileges, and (iii) all properties necessary or useful to the proper conduct of its business; and
- Reimburse all reasonable Company-related expenses of its Directors within India.

Initial Public Offering

(a) The Company and the Promoter Group will perform all such acts and deeds and do all such things as may be necessary to ensure that an initial public offering of the Company's shares (the "IPO") is made and that such shares are listed on the Bombay Stock Exchange or National Stock Exchange on or before June 30, 2012 (or such later date as Acumen Fund may, in its sole discretion, approve in writing, such approval not being unreasonably withheld);

(b) In completing the IPO, the Company will seek out and utilize the advice of a reputed investment banker unanimously approved by the Board; and

(c) The shares of the Company offered to the public pursuant to the IPO may be new shares, existing shares or any combination of the foregoing, as Acumen Fund may approve in writing (such approval not being unreasonably withheld). Acumen Fund will have the right (but not the obligation), at its sole discretion, to FIRST offer to sell all or any portion of the equity shares held by it as part of the IPO, subject to a limit of 50% of the IPO dilution.

Strategic Sale:

If the Company does not effect an IPO by June 30, 2012, Acumen Fund will have the right to sell all of its equity shares in the Company to any person, after granting the right of first refusal to the promoter group. If, however, the company has not effected the IPO by June 30, 2014, Acumen Fund will, based upon its sole discretion, have the right to cause each other equity shareholder to sell 100% of its equity shares in the Company to any such person purchasing 100% of Acumen Fund's equity shares in the Company.

(continued)

Figure 12.6 *(Continued)*

Anti-Dilution

In the event that the Company issues any equity shares, or any rights, options, warrants or instruments entitling the holder to receive any equity shares of the Company, including, without limitation, share splits, share dividends and recapitalizations (each, a "Dilution Instrument"), Acumen Fund will be entitled to acquire such number of Dilution Instruments as would enable it to maintain its proportion of shareholding in the Company after all such equity shares are issued and all Dilution Instruments and all Series A Preference Shares are converted into equity shares. Acumen Fund will be entitled to acquire any such Dilution Instruments on terms no less favorable than those offered by the Company to any other person.

Management Lock-In

The Promoter Group will not be entitled to, and will not, transfer or create any lien or encumbrance over or dispose of any equity shares or other securities in the Company or any interest in such securities save and except with the prior written approval (which shall not be unreasonably withheld) of Acumen Fund and on such terms and conditions as Acumen Fund may specify.

Until the fourth anniversary of the date of the Offering, the Promoter Group will not be entitled to, and will not, transfer or create any lien or encumbrance over or dispose of any equity shares or other securities in the Company or any interest in such securities save and except with Acumen Fund's prior written approval (which shall not be unreasonably withheld), and on such terms and conditions, including a valuation not less than INR <TBD>.

Representations and Warranties

The Shareholders Agreement will contain a detailed section on representations and warranties to be provided by the Company and the Promoters.

External Auditor

The shareholders of the Company will select and appoint an external auditor based on an arm's-length commercial considerations. The external auditor will perform such functions as the Board may direct.

Figure 12.6 *(Continued)*

Governing Law
The Shareholders Agreement will be governed by, and construed in accordance with, the laws of the Republic of India.

Disputes
In the event of any dispute arising out of the Shareholders' Agreement or any subsequent agreement related to the Company, the shareholders of the Company will attempt in good faith to resolve the dispute amicably. Any dispute which cannot be resolved within sixty (60) days from the date such dispute has arisen shall, at the option of any party to the dispute, be finally settled under the Rules of Arbitration of the International Chamber of Commerce by one or more arbitrators appointed in accordance with the said Rules. The status of the arbitration will be Mumbai (unless the parties agree otherwise) and the arbitration proceeding will be conducted in the English language only. The shareholders of the Company agree that arbitration will be the exclusive method for resolution of disputes between the parties hereto arising out of or in connection with the Offering and the Shareholders' Agreement. The arbitrators will have the power to grant any remedy or relief that they deem just and equitable, including but not limited to injunctive relief, whether interim and/or final, and any provisional measures ordered by the arbitrators may be specifically enforced by any court of competent jurisdiction. The award rendered in connection with such arbitration will be final and binding upon the shareholders of the Company and may be entered in any court having jurisdiction thereof.

Confidentiality
Each of the shareholders of the Company will keep all non-public information received in the course of the negotiation or conclusion of the present transaction, or any subsequent agreement related to the Company, confidential in accordance with customary confidentiality arrangements.

One comparison that ZHL did have was Rural Metro, a U.S.-based EMS company that was listed on the NASDAQ. The P/E ratio of Rural Metro was 2.3 as of March 31, 2006. The market capitalization/revenue ratio was 0.3. However, there were reasons to use a higher P/E for ZHL. In the United States, the EMS market was mature, making it difficult for a single EMS provider to record high growth rates. The market in India, by comparison, was nascent and highly fragmented. This provided great growth potential for a professional service such as ZHL.

The Acumen Investment Committee made the decision to make a $1.5 million equity investment in ZHL to support capital expenditures ($0.39 million in 2006, $0.9 million in 2007), marketing expenses ($0.16 million in 2006), and working capital ($0.05 million in 2007).

To Recap

Where a social venture's funding comes from—and how much the venture requires—changes across that venture's life cycle. Main sources include everything from personal funds and grants, to loans, convertible debt, and equity investment. When fund-raising, a target list of potential sources, an elevator pitch, a business plan summary presentation (targeted specifically toward interested parties), and a "leave behind" investment profile all come in handy. In the next chapter we look at the way forward for organizations with a mission at their heart.

Exercises

12.1 Funding Sources and Amount(s)

Use your budget and cash flow statements from chapter 11 to calculate the amount of money needed and when it will be needed. Create a list of funding sources to be approached each time funding is needed. In general, it is better to approach only one type of source at each stage. In addition, if you need additional funding, make sure that earlier stage funders understand how their investments will be treated relative to the new funding sources.

12.2 Elevator Pitch

Minimum Critical Specifications Checklist
Financing
• Financing sources and amounts are specified for the venture's life-cycle stages.
• Focused and disciplined use of funds in operating plans ensures that milestones are achieved.
• Venture and investor outcomes, social impact, and financial return objectives are specified and aligned.

Although there are many ways to go about creating an elevator pitch, we suggest proceeding in three steps. First, create a one-page PowerPoint slide that addresses the following:

- What an organization does (What are your products or services?)

- Who the intended beneficiaries are (Who benefits from your products or services?)

- Who the economic buyer is, if different from the beneficiary (Who pays for the products or services?)

- Why your organization's product or service is important to the beneficiaries (How, specifically, are the beneficiaries' situations improved?)

- Why the organization is the best at what it does (Why are you a better choice than the alternatives?)

- How the organization measures what it does (What metrics do you use to determine whether you are successful?)

Second, turn the PowerPoint slide that you just created into a written document that "tells a story" about the organization. This is the elevator pitch. The elevator pitch does not have to use the same order of elements as in the PowerPoint slide. For example, you could begin with a compelling story about the needs of one or more of your beneficiaries and how the organization fills the needs, and then generalize to describe the number of such beneficiaries and how the organization works to help them.

Third, memorize the elevator pitch and make sure to practice it slowly out loud so that it can be given in less than three minutes. There will be many opportunities to share the elevator pitch when encountering someone new who may be interested in possibly investing time or money in your enterprise. So, it is worth the time and effort to develop a compelling elevator pitch and memorize it so that it can be easily and comfortably delivered.

12.3 Develop a PowerPoint Business Plan Summary Presentation

As a template for presentations to potential funding sources (and to other interested parties), use the outline in this exercise to create ten to fifteen PowerPoint slides capturing the results of the exercises in chapters 4–10. It is not necessary to follow the outline exactly, but make sure all the suggested information is included. The outline should contain the following:

- Title slide with your mission statement (one slide)

- Value proposition (one slide)

- External environment (one slide)

- Market/beneficiary analysis (one to three slides)—possibly including a story about a beneficiary

- Key strategies (one slide)

- Value chain and business model (two to five slides)

- Metrics dashboard (one slide)

- Financing: needs and uses (one slide)

- Summary (one slide)

You should be able to modify or add to the PowerPoint charts in this outline to create a presentation tailored to each funding source. Selected information from the worksheet in Exercise 12.4 may also be of value in producing a "PowerPoint Deck" for use in business plan presentations.

12.4 Develop an "Investment Profile"

Use the results of the exercises in chapters 4–11 to provide the following worksheet (Figure 12.7) with information for use in creating an investment profile.

Figure 12.7   Investment Profile Worksheet

1. Provide the full name (and abbreviation/acronym if you use one) of your organization. If you are representing a single project or department in your organization, please identify that project or department.

2. List the name(s) and position title(s) of the social entrepreneur(s) representing the organization. If this person is not the founder(s) or chief executive, please list these individuals as well.

3. Provide your
   a. email address
   b. website URL (if any)
   c. phone number
   d. Twitter, Facebook, YouTube, or other URLs (if any)

4. In what year was this organization established?

5. What is your organizational (legal) form of doing business?

   _____ Nonprofit/NGO

   _____ For-profit

   _____ Hybrid (you have both for-profit and nonprofit organizations)

   _____ Government

   _____ Other (please specify): _____

6. Copy your ten-word mission statement from Exercise 4.1.

7. Please list the city (cities) and country (countries) where you "do business" (have beneficiaries). If one of these is your headquarters, please identify it. If there are no cities, just list the countries and regions.

8. In which sectors do you have impact? (choose a maximum of two)

   _____ Agriculture & Fishing   Equality & Social Justice

   _____ Cleantech & Energy   Housing

_____ Economic Development   _____ Information &
                                                   Communications
                                                   Technology (ICT)

_____ Education   Microfinance

_____ Environment   Transportation

_____ Fair Trade   Water & Sanitation

_____ Health   Other:_____

9. How many employees do you have (full-time equivalents)? How many volunteers (full or part time) do you have at any one time?

10. What is your annual budget (total of all expense drivers) for this year?

11. What are your major income (funding) sources (contributed and/or earned income drivers for this year), and what will be your total income?

12. What were the major sources of your initial funding? If you have investors, please list them and the percentages of investment for each. If you have loans, please list the lenders and the percentages of your loans held by each.

13. List major awards you have received and give the year in which you received the award.

14. What is your value proposition? (you can copy or revise Exercise 9.1)

15. Describe the target market for your organization (you can copy or revise Exercises 6.2 and 6.3). If you have pictures of your beneficiaries, please include them. Be sure to include the size of the total available market.

16. Provide a short description that illustrates your product or service. If you have a technical innovation, please describe it as well.

17. Give a one-sentence statement that quantifies the impact of your organization in terms of one quantitative metric (e.g., "we have provided jobs for 1,000 youth," or "we provide healthcare products to over 100,000 women," or "we have built 10,000 earthquake-resistant homes that house over 60,000 people").

18. List three to five of the most significant growth milestones you have achieved (funding, income, impact, or growth of beneficiaries). Provide the dates and values (e.g., amounts, numbers) for each milestone (e.g., 2008: obtained $250,000 in funding; 2009: opened three regional training centers; 2010: trained five hundred youth).

19. List three to five of your most significant, quantitative growth goals for the next three years (e.g., 2012, build twelve village power systems; 2013, build eighteen village power systems; 2014, build twenty-four village power systems).

20. Provide one to three quantitative metrics of the impact of your organization/project since its inception (i.e., what has been the total impact). One of these metrics should be the total number of people who have benefited from your organization/project. Include an explanation of how you calculate that number.

21. Provide a quote from one of your beneficiaries that illustrates the impact of your organization on the beneficiaries' lives.

22. Briefly describe the type of investments the organization is seeking (grants, public-private partnership subsidy, debt, convertible debt, and equity), the required amounts, and investment time frame. If a monetary investment is not being sought at this time, describe other types of support that are being sought, such as partnerships and technical assistance.

23. Provide as many of the following images as possible. List URLs or attach files in .jpg, .jpeg, gif, or .png formats:
    a. Logo
    b. Headshot photo of you
    c. Photo or diagram that illustrates your value proposition
    d. Photo of some of your beneficiaries
    e. Diagram or picture that illustrates your product or service, and if applicable, the technical innovation
    f. Up to five additional photos or diagrams that illustrate the organization's work and the local context

Background Resources

Bannick, Matt, Paula Goldman, and Michael Kubzansky. *Frontier Capital: Early Stage Investing for Financial Returns and Social Impact in Emerging Markets.* Omidyar Network Research Report, October, 2015.

Dees, J. Gregory, Jed Emerson, and Peter Economy. *Strategic Tools for Social Entrepreneurs: Enhancing the Performance of Your Enterprising Nonprofit.* New York: John Wiley, 2002, chapter 6.

DeThomas, Arthur, and Stephanie Derammelaere. *How to Write a Convincing Business Plan.* 3rd ed. New York: Barron's Educational Services, 2008, chapters 1, 2, 3, and 11.

Faiz, Lala, Charly Kleissner, John Kohler, and Nancy Y. Lin. *Total Portfolio Activation for Impact: A Strategy to Move beyond ESG*, Report from Miller Center for Entrepreneurship, September 2016.

Global Impact Investing Network (GIIN). "Impact Investing Trends," December 2015.

McKinsey and Company and Time Koller. *Valuation: Measuring and Managing the Value of a Company.* New York: Wiley Finance, 2015.

O'Leary, Chris. *Elevator Pitch Essentials.* Limb Press, 2008. http://www.elevatorpitchessentials.com.

SOCAP11: Impact Investing Special Edition. Cambridge, MA: MIT Press, 2011, especially Ann-Kristin Achleitner et al., "Unlocking the Mystery: An Introduction to Social Investment," pp. 41–50.

William Davidson Institute at the University of Michigan. "Acumen Fund Valuing a Social Venture," Case 1-48-428-788, May 2009.

Chapter 13

The Path Forward

In chapter 3, we described a variety of conventional business planning paradigms and suggested an alternative—one we believe is better suited to the unique challenges of building successful social ventures. Our framework intends to contribute to the gradual elaboration of a specific model of socioeconomic development—a bottom-up, market-based approach that is better equipped to solve social problems than other existing approaches to economic growth.

Chapters 4 through 12 deconstruct our business planning framework into nine modules, each with checklist criteria for assessing a venture plan's strength. These modules have continued to be refined from working with the founders of more than eight hundred social ventures through Miller Center for Social Entrepreneurship at Santa Clara University. In addition, our overall model has been tested and refined as a paradigm for teaching the fundamental building blocks of successful social venture creation with both MBA students and undergraduates—many of whom we hope will become next-generation social entrepreneurs. We seek to foster the spread of social entrepreneurship as an adaptive process—one that can help overcome instances of market and government failure, particularly when it comes to providing essential products and services like access to safe water, quality education, affordable healthcare, housing, and clean energy access, as well as livelihood opportunities, food security, and ultimately thriving communities.

The ingenuity of social entrepreneurs is opening up whole new pathways for social progress. It is a highly adaptive phenomenon built around networked and collaborative models of organizing and innovative strategies for market creation. It encompasses a variety of legal forms and new approaches to governance. It also enables access to a wider array of financing alternatives across the stages of organizational life cycles.

Consistent with the conceptual foundations of this emergent field, our approach places an organization's mission—its social value proposition—at the center of the business planning process.[1] It addresses the social entrepreneurship process systematically and encourages social entrepreneurs to think of their organizations as *real businesses*—businesses subject to the same scrutiny for the robustness of their plans and competitive position as businesses rated by Gartner, the industry research and advisory company. Gartner rates organizations on the basis of *completeness of vision* and the *ability to execute*—with the "magic quadrant" cell in a 2×2 matrix where both of these dimensions are high.[2]

We will use these broad categories as a framework for summarizing the elements of our model and identifying important distinctions between the logics of social and commercial venture businesses.

Completeness of Vision

There are three elements in our paradigm that, taken together, can be used to assess the completeness of a social venture's vision and the logic model for its theory of change:

- Mission, opportunity, and strategy

- Environment analysis

- Target market

Mission, Opportunity, and Strategy (Theory of Change)
Social ventures address complex problems and are held accountable for outcomes in settings where resources are scarce and the external environment can be at times unpredictable. In settings like these, we posit that a ten-word mission statement and a tight *resources-activities-outputs-outcomes-impact* logic model are extremely useful in marshaling resources around a shared vision. In fact, as we have seen countless times, the absence of a clear focus and specific outcome measures can dilute resources and undermine organizational effectiveness.

A clear theory of change with a disciplined approach to resource align-ment is an imperative that distinguishes social from commercial venture busi-ness planning. Where commercial venture strategies are defined in relation to financial measures such as profits or shareholder value, social businesses exist to achieve measurable changes in individual well-being or social progress and *stakeholder* value while, at the same time, becoming financially viable and increasing market penetration relative to the size of unmet needs. Moreover, Castells and Koch posit that "the outcome of the activity of the social enterprise is not only a product, but a process, such as the process of economic empowerment and psychological self-esteem of those involved in the social enterprise."[3]

External Environment

Before social entrepreneurs can intervene with the hope of creating an equi-librium change, they must understand the environmental conditions that hold an unjust or undesirable situation in place.[4]

Martin and Osberg suggest that this requires humility grounded in the paradox of both *abhorrence* and *appreciation* for the "current state."[5] In other words, it requires discernment of what anchors an unjust system. Strategies for effectively intervening in places where urgent problems exist require deep thinking, an understanding of ecosystems, and an appreciation of the needs of those with influence on desired outcomes. For social entrepreneurs seek-ing to marshal resources, these influencers can be sources of resistance or drivers of positive change. They are repositories of local knowledge and gate-ways to potential resources. As allies and partners, they can reduce market frictions, foster value chain innovations for serving previously underserved populations, and lower costs. Our business planning framework places an em-phasis on the identification of ideal partners as sources of legitimacy, re-source leverage, and means of fostering lasting social change. In contrast to commercial entrepreneurship, where *capital* generally refers to financial considerations, in a social business, *social capital*—networks of trust, reci-procity, and shared purpose—is essential to embedding lasting change in local contexts. Financial capital is critical, but without social capital, social ventures can burn through money very quickly without achieving a sustain-able enterprise, let alone any significant impact. Conversely, with strong so-cial capital, social entrepreneurs can achieve significant impact with limited financial resources and create a network of alliances for attracting and effectively utilizing financial resources.

Beneficiary (Market) Analysis

The size of market needs in contexts of extreme poverty is frequently measured in millions, and often hundreds of millions or even billions, but the composition of these markets is typically opaque to outsiders. In our framework, the process of creating the blueprint for a successful social venture and validating its business model begins with deep empathy and an appreciation of local market realities. How you sell clean cook stoves in village economies, for example, varies incredibly depending on variables like family dynamics (who manages the money), availability of fuel, cooking habits, and social dynamics. Social entrepreneurs who develop a successful model for working in one location will almost certainly find that it may or may not scale to other geographies with the same need. Often, individuals with different local realities need to be reached through totally different marketing approaches.

As with business planning for commercial ventures, discerning the demographic and psychographic attributes of potential early adopters is an essential outcome in target market segmentation. Beyond that, our framework places added emphasis on distinguishing direct and indirect "customers" as well as related beneficiaries and the motivations of "economic buyers" or "paying" customers. The default option for the poor, as direct customers, is simply to do without (i.e., nonconsumption). Economic exchange in settings of deep poverty can be a precarious proposition. It often occurs in the context of trust-based personal relationships among unbanked populations with low literacy levels and low levels of trust in government or outsiders. This requires the common elements of a marketing plan (product, price, placement, and promotion) to be reframed as challenges in overcoming market failure.

Our business planning paradigm posits that a fruitful approach to creating a sustainable enterprise and engendering transformative change is to develop solutions based on a deep appreciation of the local customs, sociopolitical structures, and norms that collectively form the basis for resident systems of economic exchange. It underscores the significance of incorporating a more "bottom-up" and participatory approach to market development—a position that contrasts with top-down methods for serving the poor that have dominated the market entry thinking of large companies and government programs.

Ability to Execute

Our paradigm includes specific processes for developing three elements in a social venture business plan that directly relate to the *ability to execute* strategies and achieve organizational goals:

- Operations and value chain innovation

- Organization and human talent

- Business model

Operations and Value Chain Innovation

During our years leading the GSBI, the biggest gaps that existed in the knowledge of social entrepreneurs were in the areas of operations. They often had inspiring visions, deep knowledge of the problem they were trying to solve, and an intuitive feel for the markets they sought to serve. Oftentimes, this was enough to get a pilot social enterprise off the ground but not enough to make that enterprise sustainable and scalable. In operations, their knowledge and skills tailed off, leaving great leaps of faith to define expense and revenue drivers—not to mention how they would actually deliver and capture value to become financially viable.

Business models are derivative. They must be grounded in *empirically based* estimates of the size of markets as well as *realistic estimates* of potential market penetration based on the effectiveness of specific strategies for customer or beneficiary engagement. For the cost per outcome to be known and effectively managed, market penetration requires value chain innovation in cost reduction and disciplined use of *unit economics* for quantifying units of business and units of benefit for all links in the supply (value) chain. We have observed that social ventures seldom have chief operations officers (COOs). In our view, once key processes and scaling strategies are defined, COOs are often more important to the viability of a social business than CEOs. A solid COO and operations team will not necessarily be able to attract the capital and partnerships necessary to scale rapidly, but if the strategy is sound, they can ensure steady organic growth. In the social entrepreneurship world, resources tend to follow great stories and charismatic leaders who can build relationships and mobilize resources. If you look under the hood of successful social ventures, though, you will always find strong operations leadership.

Organization and Human Talent

Social ventures differ from commercial businesses in the centrality of values associated with resource mobilization. This is especially evident in decisions regarding organizational design—from the choice of legal form and board composition to organization structure. It is also evident in the identification of critical skills at each level of the organization—from the need for complementary skills in executive leadership teams, to the specifying of knowledge, skills, and abilities for pivotal front-line jobs. Next to distribution challenges in underdeveloped infrastructure settings, the shortage of individuals with critical skills is often the most difficult hurdle for social ventures to overcome. Successful ventures address this hurdle by developing an expertise in hiring for fit with organizational mission and ability to learn, and by formalizing training processes. Moreover, they create an organizational culture that allows mission-aligned employees to reach their highest potential and, in this way, retain talented staff who could earn a better salary elsewhere. Their leaders place a major emphasis on strengthening the organization's capacity for continuous learning and innovation. In the high-tech region of Silicon Valley, it is common knowledge that the best technology is a benefit, but does not necessarily win. In our nine-element business planning framework, the consensus of seasoned mentors is straightforward: "Without the right team, none of the other elements of the business plan matter." In addition to insisting on clear evidence of senior leadership strengths, our seasoned Silicon Valley entrepreneurial mentors encourage their social venture mentees to

- specify the board expertise needed for members to contribute to success,

- develop a strategic rationale for choice of legal structure (for profit, nonprofit, hybrid, etc.),

- specify organizational risk factors and identify potential gaps in critical skills, and

- clarify mechanisms for creating an organization culture that can drive extraordinary results through ordinary people.

Business Model

While a business model describes the rationale for how an organization creates, delivers, and captures value, there are important distinctions between the rationality of commercial and social ventures.[6] The most notable distinctions stem from social mission and investor priorities. While commercial investors seek to maximize risk-adjusted financial returns, social investors care about a venture's impact model and are willing to make financial return trade-offs. All of the elements in a business model must evolve around the ability to create and deliver on a compelling value proposition—in the case of a social business, a social value proposition (SVP). The expense drivers associated with SVPs are strongly influenced by activities in logic models designed to produce measurable social outcomes and impact. These activities require resource mobilization through engaging stakeholders with a variety of interests in outcomes as opposed to stockholders with a narrow interest in financial returns. In a similar vein, the revenue drivers of social ventures often require major efforts to develop channels and educate direct and indirect customers, or others who stand to benefit from social outcomes.

From our work with social ventures, we have concluded that *unit economics*—the revenues and expenses associated with a unit of benefit—have been a missing consideration in social venture plans for growth (scale). Ideally, with increasing volume, unit economics become more favorable. This is often not the case, as the marginal cost of serving the poorest of the poor may actually increase. There can also be significant tensions for social entrepreneurs between their desire to serve poorer customers and economic or government policy considerations pointing them to less poor customers. For example, one venture we have worked with started out aiming to serve off-grid rural customers and ultimately pivoted toward selling to grid-connected households because that is where the government subsidies had moved. Value chain innovation is a critical factor in addressing complex social issues, achieving unit cost reductions, and increasing market penetration. Our nine-element business planning process provides a useful guide for identifying disruptive innovation opportunities and building more inclusive markets.

Entrepreneurial Adaptation

The business planning framework in this book places a major emphasis on the enterprise development and market creation challenges posed by Ted London in *The Base of the Pyramid Promise*, as illustrated in Figure 13.1.[7] In practice, we have found that the business models for adapting to these challenges continuously evolve through processes of incremental and discontinuous change. Incremental adjustments occur in periods of the organizational life cycle when ventures are able to take advantage of desirable factors in their internal and external environments. These may be characterized as periods with predictable cycles of value creation, delivery, and capture. They allow ventures to hone their business models to improve efficiency and optimize impact. In contrast, intense periods of organizational learning and business model adaptation are required when critical success factors in operating plans prove to be invalid, essential alliances fail to materialize or falter, the unit economics across innovative value chains are insufficient to incentivize stakeholders, or opportunities and threats in the external environment call fundamental business plan assumptions into question. Periods of discontin-

Figure 13.1 Venture Development and Market Creation

	Enterprise Development	Market Creation
Action Enabling	*Facilitate Enterprise Activities* **Market Intelligence:** • Cultural context, competitive landscape • Consumer demand, supplier preferences **Market Access:** • Connection to distributors, other platforms **Value Creation:** • Assess poverty impacts	*Facilitate Market Transactions* **Demand Creation:** • Awareness raising, behavior change • Microcredit, other sources of financing • Vouchers/subsidies **Supply Enhancement:** • Advisory services for producers • Improved inputs • Aggregation of outputs
Capacity Building	*Enhance Enterprise Resources* **Financial Capital:** • Grants, equity, debt, loan guarantee **Human Capital:** • Talent development, technical assistance **Knowledge Capital:** • Processes, tools, and frameworks **Social Capital:** • Legitimacy, access to networks	*Enhance Market Environment* **Value Chain Infrastructure:** • Physical infrastructure development • Quality assurance and certification • Market transparency **Legal Infrastructure:** • Policy changes and regulation enforcement **Institutional Infrastructure:** • Banking, legal, property sector enhancement

Source: Ted London, The Base of the Pyramid Promise—Building with Impact and Scale (Stanford, CA: Stanford University Press, 2016), 135.

uous change in organization strategy and business plans are commonly referred to as pivots. Both Angaza and Husk Power Systems provide excellent windows into entrepreneurial business model adaptation. We describe each of these in the snapshots below.

Social Venture Snapshot: Discontinuous Change in the Angaza Business Model

Over one billion people who do not have access to grid electricity burn kerosene as a source of light. Angaza's product solution uses solar energy—a cleaner, more reliable, and less expensive energy source. Its original business model was based on a vertically integrated value chain with Angaza designing, manufacturing, and distributing solar products to end-user customers. Realizing that these products were prohibitively expensive for those who needed them presented Angaza with an option, according to founder and CEO Lesley Marincola, to either take away quality and functionality or find a way to make the same products more affordable. Angaza took inspiration from the diffusion of cell phone technology in sub-Saharan Africa, where, Marincola noted, "in the past ten-years mobile deployment went from no connectivity to where everyone is connected through their mobile phone."[8] The leapfrogging of land lines was made possible by inexpensive handsets and the ability to buy airtime in tiny increments. This enabled Angaza to create a business model where energy could be purchased in the same way as prepaid airtime. Its pay-as-you-go, rent-to-own financing technology overcame the up-front cost hurdle, and its value proposition enabled customers who were spending up to 20 percent of their income on kerosene to have a free solution once solar payments were finished.

Marincola says, "We just realized that if we wanted to impact a hundred million people, a billion people, we needed to transition from a business-to-consumer (B2C) model to a business-to-business (B2B) model and focus directly on designing and developing the pay-as-you-go technology platform" and then offer this software to distributors. In contrast to its B2C model, distributors would then become the channel for getting to customers. This, in turn, empowered the field agents of distributors to earn more money. Marincola believes "pay-as-you-go has completely transformed the off-grid energy industry. There's a whole new market emerging. And it is amazing to see how many jobs have been created from solar distribution. We are growing exponentially. Right now we're working in over 10 countries."

In addition to its seed round financing of $1.5 million in 2013, Angaza raised $4 million of Series A funding in 2014. The decision to change from a B2C to a B2B business model has enabled it to build a technology platform for addressing needs on a global scale through partner distributors. By 2016, it had thirty such partners. In addition to licensing and royalty revenues from manufacturers, Angaza receives royalties and small transaction fees for each unit of energy sales tracked through its software in distributor energy hubs. These energy hubs produce data analytics for distributors to monitor battery capacity, solar panel efficiency, and payments. Payment data can also be monetized through MFIs and other financial institutions, as well as big companies interested in pursuing the markets for their goods among customers with more cash.

In summary, the transition from a B2C to a B2B business model has involved a change in the identification of paying customers, a change in how end-user customer needs are met, a change from a vertically integrated to a network value chain, and, significantly, different monetization strategies.

Social Venture Snapshot: Entrepreneurial Adaptation at Husk Power Systems

Husk Power Systems ("HUSK") is a global leader in the decentralized off-grid rural electrification sector. In 2008, HUSK started its journey with biomass gasification powered mini-grid operations in India and provided six to eight hours of alternating current (AC) power daily to rural customers. By 2013, customer feedback indicated that they were not content with only six to eight hours of power. Customers wanted to own appliances like TVs, fans, and refrigerators and wanted access to on-demand power. So, in 2013, HUSK embarked on a journey to find a new energy solution for providing reliable 24/7 power 365 days a year. By understanding how rural customers aspired to use power and working relentlessly to address their needs, HUSK developed an energy solution that gave them the freedom and flexibility they desired.

Between 2008 and 2013, solar PV prices had declined by more than 80 percent. So HUSK partnered with U.S.-based First Solar Inc., the largest publicly traded solar panel manufacturing company, to develop a proprietary solar-biomass hybrid system. In October 2015, HUSK deployed the first hybrid system that could generate 24/7 power by synchronizing solar and biomass gasification power plants. With this innovation, HUSK was able to reduce battery cost and provide 100 percent renewable and on-demand power (24/7) through a smart prepaid metering system as a pay-as-you-go service. In a sense, HUSK had repositioned itself from a provider of six to eight hours of biomass AC power to a mini-utility. Its solar-biomass hybrid power plants are the lowest-cost off-grid solution that can deliver 24/7 AC power to households and commercial customers such as welding machine shops, telecom towers, and rice and flour mills. By bringing AC power to rural communities, HUSK provides customers the opportunity to plug in any off-the-shelf appliance, from TVs to refrigerators to industrial machinery.

By January 2017, less than fifteen months after deploying its first system, HUSK owned and operated seventy proprietary solar PV–biomass gasification sites in India and five in Tanzania with services to fifteen thousand customers across four hundred villages in India and two hundred customers in Tanzania. In addition to providing the lowest cost of delivered energy in the mini-grid sector, its costs are at least 50 percent cheaper than solar home systems. In addition, it also generates and distributes three-phase AC power necessary for commercial customers and has the ability to set differential tariffs for residential and commercial customers as well as time-of-day discounts for daytime energy consumption.

HUSK's analysis of the off-grid sector indicates that micro-grid solutions have significant economic advantages over grid extensions for serving villages of fewer than three hundred customers at distances greater than seven kilometers from national grids. Even in developed countries like the United States and Germany, there is a proliferation of decentralized power generation. In India and Tanzania, HUSK has a chance to leapfrog grid extension solutions and provide 24/7, highly reliable and renewable power to villages in the most sustainable and economical way. This is very similar to the telecom revolution in India and Africa a few decades ago, in which cell phone technology, rather than landline connection extension, enabled more than 90 percent of people to have a reliable phone and data connectivity. In this context, the HUSK solar-biomass-battery option is approximately 33 percent cheaper than solar-diesel-battery mini-grids.

"We bring good things to life" was the jingle for a post–WWII General Electric commercial. So it is in developing countries today—when people have power, incredible things happen. Studies show that access to reliable energy promotes economic activity and improves the human development index across a variety of areas—from education and food safety to more productive livelihoods. Making this possible in every village is at the heart of everything HUSK does. It proactively works with its customers to promote productive uses of power for commercial activities that provide economic possibilities in rural areas—from the opening of appliance shops, to lathe machine shops, to restaurants selling cold drinks.

In summary, the transition from a business model based on biomass mini-grids to a business model based on proprietary solar-biomass hybrid mini-grids has involved a change in how end-user customer needs are met, the development of a partnership with First Solar to offer an integrated 24/7 solution, and a significantly different monetization strategy through a pay-as-you-go service. Looking back, HUSK board chairman Brad Mattson quotes Darwin, "It is NOT the fastest, strongest, or even smartest species that survive; it is the one most quickly to adapt." He adds, "The first business model you develop may not work—adapt!"(personal correspondence)

Metrics, Accountability in Operating Plans, and Financing

Social entrepreneurs marshal resources to pursue a focused mission in collaboration with both internal and external stakeholders. Their success in achieving both social impact and financial objectives depends on the development of innovative value chains and operating routines that incorporate metrics and accountability.

Metrics

The problems that social ventures seek to solve are complex and often growing in scale. If easy solutions existed, they would have already been implemented and the problems would no longer exist. Time after time, we have observed that the proximate relationship of bottom-up innovation to the problems that social entrepreneurs are addressing facilitates organizational learning and the potential for breakthrough solutions. Our paradigm utilizes a balanced scorecard framework to strengthen accountability for continuous improvement and innovation. It stresses the importance of identifying "owners" with accountability for each of the following metrics:

1. Financial performance
2. Key processes

3. Organization and foundational capabilities

4. Customer/beneficiary outcomes

Effective operating routines incorporate metrics in each of these areas to control variances in performance, for real-time entrepreneurial adaptation in strategy execution, and, in some instances, to identify when strategic pivots are needed.

Operating Plans

As with metrics, we added the operating plan element to our business planning paradigm after several years of work with social entrepreneurs. In this instance, the impetus was our realization that resourcing for strategic initiatives was often poorly integrated with operating budgets and organizational accountabilities. In our paradigm an operating plan translates strategic initiatives in the business plan into *milestones* with associated actions for achieving program specifications, resource requirements, due dates, and "owners." Most importantly, operating plans specify a *budget* that combines strategic initiative funding needs with the monthly income and expense targets from ongoing operations. This enables the organization to develop a *cash flow* statement that clarifies the financial viability of operating plans. In our paradigm, operating plans are an essential management tool used to focus the enterprise and match resources with specific plans, as well as to track progress and make course corrections if needed. Moreover, they are a mechanism to hold people accountable for performance.

Financing

To grow a social venture and its impact requires financing, often at multiple times. Drawing on *cash flow* statements in operating plans, this element of our paradigm enables social entrepreneurs to specify the amount and timing of funding needs. It also clarifies alternative types of funding and their appropriateness for various stages of the organizational life cycle (e.g., grants for R&D or product and service innovation, debt for working capital or to finance customers, and equity for building the organization and management team, as well as systems for scaling). In addition, the financing element of our paradigm identifies important factors in due diligence and criteria that can be used in valuation—or determining the value of a social business to investors. At a practical level, our financing guidelines for social entrepreneurs incorporate templates for investor presentations and investment profiles. While recognizing that overcoming institutional-level barriers to mainstream financial markets and institutions remains a work in progress, our focus is on building ventures that can meet the criteria for accessing the growing availability of *impact financing*. This investment capital is being provided by a different calculus than the one prevailing in financial markets or financial institutions. It supports economic empowerment and efforts to extend production and market creation to poor communities, and includes certain values (e.g., environmental preservation) in the criteria for funded economic activity. For these social impact markets to flourish, ventures must be sustainable in financial terms and provide evidence of pathways to replication.

Overcoming Market Failure

Creating solutions to complex problems in diverse local cultures is likely to meet with extremely limited success without deep local connections. The original C. K. Prahalad thesis posited that leadership in addressing the unmet needs of the four billion people at the base of the economic pyramid would be driven by the enlightened self-interest of major companies that could leverage vast resources to create more inclusive markets. In *The Base of the Pyramid Promise—Building Businesses with Impact and Scale,* Ted London acknowledges the flaws in top-down approaches to creating BOP markets.[9] His prescription for developing scalable BOP businesses offers an insightful conceptual framework for co-creating, innovating, and embedding solutions to poverty in local communities. To overcome market failure, he posits that ecosystem partnerships must be developed across a broad web of stakeholders—from multinational and host country companies to impact investors, nonprofit organizations (NGOs), development agencies, governments, and community leaders. In addition to collaborative interdependence, his framework places a major emphasis on assessing impact on poverty alleviation as a feedback loop to accelerate learning.

While our approach has been validated as a robust framework for business planning by over eight hundred ventures from more than sixty countries, as in any complex endeavor, there is much more to learn. Addressing complex or intractable problems cautions humility. We encourage others to adapt our framework to their unique needs, to improve on it, and to share their learning with us and with others. This is a *guide,* not a *prescription.* As entrepreneurs ourselves, we are inspired by the incomplete nature of this work. Our experience with organizations like Angaza and HUSK indicates that resilience and entrepreneurial adaptation are essential in building successful social ventures.

Combinatorial Innovation

> *Combinatorial innovation consists in (knowing) what is likely not to work, what methods to use, whom to talk to, what theories to look to, and above all how to manipulate phenomena that may be freshly discovered and poorly understood.*[10]
>
> Brian Arthur

The concepts and exercises in our business planning paradigm and its emphasis on social change have been strongly influenced by work with hundreds of social entrepreneurs in the laboratory-like atmosphere of the GSBI at Santa Clara University. Through this "laboratory" we have learned from social entrepreneurs more than we have taught. We have also learned from the extensive informal knowledge of dedicated Silicon Valley mentors who have worked with them—they are the "secret sauce" in the GSBI program. It is from the combination of their expertise and a curriculum that has been refined through more than a decade of continuous learning that the lessons in this book have been honed.

As the quote from Brian Arthur suggests, GSBI mentors practice "deep craft," knowing intimately the various functionalities of a successful venture and how to effectively combine them. Their value, however, stems as much from their commitment to listen with humility as it does from their expertise. To paraphrase Roger Martin and Sally Osberg, they must see themselves as both *experts* and *apprentices*.[11]

For example, in settings that are opaque to outsiders, the ability to envision a better future for the poorest among us often requires an understanding of informal markets in settings bereft of effectively functioning institutions and lacking in the critical knowledge and skills to develop and operate a successful venture. Effectively sharing knowledge from a place like Silicon Valley with Base of the Pyramid (BOP) protagonists in these settings requires collaborative engagement—working alongside and with social entrepreneurs as opposed to pontificating from on high as an "expert." In this way, the role of mentors shifts back and forth from teacher to student.

In chapter 2, we introduced the value equation concept and posited that social ventures must be built with both value and cost in mind. In our experience, innovation across the spectrum of the nine elements in the GSBI business planning paradigm makes this possible. It is, after all, an iterative process. Theories of change and strategies must be adapted to diverse environments. Their robustness depends on partnerships and the ability to embed solutions—often in both global and local ecosystems. Addressable BOP markets are frequently fragmented. They must be segmented with product features adapted to specific user needs across geographic, cultural, and economic settings. In a related vein, value propositions and their associated revenue and expense drivers in business models can be effectively executed only if the right leadership team is in place and organizations are designed for continuous learning. In resource-poor environments this requires the ability to accomplish extraordinary things through ordinary people. In turn, it requires metrics designed to support well-defined organizational routines and formal operating plans, as well as entrepreneurial adaptation and accountability to investors.

Economists refer to economic buyers as those who are willing to pay. Martin and Osberg argue that successful social ventures restructure the value equation by increasing value to beneficiaries with no increase in cost or by maintaining value at a lower cost.[12] All thirteen ventures used to illustrate our model for business planning do *both*—they increase value *and* lower cost. All thirteen of the ventures we examined add value to existing assets. All thirteen of the ventures we examined through the lens of the GSBI paradigm have borrowed technology from other contexts, including Silicon Valley, to lower capital costs. And all thirteen have created lower-cost product/service offerings that increase the life choices of the poor. Their success reflects combinatorial innovation.

Against the backdrop of the Social Progress Index and Sustainable Development Goals described in chapters 1 and 2, a unique form of entrepreneurship—social entrepreneurship—is blossoming in many regions around the world. The ventures that are emerging from this movement are driven by a rationality which prioritizes human well-being and community wealth ahead of profits. With our colleagues in Miller Center and its dedicated Silicon Valley mentors, we've been fortunate to accompany hundreds of the social entrepreneurs who are leading these efforts as they refined each element of an integrated business plan, prepared investor presentations, and in many instances secured capital for scaling their ventures. Our hope is that the lessons learned from this collaborative journey will serve as a guide for others to bridge the chasm between transformative ideas and the complex realities of creating successful ventures. Through our collective imaginations we can construct a path forward to a more sustainable, just, and prosperous world—one that works for everyone.

Background Resources

Arthur, W. Brian. *The Nature of Technology: What It Is and How It Evolves.* New York: Free Press, 2009.

Austin, James, Howard Stevenson, and Jane Wei-Skillern. "Social and Commercial Entrepreneurship: Same, Different, or Both?" *Entrepreneurship Theory and Practice* 30, no. 1 (January 2006): 1–22.

Castells, Manuel, and James Koch. "On Analyzing Social Entrepreneurship: A Methodological Note." Santa Clara University, May 2010.

Gartner Group. "Vendor Rating Methodology." 2016. http://www.gartner.com/technology/research/methodologies/research_vrate.jsp.

London, Ted. *The Base of the Pyramid Promise—Building Businesses with Impact and Scale.* Stanford, CA: Stanford University Press, 2016.

Martin, Roger L., and Sally R. Osberg. *Getting Beyond Better—How Social Entrepreneurship Works.* Boston: Harvard Business Preview Press, 2015.

Martin, Roger L., and Sally R. Osberg. "Social Entrepreneurship: The Case for Definition." *Stanford Social Innovation Review* 5, no. 2 (2007): 28–39.

Osterwalder, Alexander, and Yves Pigneur. *Business Model Generation: A Handbook for Visionaries, Game Changers, and Challengers.* New York: John Wiley and Sons, 2010.

Notes

Preface

1. Muhammad Yunus, *Creating a World without Poverty: Social Business and the Future of Capitalism* (New York: Perseus Book Group, 2007), 24.

2. Ibid., 31.

Chapter 1: Top-Down and Bottom-Up Theories of Social Progress

1. Welcoming remarks from Pamela Hartigan, Director of the Skoll Center for Social Entrepreneurship in the Said Business School at the University of Oxford, 2012 Skoll World Forum, April 10–13, University of Oxford.

2. Ted London, *The Base of the Pyramid Promise—Building Businesses with Impact and Scale* (Stanford, CA: Stanford University Press, 2016).

3. Social Progress Index 2016, Michael E. Porter and Scott Stern, with Michael Green, Social Progress Imperative, http://www.socialprogressimperative.org/wp-content /uploads/2016/06/SPI-2016-Main-Report.pdf.

4. U.S. Census Bureau, https://www.census.gov/library/publications/2016/demo/p60-256 .html.

5. Amartya Sen, *Development as Freedom* (New York: Anchor Books, Random House Publishing, 1999).

6. Thomas Piketty, *Capital in the Twenty-First Century* (Cambridge, MA: Harvard University Press, 2017).

7. Oxfam International, "Just 8 Men Own Same Wealth as Half the World," January 16, 2017, https://www.oxfam.org/en/pressroom/pressreleases/2017-01-16/just-8-men-own -same-wealth-half-world.

8. Drew Desilver, "U.S. Income Inequality, on Rise for Decades, Is Now Highest Since 1928," Pew Research Center, December 5, 2013, http://www.pewresearch.org/fact-tank/2013/12/05/u-s-income-inequality-on-rise-for-decades-is-now-highest-since-1928/.

9. Remya Nair, "IMF Warns of Growing Inequality in India and China," LiveMint, May 4, 2016, http://www.livemint.com/Politics/mTf8d5oOqzMwavzaGy4yMN/IMF-warns-of-growing-inequality-in-India-and-China.html.

10. Thomas Sowell, "Trickle Down Theory and Tax Cuts for the Rich," (Stanford, CA: Hoover Institution Press, 2012), https://www.hoover.org/research/trickle-down-theory-and-tax-cuts-rich.

11. *The Economist*, "Poverty Elucidation Day," October 20, 2014, https://www.economist.com/blogs/freeexchange/2014/10/chinas-economy.

12. "Income, Poverty and Health Insurance Coverage in the United States: 2016," https://www.census.gov/newsroom/press-releases/2017/income-poverty.html, accessed on March 19, 2018.

13. *Forbes*, "America Has Less Poverty Than Sweden," September 10, 2012.

14. Alejandro Portes, Manuel Castells, and Lauren A. Benton, eds., *The Informal Economy* (Baltimore: Johns Hopkins University Press, 1989).

15. Hernando De Soto, *The Other Path* (New York: Harper and Row, 1989).

16. C. K. Prahalad, *The Fortune at the Bottom of the Pyramid: Eradicating Poverty through Profits* (Philadelphia: Wharton School Publishing, 2010).

17. S. Sridharan and M. Viswanathan, "Marketing in Subsistence Marketplaces: Consumption and Entrepreneurship in a South Indian Context," *Journal of Consumer Marketing* 25, no. 7 (2008): 455–462.

18. S. Jain and J. Koch, "Conceptualizing Markets for Underserved Communities," in *Sustainability, Society, Business Ethics, and Entrepreneurship*, ed. A. Guerber and G. Markman (Singapore: World Scientific Publishing, 2016), 71–91.

19. Allen Hammond et al., *The Next 4 Billion* (Washington, DC: World Resources Institute, 2007).

20. *India Labor Market Update*, International Labor Office (ILO) for India, July 2016.

21. Tarun Khanna and Krishna G. Palepu, "Why Focused Strategies May Be Wrong for Emerging Markets," *Harvard Business Review*, July–August 1997.

22. R. H. Coase, "The Problem of Social Cost," *Journal of Law and Economics* 3 (October 1960): 1–44; Oliver E. Williamson, *The Economic Institutions of Capitalism* (New York: Simon & Schuster, 1985); Jain and Koch, "Conceptualizing Markets for Underserved Communities."

23. Nancy Wimmer, *Green Energy for a Billion Poor* (Vatterstetten: MCRE Verlag, 2012).

24. London, *The Base of the Pyramid Promise—Building with Impact and Scale.*

25. Matthew G. Grimes, Jeffery S. McMullen, Timothy J. Vogus, and Toyah L. Miller, "Studying the Origins of Social Entrepreneurship," *Academy of Management Review* 38, no. 3 (July 1, 2013): 460–463.

26. Julie Battilana and Matthew Lee, "Advancing Research on Hybrid Organizing—Insights from the Study of Social Enterprises," *Academy of Management Annals* 8 (2014): 397–441.

27. Shahzad Ansari, Kamal Munir, and Tricia Gregg, "Impact at the 'Bottom of the Pyramid': The Role of Social Capital in Capability Development and Community Empowerment," *Journal of Management Studies,* 49, no. 4 (2012): 813–842.

28. Geoffrey Desa and James Koch, "Building Sustainable Social Ventures at the Base of the Pyramid," *Journal of Social Entrepreneurship* 8 (2014): 146–174.

29. Jain and Koch, "Conceptualizing Markets for Underserved Communities: Trajectories Taken and the Road Ahead," 71–91.

30. Peter Buffett, "The Charitable-Industrial Complex," *New York Times,* July 26, 2013.

Chapter 2: The Market at the Base of the Pyramid

1. A. Hammond, W. Kramer, J. Tran, R. Katz, and W. Courtland, *The Next 4 Billion: Market Size and Business Strategy at the Base of the Pyramid* (Washington, DC: World Resources Institute, 2007).

2. World Bank Group, "Global Consumption Database," 2018, accessed January 2018, http://datatopics.worldbank.org/consumption.

3. Pew Research Center, "Cell Phones in Africa: Communications Lifeline," April 2015.

4. James Koch and Al Hammond, "Innovation Dynamics, Best Practice, and Trends in the Off-Grid Clean Energy Market," *Journal of Management for Global Sustainability* 1, no. 2 (2014): 31–49.

5. *Wall Street Journal,* January 19, 2016.

6. Amartya Sen, *Development as Freedom* (New York: Anchor Books, Random House Publishing, 1999).

7. United Nations Development Programme, "The Millennium Development Goals Report 2015," accessed January 2018, www.undp.org/content/undp/en/home/librarypage/mdg/the-millennium-development-goals-report-2015.html.

8. United Nations, "Goal 1: Poverty," accessed January 2018, http://www.un.org/sustainabledevelopment/poverty/.

9. United Nations, "Goal 2: Hunger," accessed January 2018, http://www.un.org/sustain abledevelopment/hunger/.

10. United Nations, "Goal 3: Health," accessed January 2018, http://www.un.org /sustainabledevelopment/health/.

11. United Nations, "Goal 4: Education," accessed January 2018, http://www.un.org/sustain abledevelopment/education/.

12. United Nations, "Goal 5: Gender Equality," accessed January 2018, http://www.un.org /sustainabledevelopment/gender-equality/.

13. United Nations, "Goal 6: Water and Sanitation," accessed January 2018, http://www .un.org/sustainabledevelopment/water-and-sanitation/.

14. United Nations, "Goal 7: Energy," accessed January 2018, http://www.un.org /sustainabledevelopment/energy/.

15. United Nations, "Goal 8: Economic Growth," accessed January 2018, http://www.un .org/sustainabledevelopment/economic-growth/.

16. United Nations, "Goal 9: Infrastructure Industrialization," accessed January 2018, http://www.un.org/sustainabledevelopment/infrastructure-industrialization/.

17. United Nations, "Goal 10: Reduced Inequality," accessed January 2018, http://www.un .org/sustainabledevelopment/inequality/.

18. United Nations, "Goal 11: Sustainable Cities and Communities," accessed January 2018, http://www.un.org/sustainabledevelopment/cities/.

19. Ibid.

20. Ibid.

21. United Nations, "Goal 12: Responsible Consumption and Production," accessed January 2018, www.un.org/sustainabledevelopment/sustainable-consumption-production/.

22. United Nations, "Goal 13: Climate Action," accessed January 2018, http://www.un.org /sustainabledevelopment/climate-change-2/.

23. United Nations, "Goal 14: Life below Water," accessed January 2018, http://www.un .org/sustainabledevelopment/oceans/.

24. United Nations, "Goal 15: Life on Land," accessed January 2018, http://www.un.org /sustainabledevelopment/biodiversity/.

25. United Nations, "Goal 16: Peace, Justice, and Strong Institutions," accessed January 2018, http://www.un.org/sustainabledevelopment/peace-justice/.

26. Ibid.

27. United Nations, "Goal 17: Partnerships for the Goals," accessed January 2018, http://www.un.org/sustainabledevelopment/globalpartnerships/.

28. Roger L. Martin and Sally R. Osberg, *Getting Beyond Better—How Social Entrepreneurship Works* (Boston: Harvard Business Preview Press, 2015).

29. Skoll Foundation, "Marine Stewardship Council," accessed January 2018, http://skoll.org/organization/marine-stewardship-council/.

30. Skoll Foundation, "Living Goods," accessed January 2018, http://skoll.org/organization/living-goods/.

31. Skoll Foundation, "International Development Enterprises (India)," accessed January 2018, http://skoll.org/organization/international-development-enterprises-india/.

32. Skoll Foundation, "Kiva," accessed January 2018, http://skoll.org/organization/kiva/; Skoll Foundation, "Medic Mobile," accessed January 2018, http://www.skoll.org/organization/medic-mobile.

33. Sanjay Jain and James Koch, "Articulated Embedding in the Development of Markets for Underserved Communities: The Case of Clean-Energy Provision to Off-Grid Publics," Academy of Management Annual Conference, Vancouver, BC, August 2015.

34. Geoffrey Desa and James Koch, "Scaling Social Impact: Building Sustainable Social Ventures at the Base of the Pyramid," *Journal of Social Entrepreneurship* 5, no. 2 (2014): 164–174.

35. Ted London, *The Base of the Pyramid Promise—Building with Impact and Scale* (Stanford, CA: Stanford University Press, 2016).

Chapter 3: Paradigms for Social Venture Business Plans

1. William A. Sahlman, "How to Write a Great Business Plan," *Harvard Business Review*, July–August (1997): 98–108.

2. Arthur R. DeThomas and Lin Grensing-Pophal, *Writing a Convincing Business Plan* (New York: Barron's Educational Services, 2001).

3. Alexander Osterwalder and Yves Pigneur, *Business Model Generation: A Handbook for Visionaries, Game Changers, and Challengers* (New York: John Wiley and Sons, 2010), 15.

4. Ibid., 16–17.

5. Ian C. MacMillan and James D. Thompson, *The Social Entrepreneur's Playbook: Pressure Test Your Start-Up Idea* (Philadelphia: Wharton Digital Press, 2013), ix.

6. Ayse Guclu, J. Gregory Dees, and Beth Battle Anderson, *The Process of Social Entrepreneurship: Creating Opportunities Worthy of Serious Pursuit* (Duke University Fuqua School of Business, Center for the Advancement of Social Entrepreneurship, 2002).

Chapter 5: The External Environment

1. R. H. Coase, "The Problem of Social Cost," *Journal of Law and Economics* 3 (October 1960): 1–44.

2. T. Khanna and K. Palepu, "Is Group Affiliation Profitable in Emerging Markets? An Analysis of Diversified Indian Business Groups," *Journal of Finance* 55, no. 2 (2000): 867–891.

3. T. Khanna and K. Palepu, "Why Focused Strategies May Be Wrong for Emerging Markets," *Harvard Business Review*, July–August 1997.

4. J. Mair and I. Marti, "Entrepreneurship in and around Institutional Voids: A Case Study from Bangladesh," *Journal of Business Venturing* 24, no. 5 (2009): 419–435.

5. H. De Soto, *Mystery of Capital: Why Capitalism Triumphs in the West and Fails Everywhere Else* (New York: Basic Books, 2003).

6. J. W. Webb, G. M. Kistruck, R. D. Ireland, and D. J. Ketchen Jr. "The Entrepreneurship Process in Base of the Pyramid Markets: The Case of Multinational Enterprise/Nongovernment Organization Alliances," *Entrepreneurship Theory and Practice* 34, no. 3 (2010): 555–581.

7. J. W. Webb, R. D. Ireland, and D. J. Ketchen, Jr., "Towards a Greater Understanding of Entrepreneurship and Strategy in the Informal Economy," *Strategic Entrepreneurship Journal* 8 (2014): 1–15.

8. C. K. Prahalad, *The Fortune at the Bottom of the Pyramid: Eradicating Poverty through Profits* (Philadelphia: Wharton School Publishing, 2010), chapters 4, 5, and 6.

9. Ibid.

Chapter 6: The Target Market Statement

1. Charles Baden-Fuller and Stefan Haefliger, "Business Models and Technological Innovation," *Long Range Planning* 46 (2013): 419–426.

2. M. Viswanathan, "Understanding Product and Market Interactions in Subsistence Marketplaces: A Study in South India," *Advances in International Management* 20 (2006): 21–57; M. Viswanathan and S. Sridharan, "Product Development for the BoP: Insights on Concept and Prototype Development from University-Based Student Projects in India," *Journal of Product Innovation Management* 29, no. 1 (2012): 52–69.

3. S. Jain and J. Koch, "Conceptualizing Markets for Underserved Communities: Trajectories Taken and the Road Ahead," in *Sustainability, Society, Business Ethics, and Entrepreneurship*, ed. Amy Guerber and Gideon Markman (Singapore: World Scientific Publishers, 2016), 71–91.

4. Jim Koch, McKinsey Global Institute, "The *Bird of Gold:* The Rise of India's Consumer Market," May 2007, https://www.mckinsey.com/~/media/McKinsey/GlobalThemes/ AsiaPacific/The bird of gold/MGI_Rise_of_Indian_Consumer_Market_full_report.

Chapter 8: Organization and Human Resources

1. William A. Sahlman, "How to Write a Great Business Plan," *Harvard Business Review*, July–August (1997): 74.

2. Arthur DeThomas and Stephanie Derammelaere, *How to Write a Convincing Business Plan*, 3rd ed. (New York: Barron's Educational Services, 2008), 154–159.

3. The United Nations, "About Cooperatives," accessed January 2018, http://www.un.org /en/events/coopsyear/about.shtml.

Chapter 9: Business Model

1. Richard G. Hamermesh, Paul W. Marshall, and Taz Pirohamed, "Note on Business Model Analysis for the Entrepreneur," Harvard Business School Report 9-802-048, January 22, 2002.

2. Ted London and Stuart Hart, *Next Generation Business Strategies for the Base of the Pyramid—New Approaches for Building Mutual Value* (Upper Saddle River, NJ: FT Press, 2011).

3. CBS News, "The Future of Money," accessed January 2018, http://www.cbsnews.com /videos/the-future-of-money/.

Chapter 10: Metrics and Accountability

1. Sasha Dichter, Tom Adams, and Alnoor Ebrahim, "The Power of Lean Data," *Stanford Social Innovation Review* 14, no. 1 (2016): 36–41.

2. Peter Scholten, Jeremy Nichols, Sara Olsen, and Bert Galimidi, *Social Return on Investment (A Guide to SROI Analysis)*, FM State of the Art Series, 2006.

3. Sankara Annual Report 2013–2014, Appendix 2, Snapshot of Sankara's Outcome Metrics.

4. Global Innovation Exchange, "Scaling Pathways: Case Study—Vision Spring," accessed January 2018, https://www.globalinnovationexchange.org/resources/scaling-pathways -case-study-visionspring.

Chapter 12: Financing

1. Matt Bannick, Paula Goldman, and Michael Kubzansky, *Frontier Capital: Early Stage Investing for Financial Returns and Social Impact in Emerging Markets*, Omidyar Network

Research Report, October 2015; Lala Faiz, Charly Kleissner, John Kohler, and Nancy Y. Lin, *Total Portfolio Activation for Impact: A Strategy to Move beyond ESG*, Report from Miller Center for Entrepreneurship, September 2016.

2.   Bannick, Goldman, and Kubzansky, *Frontier Capital*; Faiz, Kleisner, Kohler and Lin, *Total Portfolio Activation for Impact*.

3.   McKinsey and Company and Time Koller, *Valuation: Measuring and Managing the Value of a Company* (New York: Wiley Finance, 2015).

4.   William Davidson Institute at the University of Michigan, "Acumen Fund Valuing a Social Venture," Case 1-48-428-788, May 2009.

5.   Ibid.

Chapter 13: The Path Forward

1.   James Austin, Howard Stevenson, and Jane Wei-Skillern, "Social and Commercial Entrepreneurship: Same, Different, or Both?" *Entrepreneurship Theory and Practice* 30, no. 1 (2006): 1–22.

2.   Gartner Group, "Vendor Rating Methodology," 2016, http://www.gartner.com /technology/research/methodologies/research_vrate.jsp.

3.   Manuel Castells and James Koch, "On Analyzing Social Entrepreneurship: A Methodological Note," Working Paper, Santa Clara University, May 2010, p. 2.

4.   Roger L. Martin and Sally R. Osberg, "Social Entrepreneurship: The Case for Definition," *Stanford Social Innovation Review*, April 2007.

5.   Roger L. Martin and Sally R. Osberg, *Getting Beyond Better—How Social Entrepreneurship Works* (Boston: Harvard Business Preview Press, 2015).

6.   Alexander Osterwalder, *Business Model Generation: A Handbook for Visionaries, Game Changers, and Challengers* (New York: John Wiley and Sons, 2010).

7.   Ted London, *The Base of the Pyramid Promise—Building with Impact and Scale* (Stanford, CA: Stanford University Press, 2016).

8.   All of the Marincola quotes in this paragraph and the next are taken from: "The Tech Awards—The First 15 Years; 2016 Laureate: Angaza," accessed April 2018, https://www .youtube.com/watch?v=BM49xEshtFs.

9.   London, *The Base of the Pyramid Promise*, 135.

10. W. Brian Arthur, *The Nature of Technology: What It Is and How It Evolves* (New York: Free Press, 2009).

11. Martin and Osberg, *Getting Beyond Better*.

12. Ibid.

Acknowledgments

The basic business plan paradigm contained in this book drew heavily from Silicon Valley approaches to business model innovation. It was initially formulated by Pat Guerra in collaboration with Al Bruno and the authors and is based on our collective experiences in leading and managing various ventures (both social and profit maximizing). The paradigm was then used as a framework for both curriculum design and desired outcome documentation, first for the GSBI in-residence program and later for the GSBI online program.

Over the first ten years of the GSBI, several dozen lecturers presented on various elements of the paradigm, and the attending social entrepreneurs and their mentors provided feedback on how to improve that material. In addition, the material was adapted for an MBA course on social entrepreneurship and has benefited from the feedback of more than one hundred MBA students. While it is not possible to acknowledge the specific lecturers, social entrepreneurs, mentors, and MBA students for their specific contributions, this book has benefited from them all.

In addition to GSBI materials created by the authors, the notes from the following GSBI lecturers provided the basis for some of the material contained in this book: Al Bruno, Bob Finnochio, Pat Guerra, Tyzoon Tyebjee, Charly Kleissner, John Kohler, Mike Looney, Brad and Vicky Mattson, Geoffrey Moore, Sara Olsen, Jeff Miller, Kevin Starr, Regis McKenna, Al Hammond, and Jose Flahaux. We thank all of these individuals for their valuable insights.

We are especially grateful for the Skoll Foundation's generous support of the GSBI and the inspired leadership of its founding CEO, Sally Osberg. Given our shared commitment to driving large-scale change, it is not surprising that six of the exemplary GSBI case studies we use to illustrate the GSBI business planning framework have subsequently gone on to become Skoll awardees.

The authors greatly appreciate the work of Danielle Medeiros, Cathryn Meyer, and Visswapriya Prabakar, whose Sankara examples, from their final project in Professor Koch's Winter 2015 Management 548 class, are used with their permission. As previously mentioned, Nancy Wimmer provided detailed feedback on the Grameen Shakti examples. Geoffrey Desa, Al Hammond, Jean Hazell, Ted London, Madhu Viswanathan, and Michael Gordon provided useful feedback on early versions of this book. In addition, Sherrill Dale, Andy Lieberman, and Cassandra Staff provided immeasurable help in organizing and implementing the GSBI and therefore also contributed to the content of this book. Early versions of this book also benefited greatly from the formatting and graphic design skills of Santa Clara University students Tiffany Lu and Arshi Jujara.

Finally, the authors are very grateful to those associated with Berrett-Koehler for their suggestions. Nic Albert's revisions greatly increased the clarity and readability of the book. Lasell Whipple redesigned the cover to convey the spirit of our work, and Deborah Grahame-Smith and Edward Wade did a masterful job of production editing. We are especially grateful for the wise and steadfast guidance of editorial director Neal Maillet. While Neal may believe that Berrett-Koehler chose to publish our manuscript, in reality, it is equally true to say that the authors chose Berrett-Koehler. The BK mission of "connecting people and ideas to create a world that works for all" aligns with our values and the many people in Miller Center for Social Entrepreneurship at Santa Clara University, where the tools we describe in this book continue to be refined to foster a more just and sustainable world.

Index

About the Authors

Eric Carlson recently retired as Dean's Executive Professor of Entrepreneurship in the Santa Clara University (SCU), Leavey School of Business, and as the director of the Global Social Benefit Incubator (GSBI®). Prior to his fifteen-year association with SCU, he spent twenty-nine years in research, product development, and executive management in Silicon Valley. During that time he served as CEO of two software companies. He served on several  corporate and nonprofit boards of directors. He also served ten years on the Los Gatos Town Council, including two terms as mayor. Carlson has a BA (economics) from Carleton College in Minnesota, and an MS (city and regional planning) and PhD (computer science) from the University of North Carolina at Chapel Hill. Eric married the former Marilyn Garbisch in 1967. After six years in Chapel Hill, they moved to Los Gatos, California, where they still live, and they spend summers on Ten Mile Lake in Minnesota. They have two children and four grandchildren.

James Koch is Professor of Organizational Analysis and Management, Emeritus, and former dean of the Leavey School of Business at Santa Clara University, where he also served as acting dean of the School of Engineering. He is the founder of Miller Center for Social Entrepreneurship (previously the Center for Science, Technology, and Society), cofounder of the Tech Awards—Technology Benefiting Humanity, and cofounder of the Global Social

Benefit Incubator. In addition to entrepreneurship and social innovation, his research and consulting focus on organizational change and the design of high-performance work systems. Prior to coming to Santa Clara, he was director of Organization Planning and Development at PG&E. He began his academic career at the University of Oregon where he was associate dean of the MBA and PhD programs. Jim has served on a number of for-profit and nonprofit boards, including Commonwealth Club of California and the Board of Trustees of Bay Area Council Economic Institute. He received his MBA and PhD in Industrial Relations from UCLA. Jim and his wife, Anne, were married in 1969. They have two children and five grandchildren.

Berrett–Koehler
Publishers

Berrett-Koehler is an independent publisher dedicated to an ambitious mission: *Connecting people and ideas to create a world that works for all.*

We believe that the solutions to the world's problems will come from all of us, working at all levels: in our organizations, in our society, and in our own lives. Our BK Business books help people make their organizations more humane, democratic, diverse, and effective (we don't think there's any contradiction there). Our BK Currents books offer pathways to creating a more just, equitable, and sustainable society. Our BK Life books help people create positive change in their lives and align their personal practices with their aspirations for a better world.

All of our books are designed to bring people seeking positive change together around the ideas that empower them to see and shape the world in a new way.

And we strive to practice what we preach. At the core of our approach is Stewardship, a deep sense of responsibility to administer the company for the benefit of all of our stakeholder groups including authors, customers, employees, investors, service providers, and the communities and environment around us. Everything we do is built around this and our other key values of quality, partnership, inclusion, and sustainability.

This is why we are both a B-Corporation and a California Benefit Corporation—a certification and a for-profit legal status that require us to adhere to the highest standards for corporate, social, and environmental performance.

We are grateful to our readers, authors, and other friends of the company who consider themselves to be part of the BK Community. We hope that you, too, will join us in our mission.

A BK Business Book

We hope you enjoy this BK Business book. BK Business books pioneer new leadership and management practices and socially responsible approaches to business. They are designed to provide you with groundbreaking and practical tools to transform your work and organizations while upholding the triple bottom line of people, planet, and profits. High-five!

To find out more, visit **www.bkconnection.com**.

Berrett–Koehler
Publishers

Connecting people and ideas
to create a world that works for all

Dear Reader,

Thank you for picking up this book and joining our worldwide community of Berrett-Koehler readers. We share ideas that bring positive change into people's lives, organizations, and society.

To welcome you, we'd like to offer you a free e-book. You can pick from among twelve of our bestselling books by entering the promotional code **BKP92E** here: http://www.bkconnection.com/welcome.

When you claim your free e-book, we'll also send you a copy of our e-newsletter, the *BK Communiqué*. Although you're free to unsubscribe, there are many benefits to sticking around. In every issue of our newsletter you'll find

- A free e-book
- Tips from famous authors
- Discounts on spotlight titles
- Hilarious insider publishing news
- A chance to win a prize for answering a riddle

Best of all, our readers tell us, "Your newsletter is the only one I actually read." So claim your gift today, and please stay in touch!

Sincerely,

Charlotte Ashlock
Steward of the BK Website

Questions? Comments? Contact me at bkcommunity@bkpub.com.

Certified

Corporation
bcorporation.net